THE CIVIL WAR AT CHARLESTON

By

Arthur M. Wilcox

And

Warren Ripley

PREFACE

The stories in this publication describe the Civil War in the Charleston area 1860-1865.

They originally were published in a series of six special sections of the two Charleston newspapers during the Civil War Centennial, 1960-1965.

Following publication, they were combined into a single tabloid which sold more than 60,000 copies through the years.

Revised and brought up to date, they are now republished on better grade paper and in more convenient size for home and school use.

Copyright, Evening Post Publishing Co. 1966
Second Edition   1966
Third Edition   1967
Fourth Edition   1969
Fifth Edition   1970
Sixth Edition   1971
Seventh Edition   1973
Eighth Edition   1975
Ninth Edition   1980
Tenth Edition   1983
Eleventh Edition   1984
Twelfth Edition   1986
Thirteenth Edition   1988
Fourteenth Edition   1989
Fifteenth Edition   1991
Sixteenth Edition   1992
Seventeenth Edition   1993
Eighteenth Edition   1994
Nineteenth Edition   1997
Twentieth Edition   1998
Twenty-first Edition   2000
Twenty-second Edition   2001
Twenty-third Edition   2006

Table

ACKNOWLEDGEMENTS

Information for stories in this publication was obtained from Army and Navy official records, contemporary newspaper accounts and similarly reliable sources.

Appreciation for assistance is extended to the South Carolina Historical Society, the Charleston Library Society and the Charleston Museum.

Published By
The Post and Courier

S.C. Secedes

Tumultuous events led up to the secession of South Carolina, but the act itself was performed in an atmosphere notable for its dignity and decorum.

The immediate cause of the departure of South Carolina from the Union was the election of Abraham Lincoln.

In April, 1860, the Democratic Party, convening at Charleston, split wide open over the issue of slavery.

Delegates from South Carolina and seven other Southern states walked out of the meeting.

Two weeks later in Chicago, the Republicans nominated Lincoln. South Carolinians promptly pledged secession in case he should be elected.

Election day was Nov. 6. On Nov. 10, the state legislature, responding to public anger over a Republican victory, voted to call a convention to consider a secession ordinance.

Not a dissenting vote was cast in either house.

From that time, secession was a foregone conclusion in the minds of most South Carolinians. They took pains, however, to approach the formal question of separation with ostentatious caution.

Even though the outcome of the vote was settled in advance, the state sent to the Secession Convention her best and wisest men.

"They have really tried to send the ablest men, the good men and true," wrote Mrs. James Chestnut, wife of one of South Carolina's U.S. senators and a keen and accurate reporter of the times.

The people of South Carolina were determined to have their freedom at all costs. They were aware that they were making history of a kind that might be charged against them. They were resolved to avoid any show of recklessness.

While sobriety and restraint prevailed within Institute Hall as the Ordinance of Secession was being signed on Dec. 20, 1860, wild excitement swept the streets outside.

When, at last, the president of the convention arose to proclaim the State of South Carolina an "independent commonwealth," jubilation followed.

Business was suspended.

The pealing of church bells mingled with the roar of saluting guns.

Old men ran shouting through the city.

Everyone entitled to wear a uniform went home and put it on.

Representatives were promptly dispatched to all parts of the South to carry the message that South

ROBERT BARNWELL RHETT

Carolina was independent and to invite her sister states to join her.

Six other Southern states agreed to send delegates to a meeting at Montgomery, Ala., to discuss proposals for a new confederacy.

The meeting assembled on Feb. 4, 1861.

At the same moment, another assembly, termed a "peace convention," was being called to order in Washington. The leaders of the peace convention were Virginians, reluctant to quit the Union, anxious to compromise its troubles. The Virginians asked South Carolina to join the conference. But South Carolinians were too far gone down the road to separation to consider turning back. They rejected the invitation.

At Montgomery, they became the moving spirits behind the plan to form a new nation.

One of the loudest voices in the convention at first was that of Robert Barnwell Rhett, editor of the radical Charleston Mercury.

Rhett went to Montgomery with ambitions to shape the new government and to be its chief executive when it was formed. Instead, he found himself on the outside of the new regime, looking in.

His extreme views did not sit well with his own delegation or those of other states.

A more modest South Carolinian played the influential part in which Rhett had hoped to be cast. He was Christopher G. Memminger, a conservative banker who offered resolutions for a committee on a provisional constitution and became its chairman.

He had already published a plan for a government and he greatly influenced the Provisional Constitution that was finally developed.

The Provisional Constitution was adopted Feb. 8. It was patterned after the U.S. Constitution with differences where slavery and tariffs were concerned.

The next day, the first leaders of the new government were chosen. Jefferson Davis got the job of president that Rhett had wanted so much.

The formation of the new Confederacy was a turning point in the military operations which South Carolina had undertaken in Charleston Harbor. Almost as soon

Seceders from Democratic Convention met at St. Andrew's Hall. (Top Photo)

South Carolina Institute Hall (Left)

as Davis had taken the oath of office, he was under pressure to do something about Fort Sumter.

Gov. F.W. Pickens of South Carolina had been slow to take the responsibility of ordering an assault. But he was quick to try to pin responsibility on President Davis.

In response to Gov. Pickens' urging, Davis lost no time in ordering a professional soldier to take command at Charleston in the name of the Confederacy. The new commander was Brig. Gen. P.G.T. Beauregard, a competent engineer and artillery expert.

With the arrival of Gen. Beauregard at Charleston, the doom of the Federal garrison at Sumter was sealed.

A.M.W.

Volunteer company inspected at Fort Moultrie.

(Sketch of Richland Volunteer Rifle Company shortly after the occupation of Fort Moultrie by South Carolina forces Dec. 27, 1860.)

Dress uniforms of Charleston militia units.

(Left to right: Highlander, Montgomery Guard, Lafayette Artillery, Citadel Cadet, Palmetto Guard, unidentified, German Artillery, Scottish Fusileers, and Charleston Zouave.)

Militia Units Were Colorful, Varied

"Mere social clubs" manned by clerks and tender youths unused to rough living, said competent observers speaking of South Carolina militia units in 1860-61. The citizen soldiers, however, were the only substantial body of organized and disciplined troops available to a state which had set her course toward independence.

From first to last during this period, Charleston furnished 28 companies of those part-time soldiers, horse, foot and artillery, not including four companies of armed firemen.

Many of these companies later volunteered "for the war." 42 in all, including 5,000 or 6,000 officers and men, served the Confederacy.

When South Carolina seceded Dec. 20, 1860, her people did not expect to have to fight.

On paper, the state had an army. Militia laws passed in 1841 provided that all male citizens 16 to 60 were liable to service. Those 18 to 45 might be called for three months duty anywhere in the state and for two months outside the state.

Companies had to assemble once a quarter for drill. Regiments had to be reviewed once a year. Officers and men were subject to fines for failures to perform their duties.

All very good — on paper. The trouble was that many of the companies were military units in name only. Some had no uniforms and no weapons. Officers were primarily interested in political advancement. As a matter of fact, anybody who wanted to be an officer had to have in him a strong streak of the politician. Officers were elected and militia soldiers did not vote for martinets.

No wonder that one patriotic South Carolinian noted with scorn that "city companies frittered into social clubs and rural militia musters into picnics."

Some of the militiamen, though, had the wisdom to interpret the signs of trouble which gathered strength late in 1860. Companies began to meet more frequently and drill more seriously. Old companies were revived. New companies were formed.

Veterans of the Mexican War or service in the regular army were employed to teach the fundamentals of soldiering. The companies advertised for recruits and planned ingenious ways to raise funds for arms and equipment.

By Christmas 1860, enthusiasm for soldiering had become a craze in Charleston. The militiamen were the darlings of the community. Citizens of all classes joined to fight the Yankees and enjoy the admiration of their neighbors.

The best families of Charleston led this parade, taking their places in the ranks as well as accepting commissions. One company of soldiers had an aggregate wealth of more than a million dollars. One was composed largely of students of Charleston College.

One of the smartest of the new units was the Charleston Zouave Cadets, formed late in 1860. In some ways, this outfit was not typical. For one thing, each man had a proper uniform. For another thing, its ranks — theoretically, at least — were filled entirely with teetotallers.

"Any person of MORAL CHARACTER AND GENTLEMANLY DEPORTMENT, and who is 17 years old and measures 5 feet 4 inches in height may become an active member," said a Zouave recruiting broadside.

"Anyone may become a subscribing member on the payment of $5 a year. These are privileged to use the bowling alley and gymnasium at all times excepting on Tuesday and Friday evenings."

New Zouaves were warned not to violate the "Golden Rules."

This meant no drinking in uniform. No patronage of saloons. Don't enter a house of ill-fame. No gambling.

In return for hewing to a sharp moral line, Zouaves were promised a snappy uniform of French Army type. It was to include a blue jacket, scarlet pants and scarlet cap, "the jauntiest little headgear ever worn by a practical fighting man."

Peculiar as the qualifications for new recruits must have seemed to some Charlestonians, the Zouaves apparently had little trouble filling up their ranks. By November 1860, they were able to turn out a respectable 40 men for drill. At this time, too, they received their flag — red with a palmetto tree in the center and nearby a crouched tiger. "A single star completes the symbolism," the Daily Courier noted with approval.

The Zouaves never got their fancy uniforms. They showed up for their first dress parade early in December clad in a uniform of gray cloth, "neat, serviceable and pretty."

This was the uniform in which they answered the long roll of the alarm drums on Dec. 27, 1860, when it was discovered that Maj. Robert Anderson and his command had fled to Fort Sumter.

Between the time that Anderson reached Sumter and the first shots were fired on the Federal garrison there, the militiamen continued in state service, though not always on active duty.

They were on duty in the harbor when the Star of the West showed up and was turned back and they saw temporary service again during the bombardment.

Some stayed on duty through the spring of 1861. Contemporary photographs show Zouaves in garrison at Castle Pinckney following the Battle of Manassas.

Under the stress of war, the militia organizations first blurred and then disappeared. The roll of militia companies for South Carolina is long, about 500. These organizations took with them into Confederate service about 60,000 men, 20 per cent of the white population.

About one fifth of these men did not return. Those who did come back found no cheering throngs.

After a while, for practical as well as sentimental reasons, some of the companies were revived. Some exist today.

Most of them, however, like so many of the soldiers who marched away under their banners, simply disappeared on one front or another and were never heard from again.

A.M.W.

Zouave Cadets on guard duty at Castle Pinckney. Late 1861.

Castle Pinckney shortly after occupation by South Carolina troops Dec. 27, 1860.

Castle Pinckney Is Captured

Castle Pinckney, first fort captured by the South, is considered by some to be the site of the initial overt act of the war.

Yet with this one exception, the fort has played a disappointing role in history.

The first fortification on the site was an earth and timber structure erected in 1798. This work, built on wood pilings, apparently was none too stable for it was battered down in the hurricane of 1804.

The masonry fort, the lower portion of which remains today, was built between 1809 and 1811. It was garrisoned several times during the succeeding years, but saw no action until 1860.

In December of that year, its occupants were a repair party composed of Lt. R.K. Meade, four mechanics and 30 laborers, and an ordnance sergeant and his family. The sergeant's job was to serve as caretaker, keep the lacquer bright on the guns and solid shot, and to trim the lamp which served as a navigation light.

The armament at this time consisted of four 42-pounders, fourteen 24-pounders, and four 8-inch seacoast howitzers, one 10-inch mortar, one 8-inch mortar and four light artillery pieces.

The laborers could not be depended upon to fight, so Castle Pinckney was virtually undefended and South Carolina forces looked upon it as a plum to be plucked at their convenience.

The time came at the end of December.

During the evening of Dec. 26, Union forces at Fort Moultrie were transferred to a more defensible position at Fort Sumter. They moved out after spiking the guns of Moultrie and leaving the carriages in flames.

In retaliation, South Carolina Gov. F.W. Pickens ordered the taking of Castle Pinckney, ostensibly to prevent further destruction of public property.

The assignment went to Col. J.J. Pettigrew who on Dec. 27 formed detachments of the Washington Light Infantry, the Meagher Guards and the Carolina Light Infantry on the Citadel Green in preparation for the assault.

Dressed in winter uniform with knapsacks, blankets and revolvers, the men, about 150 strong, marched to the shore and boarded the steamer Nina which crossed the short stretch of harbor and tied up at the Castle Pinckney wharf about 4 p.m.

As soon as the vessel touched, a small assault force dashed down the wharf and around the side of the fort to the main gate hoping to get inside before it was closed.

They were too late.

Meade had closed the gate as soon as it was apparent an attack was imminent. He also ordered the laborers, who had rushed to the ramparts, to return to their quarters.

The assault party called for scaling ladders and as soon as they were brought from the ship, Col. Pettigrew led the ascent.

He climbed over the parapet to be confronted by Lt. Meade who identified himself as the commanding officer when Pettigrew announced that he was taking charge of the work on orders of the governor.

Pettigrew then started to read his orders, but was interrupted by Meade who refused to acknowledge the authority of the governor to take over the work. However, the lieutenant added that he had no means of resistance and could only offer his protest.

He then refused to accept receipts for the public property and declined to give his parole since he did not

Occupation of Castle Pinckney by South Carolina forces.
(Contemporary sketch is inaccurate. Troops carried no flag. Union officer, left, was on the wall, not the wharf.)

Castle Pinckney as it looks today.

consider himself a prisoner of war. After receiving a promise of considerate treatment for the ordnance sergeant and his family, Meade and four men, presumably the mechanics, left Castle Pinckney for Fort Sumter.

While this highly formal, although somewhat ludicrous, scene was being played on the terreplein, other men had scaled the walls and opened the gates.

The South Carolina forces then were formed on the parade and a Palmetto flag, borrowed from the Nina because no soldier had thought to bring one, was raised over the fort.

Although a bloodless capture, the action is considered by many to be the first overt act of the war since it occurred prior to either the firing on the Star of the West or the opening shot against Fort Sumter.

During the remainder of the war, Pinckney was relegated to a strictly secondary role.

The latter part of 1861 saw her serving as a military prison for Yankees captured at First Manassas. Some of her guns were later removed to strengthen other fortifications in the harbor and apparently she took little or no part in the heavy fighting around the harbor entrance during 1863 and 1864.

At the evacuation of Charleston, Feb. 17-18, 1865, the fort was abandoned by its Confederate garrison. It was occupied during the morning of the 18th by the 21st U.S. Colored Troops. They hauled down the Confederate garrison flag and raised the Stars and Stripes to fly once again over the little fort.

W.R.

Guns dismounted after carriages burned.

Guns bear on Fort Sumter after carriages rebuilt.

State Troops Occupy Moultrie

Fort Moultrie, scene of a valiant defense by South Carolinians during the Revolution, was taken by their descendants in 1860 without firing a shot.

Palmetto State troops took over the fort Dec. 27 after its evacuation by Maj. Robert Anderson the previous evening.

Charleston's first inkling that something was amiss came on the morning of the 27th when the guard ship Nina came racing to the city with word that Union troops had been seen on the ramparts of Fort Sumter which previously had been occupied only by a force of workmen.

A short time later, South Carolinians were treated to another shock — smoke began to curl up from the walls of Fort Moultrie.

The smoke came from burning gun carriages, set afire by a small detachment left behind as a rear guard. These men manned several of the fort's cannon to cover the crossing of their comrades, then spent the remainder of the night in removing stores, cutting down the flagpole, and making preparations to burn the carriages of guns facing Fort Sumter.

The following afternoon they were recalled to Sumter, leaving an engineer sergeant as overseer and sole occupant of the fort.

That evening, the 27th, Lt. Col. William G. deSaussure, acting under the orders of the governor, embarked detachments of four artillery units aboard the steamboats Nina and General Clinch.

The men, some 225 strong, were taken from the Washington, German, Lafayette and Marion Artillery units with a few from one of the infantry outfits.

Landing on Sullivan's Island, the men marched the short distance to the fort and the overseer surrendered it upon demand to the South Carolinians.

Although in the hands of Southern forces, the fort was not occupied that night because rumors had been spread that the area had been mined.

The rumors were entirely unfounded, but the state troops took no chances and waited until the following day before taking over the fortification.

Although Anderson had spiked the guns bearing on the channel and had burned many of the gun carriages, the South Carolina forces picked up an impressive total of ordnance.

They had captured 56 weapons including light and heavy pieces. The breakdown amounted to sixteen 24-pounders, nineteen 32-pounders, ten 8-inch columbiads, one 10-inch seacoast mortar, four 6-pounders, two 12-pounders, and four 24-pounder howitzers. In addition, they took over considerable ammunition and engineer equipment.

After occupation, the South Carolina forces began immediate work to protect the weapons bearing on Fort Sumter since, without protection, that formidable fortification could make short work of Moultrie.

The strengthening of Fort Moultrie continued during the early part of 1861. Burned carriages were replaced and vents of the guns, spiked fortunately with soft wrought-iron nails, were easily cleared enabling Moultrie to join the ring of cannon that poured shot and shell into Fort Sumter during the two-day April siege which resulted in the surrender of Anderson's forces.

W.R.

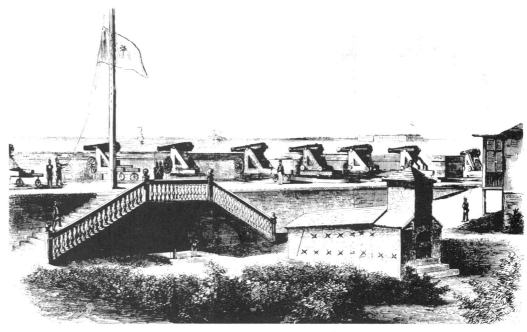

Interior of Moultrie after occupation by S.C. troops.

(Northern magazines using this sketch after Anderson abandoned Moultrie, simply took an existing drawing and added the S.C. flag. In reality, Anderson had burned the gun carriages and cut down the flagstaff.)

Fort Moultrie as it looks today. Fortification is now property of the National Park Service.

South Carolina volunteer troops try out captured arms at the Arsenal.

Arsenal Falls In Bloodless Coup

The United States Arsenal at Charleston fell to South Carolina troops in a bloodless coup the morning of Dec. 30, 1860, its enlisted commander being in no position to put up a fight.

F.C. Humphreys, who officially was called "military storekeeper, ordnance," but generally referred to as an ordnance sergeant, was in charge of the entire Arsenal which encompassed a city block. His "command" consisted of nine enlisted men and six hired hands.

Some weeks before, a colonel had been named commander of the Arsenal. However, about 10 days after assuming command, he was recalled to Washington, leaving Humphreys in charge.

Although the Arsenal actually surrendered Dec. 30, to all intents it had been held by South Carolina troops for more than a month.

During November, Col. John L. Gardner, who was later relieved as commander of Charleston's forts by Maj. Robert Anderson, had attempted to remove all of the fixed ammunition for small arms from the Arsenal for use at the forts.

The move was discovered after only two or three cartloads were aboard the schooner for transport to Fort Moultrie and, to prevent a clash with the citizenry, the ammunition was returned to the Arsenal.

This led Humphreys to agree to an offer by South Carolina's governor to station a guard of state troops at the Arsenal to protect it from any "insurrectionary movement on the part of the servile population...," to quote Humphreys' report to Washington.

The guard also, of course, effectively prevented any more attempts to send much-needed ammunition and other stores to the U.S. troops stationed at Moultrie.

On the 28th of December, the guard was reinforced and refused permission to anyone to enter or leave the Arsenal grounds without the countersign.

Humphreys reported this new move to Washington, protesting the indignity offered him and his men and stating that if, upon proper request to state authorities, the troops were not removed, he would haul down his flag and surrender.

He was saved the trouble.

On the 30th, acting under orders from the governor and on the pretext of preventing "any destruction of public property that may occur in the present excited state of the public mind...," Col. John Cunningham of the 17th Infantry Regiment took a detachment of the Union Light Infantry to Humphreys' quarters and demanded surrender of the Arsenal.

Humphreys stated that he was forced to comply because he had insufficient strength to resist, but that he did so under protest and demanded the right to salute his flag upon lowering it with 32 guns, one for every state remaining in the Union.

He also received permission for him and his men to occupy their quarters until instructions could be obtained from Washington.

By taking the Arsenal, South Carolina picked up some 22,430 pieces of ordnance, ranging from cannon to pistols and valued at roughly $400,000. The military storehouse was used by the Confederacy throughout the war and reverted to United States control after the cessation of hostilities.

Within a few years, however, the government found it no longer needed the property and it was turned over to the Rev. Dr. A. Toomer Porter who had established a school in 1867.

Porter Military Academy utilized the site until 1963 when the tract was sold to the Medical University of South Carolina.

During its long occupation as a military school, the property changed very little and many of the buildings which echoed to the tramp of cadets moving to class, once shuddered to the shock of 32 guns, as Humphreys lowered the United States flag, and a single discharge as South Carolina troops saluted the hoisting of the Palmetto banner.

W.R.

U.S. Arsenal after it was reoccupied by Union forces in 1865.

Anderson In Tough Spot

"Why did that green goose Anderson go into Fort Sumter?" demanded a Charleston lady of her diary early in April, 1861.

"Then everything began to go wrong." But everything had begun to go wrong long ago. For Maj. Robert Anderson, a Southern officer sent to hold the fort at Charleston, trouble began the day he reported in at Fort Moultrie, across the channel from Fort Sumter.

Moultrie, not Sumter, was the fort Maj. Anderson had been sent to hold. From a military point of view, however, Fort Moultrie seemed impossible to hold — and not worth the trouble anyway.

Capt. Abner Doubleday, the senior company commander, said it was not really a fort at all, only a sea battery. It was ridiculously undermanned. Designed for 300 men, it had about 75 on the rolls.

Its brick walls were no higher than the ceiling of somebody's good-sized parlor. Sand had drifted deep against them. In some places the masonry had entirely disappeared from sight.

Foraging cows climbed the drifts and wandered along the parapets to the scandal of the garrison.

Nobody had ever dreamed that the little fort might some day be in danger of attack from the people it was supposed to protect. It was practically defenseless from the rear. Charlestonians had built cottages close to the walls. A sentry walking his beat had to turn his head to avoid peeking in the windows.

Rubbing elbows so closely with civilian neighbors had not troubled the garrison until politics began to boil toward the end of 1860. Then the position of the federal soldiers became anomalous, as Sgt. James Chester put it so delicately.

As secession fever grew in Charleston, resentment against the federal soldiers began to make itself heard. The little cottages which peeped over the walls began to look less neighborly every day. They began to look more like places where sharpshooters could lie at ease and pick off soldiers in Moultrie at their leisure.

Charlestonians looked with proprietary eyes upon all the forts in Charleston Harbor. They were particularly proprietary about Moultrie because of its historical significance. Over in the city, they began to talk about taking over from the Yankees.

Anderson and his men heard the talk. While it grew loud in November and December of 1860, the gate at Moultrie remained wide open to civilians who wanted to wander through the post looking it over.

Militia officers in uniform prowled the place and made notes on what was going on. Anderson's energetic engineer officer was trying to put the fort in defensible condition. Some of the South Carolinians said they were pleased to see it would be in such good order when it was turned over to them.

Eventually, Anderson reacted to the growing pressure. He behaved with soldierly simplicity. He shut the gates and began to plan for defense. His predecessor in command at Moultrie, Col. John L. Gardner, had also had some notions about defense. Col. Gardner was a superannuated officer who had fought in the War of 1812 but he had gotten his back up a bit and sent to the arsenal in the city for some ammunition for the garrison's muskets. This made the South Carolinians angry. They pulled strings in Washington. Col. Gardner was relieved.

When Maj. Anderson tried the same thing, he ran into the same kind of resentment. The War Department did not want more trouble at Charleston than was already brewing. When Anderson applied for reinforcements and funds to strengthen the walls, he learned to his dismay that he was almost on his own as far as Washington was concerned.

With the place crawling with secessionists and rumors flying that the Southerners were getting ready to march in, talk in the messes at Moultrie began to turn to slipping over the water to Fort Sumter.

Capt. Doubleday said Moultrie couldn't be defended with only 75 men or so.

Anderson could see that as well as anybody but he had been assigned to Fort Moultrie and he said he would stay there.

Sometime in December, however, he began to make plans to quit Fort Moultrie.

He got a nudge in the direction of Sumter on the 11th when a sharp young major from headquarters by the name of Buell came down and discussed the possibilities of abandoning Moultrie.

Buell was speaking for the War Department and he left permission for Maj. Anderson to occupy any of the forts in the harbor if the pressure grew too great.

This concession was carefully hedged with restrictions and warnings not to make the South Carolinians angry, but Maj. Anderson concluded he now had authority to leave Moultrie if he thought it necessary.

A.M.W.

Sand against walls hindered defense of Moultrie.

Evacuation of Fort Moultrie by Maj. Anderson's command. Troops and stores loading for Fort Sumter.

Anderson Moves To Fort Sumter

Few secrets of the Civil War were better kept than Maj. Robert Anderson's move to Fort Sumter.

Even his own officers, with two or three exceptions, knew nothing about it until half an hour or so before the move.

Since his arrival in Charleston during the latter part of November, Anderson had been repairing and increasing the defensive power of Fort Moultrie. However, he knew from the start that no matter what he did, Moultrie, with his small force of some 75 men and officers, could never withstand a land attack.

Consequently, he decided to move to Fort Sumter where his small garrison could give an adequate account of itself instead of being massacred in Fort Moultrie. But to announce his intentions to his men, even his officers, would be inviting an inadvertent "leak" to the Southerners, many of whom were very close friends of members of his command and their families.

However, he did have to take several officers into his confidence — his engineer officer supplied the rowboats and barges necessary for the transfer of the men and equipment, and another officer went with the men's families aboard schooners.

These vessels, three of them, had been chartered by Anderson ostensibly to take the women and children to Fort Johnson where they would be out of harm's way in case of an attack on Moultrie.

However, the officer in charge was ordered to lie off Fort Johnson until he heard a gun signaling the successful transfer to Sumter.

During the daylight hours of Dec. 26, the schooners were loaded, not only with the belongings of the women and children, but also with stores for Fort Sumter.

Then, late in the afternoon, while Anderson and some of his officers stood on the ramparts of Fort Moultrie watching the schooners sail, Capt. Abner Doubleday, one of Anderson's two battery commanders approached the group. Anderson turned to him, said he had just told the others of his intention to move to Sumter, and gave Doubleday 20 minutes to form his men and be ready to make the move.

Twenty minutes later, the entire command, with the exception of a small rear guard, marched quietly through the streets of Moultrieville about a quarter of a mile to the boats which had been concealed behind a seawall.

Anderson and one company shoved off while Doubleday's men loaded their boats. It was twilight when they started the short trip to Fort Sumter — light enough for Doubleday to see a Southern guard boat bearing down on them. It cruised the waters between Moultrie and Sumter to prevent such a transfer as this.

Realizing he could not retreat, Doubleday ordered his men to take off their coats and put them over their rifles in the bottom of the boat. He then opened his own coat to conceal the buttons, hoping they could pass for a party of laborers returning to the fort.

The ruse worked. The guard boat, which was towing

(Continued On Page 9)

Smoke drifts over Fort Moultrie as gun carriages burn.

(Continued From Page 8)

ANDERSON MOVES

a barge, stopped for a quick look, then the paddle wheels picked up again as the vessel steamed into the gathering twilight.

Doubleday's men picked up the stroke and soon landed at the fort where they were greeted by the workmen who were repairing it. Many of them wore the cockades of secession, so Doubleday's men formed ranks and drove them into the fort at bayonet point where they were held until Anderson and the other men arrived. They had escaped notice of the guard boat by hugging the shore. However, the move had delayed them a bit permitting Doubleday to land first.

With the fort in Union hands, Anderson ordered the signal cannon fired to bring in the schooners with the women and children. They were landed and the stores unloaded. The schooners transferred the workmen to Fort Johnson and then returned to Fort Moultrie for more supplies.

At that fort, the rear guard had been manning cannon bearing on the harbor with orders to fire if the guard boat attempted to hinder the crossing.

Now that the crossing had been accomplished, the rear guard spiked the cannon, chopped down the flagpole and prepared the carriages of a number of guns for burning in the morning. Then they continued sending supplies until the middle of the following afternoon when they were ordered to Fort Sumter by Anderson.

W.R.

Union troops entering Fort Sumter the night after Christmas, 1860.

South Builds Floating Battery

An ironclad vessel was used in Charleston Harbor almost a year before the historic clash of the Monitor and Virginia in Hampton Roads.

Called officially "The Floating Battery," but better known to Northerners as "The Raft" and to Southerners as "The Slaughter Pen," the vessel was built during the early part of 1861.

Although most of the world's warships were wooden, the concept of an armored vessel was not new. Various European countries, particularly the French, had been experimenting with ironclad vessels for some years. They were heavy, unwieldy and slow, but against forts they were considered excellent.

This latter quality of the ironclads intrigued the South Carolinians who were starting out as a new nation with an enemy manning a fort covering the entrance to one of their main harbors.

They studied the armored vessel concept, then adapted it to their own use. There was no need for a maneuverable vessel, they reasoned, since its main purpose was to smash Fort Sumter and the fort wasn't going to move.

With this in mind, they set out in January 1861 to build an armored, floating battery.

Construction was under the direction of Lt. J.R. Hamilton, a former officer in the United States Navy,

and was carried out on the city's waterfront within sight of Fort Sumter.

Although records of its dimensions are sketchy, one historian reports that the battery was about 25 feet wide and approximately 100 feet long. It apparently was built of pine logs, buttressed in front with palmettos and the whole strapped with iron.

In appearance, it resembled a barge with a three-sided peak-roofed barn placed across the bow and a platform of sandbags extending off the entire width of the stern.

The "barn" had only one long side which was placed toward the front and was pierced with four "windows" for cannon. The open side faced the rear or the interior of the barge.

Toward the rear, below the water line and protected above by sandbags, was the powder magazine. Shot, according to contemporary sketches, was stored behind the guns in bin-like holes in the deck. Beneath the sandbagged platforms at the rear, which served to counterbalance the weight of the guns, and on a separate raft, was a small hospital.

Construction of the floating battery created considerable comment in both North and South. New Yorkers were invited by the New York Herald to visit their offices and see a palmetto log of the type being used in

the floating battery. Another palmetto log, according to that newspaper, was brought north for sale to Barnum who, however, refused to pay the $150 requested.

Washington was kept advised of the progress on the "raft" by the garrison at Fort Sumter.

An engineer officer, Capt. J.F. Foster, apparently thought little of the battery. He wrote his superiors: "...I think it can be destroyed by our fire before it has time to do much damage...." A few days later he wrote:"...I do not think this floating battery will prove very formidable...."

He also passed along a rumor that the battery was a failure since it drew too much water. About a month later, he qualified this by saying he had heard that "...the raft does not meet expectations...." He also reported that it was being covered with railroad strap iron of approximately an inch thickness instead of railroad "T" rail which would have been much thicker.

Foster also gave a clue to the type of at least two of its four guns for he reported March 6 that "two 8-inch columbiads are lying on the wharf ready to be put on board...."

Maj. Robert Anderson, commander of Fort Sumter,

(Continued On Page 10)

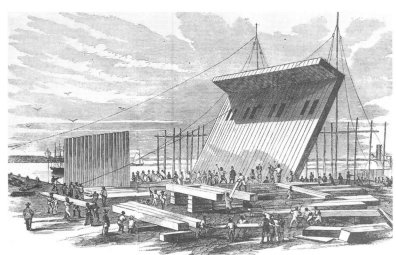

South Carolinians erecting floating battery.

Floating battery nears completion.

(Continued From Page 9)

SOUTH BUILDS

also was considerably interested in the monster being fitted out against him and asked Washington for instructions if the battery was brought near the fort prior to the opening of hostilities.

He was told that if he was convinced the battery was advancing to attack him, he would be justified in firing, but if it were simply being emplaced at a good distance for possible future use, then he was to use forbearance.

The South Carolinians apparently watched construction of the battery with mixed feelings. Civilians were delighted with the new weapon and visited it in crowds March 15 when a salute of seven guns was fired to celebrate its completion.

Troops who were to man it, however, took a somewhat dimmer view. They dubbed it "The Slaughter Pen" and feared it would tip over in action. Its eventual use from a grounded position may have been out of deference to public opinion.

The battery was emplaced at the west end of Sullivan's Island (Cove Inlet) during the night of April 10 or early morning hours of April 11 and fired from this position during the bombardment of Fort Sumter April 12-13.

It was under the command of Lt. Hamilton and manned by members of Company D of the Artillery Battalion.

Although apparently reasonably successful, its later history is vague.

A Coast and Geodetic survey chart of 1863 shows it anchored in the harbor between Middle Ground and Fort Johnson. Charts of 1865 fail to show it, indicating

that it had been moved or destroyed by then.

There is evidence that it went to pieces during a storm in the latter part of 1863. One writer, who served on Morris Island, stated that fuel was scarce until one morning after a storm the beach was strewn with logs which were said to have been from the floating battery.

Another, writing of a trip to Charleston immediately after the war in 1865, described the entrance to Charleston as follows: "...Just beyond the ruin (of Fort Sumter) at the left, lies the wreck of the famous old floating battery... A portion of one of its sides, with four portholes visible, still remains above the water...."

This side with the four "portholes" apparently was the front of the battery through which cannon pounded Fort Sumter at the opening of the Civil War four long years before.

W.R.

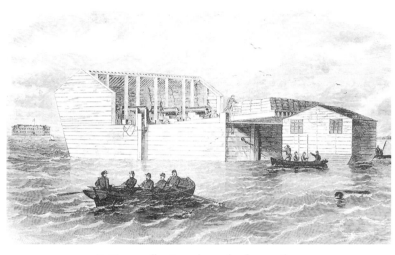

Battery afloat and ready for action.

In action. Gun crews bombarding Fort Sumter.

Steamer Fails To Aid Sumter

When historians talk of the "first shot" of the Civil War it is a matter for disagreement. The men on the spot in Charleston Harbor Jan. 9, 1861, thought they knew when the first shot came.

It was fired when a Citadel cadet at a battery half concealed in the sand hills of Morris Island sent a ball whistling across the bow of a steamer named Star of the West.

The Star of the West wore a huge U.S. ensign on her foretruck when she steamed up the Main Ship Channel on Jan. 9. Her 'tween decks were crowded with U.S. soldiers. Otherwise, she was out of character as a ship employed on a vital military mission.

The Star of the West was a passenger liner, diverted from her run between New York and New Orleans for this business of bringing reinforcements to Maj. Robert Anderson in Fort Sumter. She had no guns, no protection and no business venturing where shots might be fired at her.

That was exactly why Gen. Winfield Scott, the aging

general-in-chief at Washington had picked her for this task. Gen. Scott had an idea the Star of the West could do what a warship could not do — steam into Charleston Harbor without arousing the suspicions of the South Carolinians.

Army headquarters had ordered strict security thrown about the Star's mission, but somebody had leaked the news. The politicians had it first and then the newspapers. Long before the Star of the West arrived off Charleston Bar, it was gossip in the streets of Charleston that the Yankees had decided to send reinforcements to Fort Sumter.

The South Carolina authorities were still red-faced over their blunder in permitting Maj. Anderson and the soldiers at Fort Moultrie to set up housekeeping in Sumter on the day after Christmas. They took pains to prevent another embarrassing slipup. Guardships were stationed in the Main Ship Channel which curved past Fort Sumter and southward along the shore of Morris Island. The Vigilant Rifles, a company of firemen

turned soldiers, were on duty on the island. They were routed out of their barracks and sent to camp in the open at the south end of Morris. The newly-erected battery which Citadel cadets had just built near the northern end of the island was alerted.

The Southerners had already smashed the expensive fresnel lenses in the lantern of the Charleston lighthouse and pulled down the lighthouse itself. Now they hauled away the lightship off Rattlesnake Shoal and picked up the buoys which marked the way across the bar.

When the Star of the West arrived off Charleston about 1 a.m. on the 9th, after three days at sea, Capt. McGowan found the coast dark. He spent an exasperating night standing off and on the low-lying coast, groping for a safe passage. First light came before her leadsman on a platform near the bow found the path.

Then the Star steamed boldly across the bar, flushing the South Carolina guardship Gen. Clinch before her. The Clinch fled up the channel, signaling the alarm with flares and rockets.

With daylight coming on, Lt. Charles J. Woods, the commander of the troops aboard the Star of the West, took pains to make the ship look like a peaceful merchantman. His non-coms herded the curious soldiers below. They sat there for the next hour or so listening to the swish of the engines and hearing the thump of cannonballs against the planking but missing the rest of the show entirely.

As the Star moved slowly up the channel, Lt. Woods studied the shore of Morris Island. Ahead, a little on the port bow, there were the ramshackle buildings of an old hospital. Above the hospital towered a flagstaff. From the staff flew a banner such as Lt. Woods had never seen before. It was red, with a white palmetto tree upon it.

The Star drew abreast the red flag. There was a puff of smoke from the dunes at the foot of the staff.

The Star of the West.

(Continued On Page 11)

(Continued From Page 10)

STEAMER FAILS

A swish and a splash announced the arrival of a shot across the bow.

The Star of the West was flying her regular colors at the gaff. Lt. Woods, startled and angered by the greeting from the shore, ordered the biggest flag aboard — a standard garrison flag — displayed at the foretruck. The flags made no impression on the inhospitable battery in the dunes.

A shot struck the side of the Star below the feet of the leadsman. Another slammed in farther aft. There was little damage. The range was long for the old-fashioned 24-pounders served by green Southern boys and the shooting was poor. Already the Star was moving out of range. Lt. Woods and Capt. McGowan turned their attention to Fort Moultrie up ahead. To reach Sumter, the Star would have to pass within a thousand yards of the gunners there.

A gun was fired from Moultrie. Lt. Woods looked at Sumter hoping for a sign of recognition or assistance. The Stars and Stripes were flying there, but no gunfire came from Sumter's walls. Another shot from Moultrie. Another.

Woods decided not to take the chance. Capt. McGowan, shaken by the encounter with the battery in the dunes, ordered the wheel put over. The Star began to turn to starboard. Riding the ebb tide, she swept down the channel. There were a few more rounds from the battery in the dunes, but the Star was moving fast. Soon she was beyond range.

A.M.W.

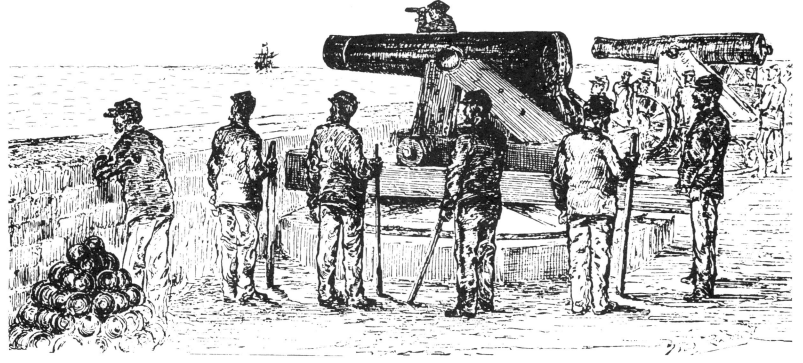

Fort Sumter garrison watches firing on Star of the West.

Anderson Debates Aiding Vessel

From the parapet of Fort Sumter, a mile and a half northwest of the Morris Island Battery, Maj. Robert Anderson and his Federal garrison heard the first gun with anger and disbelief.

Since first light — which came about 10 minutes after six that morning — the lookouts at Sumter had been watching a strange steamer off the bar and speculating upon her identity.

Capt. Abner Doubleday, the senior captain and second in command at Sumter, had trained his glass upon the steamer. He had made out a U.S. flag flying at her gaff.

When he saw the cannonball from Morris Island splash near the strange vessel's bow, Capt. Doubleday raced down the stone steps which led to the gloomy interior of the fort. He cut across the parade ground to the room where Maj. Anderson slept in his big sleigh bed and roused the major from sleep. Doubleday thought the ship might be the relief vessel which newspapers sent to the garrison had reported was coming.

Anderson, too, had heard the rumors, but he did not believe them. He had nothing official from Washington on the subject. His faith in headquarters left him no room to believe that his superiors might leave him uninformed of such an important undertaking. Just the same, he told Capt. Doubleday to turn out the garrison.

While the long roll echoed through casemates and passageways, the two officers climbed to the barbette tier of guns, the highest level of the fort.

With the crews of the few guns for which he had men available, Maj. Anderson watched composedly as the steamer threaded her way between the splashes of the Southern shells. Now the Stars and Stripes was clearly visible. An old-fashioned walking beam drove the steamers paddle wheels.

The sight of the walking beam appeared to confirm Maj. Anderson's impression that this was not a relief ship. Warships did not have walking beams. Surely Washington — if it was going to send anything at all — would send nothing but a full-fledged man-of-war.

Some of the other officers, however, were confident that the steamer was bringing them the help they wanted so badly. They looked expectantly at their commander. He ordered the guns hauled into firing position, but he did not give the command to fire.

The gunners, patient and puzzled, waited at their stations. The officers stamped up and down the terreplein in angry impatience. Maj. Anderson wrestled in silence with his decision.

Shoot or be silent?

Start a war or let somebody else start it?

Pressed by his officers, Maj. Anderson agreed to try to signal the steamer by lowering and raising the flag. But the halyards were twisted and the flag could not be used.

A few moments later a gun was fired from Fort Moultrie. The Star of the West turned and raced down the channel.

"Hold on," said Maj. Anderson. "Do not fire."

A.M.W.

Citadel Cadets Fire on Ship

The first shot at the Star of the West had been fired by a young Citadel cadet named G.W. Haynesworth. He and 39 fellow cadets had been assigned to Morris Island Battery — afterwards known as the Star of the West Battery — because they were better grounded in artillery tactics than in other military business.

Sharing their quarters in the abandoned smallpox hospital were two militia units, the Zouave Cadets and the German Riflemen. They were typical militia outfits, assigned to serve as infantry support for the guns in case the Yankees should get it in their heads to try an amphibious assault.

This fear had some foundation. The battery which the cadets manned was of the crudest kind. It consisted of parapets of sand over which the guns peered. There was no protection for the crews. The broadside of a light warship might have swept the whole affair into ruins. A landing force would have found it open and unprotected in the rear.

Worst of all, the Southerners felt the brooding presence of Fort Sumter whose guns looked down upon their backs from 3,000 yards away. Actually, the battery was out of range of Sumter's guns, but neither side knew it.

The clamor of the guard ship hastening up the channel was plenty of warning for the gun crews on Morris Island. A few preliminary taps and the drummers started the compelling long roll that was the call to action stations.

The identity of the strange vessel was uncertain, but it did not really matter. Maj. P.F. Stevens, the battery commander, had positive orders from Gov. F.W. Pickens: Fire into any strange vessel which attempts to pass up the channel. Maj. Stevens sighted one of the guns himself. Then he turned the piece over to young Mr. Haynesworth.

Haynesworth snapped one end of his firing lanyard into the ring of the friction primer protruding from the vent of the gun. Then he uncoiled the lanyard to full length and drew it taut.

At 7:15 a.m., Maj. Stevens gave the command, "Fire."

A.M.W.

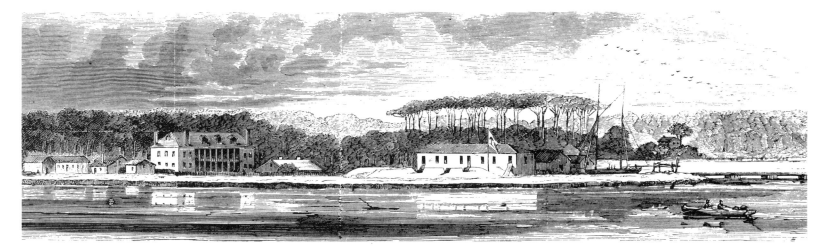

Sketch of Fort Johnson drawn by an officer in Maj. Anderson's command at Fort Sumter.

Fort Johnson Erected 1708

Fort Johnson, which lobbed the opening shot of the Civil War at Fort Sumter, has played an important, though generally bloodless, role in Charleston history.

The first fort was erected about 1708 and named for Sir Nathaniel Johnson, governor of the Carolinas under the proprietary government. Prior to this, the site had been known as Windmill Point.

A second fort, built in 1759, apparently was an enlargement of the first.

The fortification saw action in 1775. At this time, three companies, commanded by Lt. Col. Isaac Motte, sailed from the city under the cover of darkness. The captain of the ship, however, refused to run in close to Johnson, so the men were forced to wade ashore across about a quarter of a mile of mud flats.

By daylight, although only a portion of the force was ashore, it was determined to attack the fort. When the leaders arrived, however, the gates were found open and the guns dismounted.

The work on the guns had been done during the previous night by a party from the British sloop Tamar who left the fort not long before the South Carolinians arrived.

A few weeks later, Johnson fired three shots at the Tamar and another British sloop. The shots were fired at extreme range and missed their targets. The vessels were firing on attempts by the South Carolinians to block the Hog Island Channel.

June the following year saw Sir Peter Parker's attack against the fort on Sullivan's Island across the harbor. However, the vessels stayed out of range and Fort Johnson did not participate in this engagement.

Four years later, a British siege map showed Fort Johnson "destroyed," whether by enemy action or storms has not been determined.

Fort Johnson as it looks today.

A third fort was built in 1793 a little to the rear of the previous work but was abandoned in 1800 when a severe storm breached the seawall. By 1807 it was reported in ruins and, although apparently some work was done in the area during the years, by 1815 it was again reported in ruins, a severe storm in 1813 having almost destroyed it.

An 1821 survey refers to the site as the "remains of Old Fort Johnson" and by 1827 scarcely a vestige remained. It was dropped from later reports of United States fortifications although two permanent buildings for officers and men were built at the site and remained after hostilities started in 1861.

Four days after Maj. Robert Anderson's move to

(Continued On Page 13)

Exterior view of Fort Johnson at the end of the war. 1865 photograph.

Fort Sumter Dec. 26, 1860, and three after the capture of Castle Pinckney and Fort Moultrie, South Carolina forces got around to occupying Fort Johnson which the Federals had considered in too bad repair to be used by troops.

There was, however, a fuel dump at Fort Johnson and Anderson's small garrison was to sorely miss it

during their occupation of Fort Sumter.

During the next three months, the South Carolinians erected two mortar batteries at the fort and a battery of three guns, only one of which bore on Fort Sumter. The east mortar battery, consisting of two weapons, was the one that fired the opening shot.

The next three years saw considerable building activity at Fort Johnson which, including its outpost forts, turned it into an entrenched camp of considerable strength mounting some 26 guns and mortars.

Although the fort did a certain amount of firing during the war, its major action occurred July 3, 1864, when within a short time Fort Johnson defenders repulsed a Union force from Morris Island of two regiments of infantry and some 60 artillerymen.

The attacking force, in small boats, lost at least seven killed, 16 wounded and 140 captured compared to the Confederate's one killed and three wounded.

Fort Johnson was evacuated along with the harbor's other forts during the night of Feb. 17-18, 1865.

W.R.

Fort Sumter Ringed By Fire

Hard on the heels of the creation of the new Confederacy, "Peter" Beauregard — Brig. Gen. Pierre G.T. Beauregard, CSA, late major, U.S. Army — came up from Montgomery to take command at Charleston.

He looked searchingly at the works erected by the South Carolinians against Maj. Robert Anderson and heard the reports of the officers in charge. He did not entirely like what he saw and heard. The Carolinians were eager, but they were amateurs at war.

They had concentrated their forces at Fort Moultrie and at Cummings Point, the two places nearest Fort Sumter. In their concern for the fort, they had almost overlooked the channel entrances.

Beauregard saw two sides to the problem of Fort Sumter.

First, he must prevent a relief expedition from getting through to Maj. Anderson.

Second, he must be able to batter the fort into submission if it became necessary, and it looked like it would.

To Gen. Beauregard, Fort Sumter looked like "perfect Gibraltar." Properly armed and garrisoned, he said, it would be impervious to anything but constant shelling night and day from the four points of the compass.

His idea was to make Fort Sumter the center of a "ring of fire" which would isolate it from the sea as well as reduce it to ruins.

While he explained this, the Carolinians listened with respect and confidence. As a field commander, "Peter" Beauregard was to be star crossed. As an engineer and gunner, he was to enjoy the reputation of a master throughout the war about to begin.

The tempo of operations promptly began to change in Charleston Harbor. Even the anxious Federal officers with their spyglasses at Fort Sumter could see that new energy had been added to the high command at Charleston.

"Renewed activity was soon manifested at every point in the harbor of Charleston," Dr. Samuel Crawford, the observant surgeon at Fort Sumter noted. "New batteries sprang up along the shore, steamers carrying men and materials passed and repassed day and night under the guns of Sumter."

The new commander dispersed the clusters of guns threatening Sumter. A system of detached batteries was erected along the shores of Morris and Sullivan's Islands. Mortar batteries were moved back as far as possible beyond the range of the guns of the fort.

Beauregard marked out on a map the location the "floating battery" was to take at the western tip of Sullivan's Island.

Requisitions went out over the telegraph wires to Montgomery. Additional mortars came from Savannah and Pensacola and were placed at Fort Johnson and Mount Pleasant. A new mortar battery at Mount Pleasant closed the "circle of fire."

To Beauregard's discerning eye, the work the Carolinians had undertaken to strengthen Fort Moultrie appeared defective. It was torn down and done over again.

While all this was going on, the men who were to man the guns were not forgotten. There were about 3,000 of them scattered around Charleston Harbor when Beauregard arrived, as many more to come later.

Most of them were "volunteers," in service for what the vast majority thought would be a lark. The rest were "regulars" — in name only.

When choleric Roswell Ripley, the lieutenant colonel commanding at Fort Moultrie, got orders on March 6 to send a pair of guns to a battery commanding Maffit's

Ironclad battery being erected at Cummings Point.

Channel, he was forced to reply that this trivial operation was beyond his means.

"I have not a single artificer to send," he said, "some 290 indifferent artillerymen....and 318 helpless infantry recruits, almost without arms, without clothing and totally and entirely unfit to meet the enemy."

The situation in which Lt. Col. Ripley found himself prevailed everywhere to a lessor or greater degree. Without competent officers to drill them, the ignorant soldiers ran wild. They neglected their duties and killed one another playing foolish games with loaded muskets and pistols. One was stabbed in the eye with a bayonet while roughhousing with some barrack mates. He died.

It took more time to whip the men into shape than to relocate the guns. On March 8, a clumsy gun crew exercising with "blank" charges at Morris Island, bounced a shot off the wharf at Fort Sumter, doing no harm but leaving "a long white scar" in the paving. There were apologies and the incident was smoothed over. Investigators reported the gun had been left loaded with a live round at a previous drill. Nobody had

thought to check to see that the bore was clear before starting the next day's drills.

Nonetheless, things did improve right along. Daily practice with handspike and rammer, interspersed with a few real shots to get the range, had its effect. Everywhere the shooting eyes of the troops improved.

By March 26, Gen. Beauregard was able to report that "My defensive and offensive batteries... will all be finished and armed tomorrow night or the day after."

Capt. Foster, the engineer officer at Sumter, spent much of his time on the parapet sizing up things around the harbor. His spyglass kept him almost as well posted as if he had been able to peep into the reports flowing into Gen. Beauregard's office.

In early April, things looked about like this to Capt. Foster:

SULLIVAN'S ISLAND

The floating battery — two 42-pounders, two

(Continued On Page 14)

Confederate mortar battery on Morris Island.

(Continued From Page 13)

FORT SUMTER

32-pounders.

Next to it, a potent 9-inch Dahlgren gun.

Next to that, a battery of two 32-pounders, two 24-pounders.

Just west of Fort Moultrie, three 10-inch Mortars.

Behind Moultrie, two 10-inch mortars.

In Moultrie, three 8-inch columbiads, two 8-inch seacoast howitzers, five 32-pounders, four 24-pounders.

MOUNT PLEASANT

Two 10-inch mortars.

MORRIS ISLAND

A battery of two 42-pounders and one rifled Blakely gun.

A battery of four 10-inch mortars.

An ironclad battery, three 8-inch columbiads.

A battery of three 10-inch mortars.

That made 30 guns and 18 mortars bearing on Fort Sumter from the "four points of the compass" mentioned by Beauregard.

It was more than enough for the task at hand.

A.M.W.

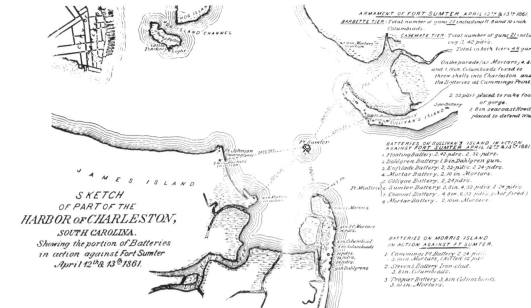

Southern fortifications bearing on Fort Sumter April 12-13, 1861.

10-inch columbiad mounted as a mortar at Fort Sumter to fire on Charleston. It was not used during the bombardment.

(The artist, not present at Sumter, has shown the cannon bearing to seaward. Actually, Charleston should lie at the reader's left.

Federal Garrison Prepares Defenses

The first thing Maj. Robert Anderson did after arriving at Fort Sumter Dec. 26, 1860, was to take steps to prevent the angry South Carolinians from carrying the fort with a rush.

He had only 65 enlisted men to defend an area intended for 650. There were not even guns enough mounted to fill all the embrasures through which an enemy might come pouring. Maj. Anderson ordered the embrasures filled up with bricks and stones.

This was an easy order to give but hard to carry out with the few hands available. But the little garrison turned to the task with a will, working feverishly at first and then more slowly and methodically as the hesitancy of the South Carolinians became evident.

Stumbling through the gloomy interior of the big, uncompleted fort, piled high with guns, carriages, shot, shell, derricks, timbers, blocks and tackle and coils of rope, the soldiers and workmen hired by the engineers mixed mortar and hauled brick for weeks on end.

Eventually, order was brought out of chaos. Guns were mounted, shells brought up, splinter proof

(Continued On Page 15)

Measures to defend Fort Sumter sallyport.

(Continued From Page 14)

FEDERAL GARRISON

protection arranged for the casemates which opened on the parade ground. By the middle of February 1861, Maj. Anderson felt fairly secure in his lonely post.

Still the soldiers found it impossible to survey what was going on around them in Charleston Harbor without feeling apprehensive. The secessionists were very busy, too, and they had the advantage of unlimited material and labor.

The guns of Fort Moultrie, which the Federal soldiers had put out of commission temporarily, were in position again. The South Carolinians were strengthening the fort with sandbags and timber works. Every detail of this labor the Federal officers scrutinized with anxious care. After dark on long winter nights, they worked on reports to Washington which they hoped would attract attention to the seriousness of their plight.

Besides preparing to defend themselves, Maj. Anderson thought he and his men might discourage attack by being ready to take the offensive themselves.

They mounted a gun to fire on the City of Charleston. They tried the range. With a two-pound charge, the ball flew high and far. The Federals were satisfied they could land shells in the streets of Charleston if they chose.

This was a comfort, but a small one in the face of difficulties with which the garrison was surrounded.

Food was short. Fresh provisions came from Charleston for a while, but the hardworking soldiers ate it up about as fast as it came. Early in January, the main supply of staples at the fort were a few barrels of pork and a few barrels of flour. This represented about four months supply, enough to carry the soldiers to about the end of April.

Presently, the fresh food stopped coming through and the garrison resigned itself to a dreary, unhealthy diet of salt pork and biscuit.

Officers and men kept busy enough during the daylight hours, but the long nights were dark, unrelieved by the glimmer of candles or the friendly glow of fires. There were no candles.

There was little fuel. Mrs. Capt. Doubleday came to visit her husband in the fort and he broke up a good mahogany table to build a fire to keep her warm. The soldiers ripped down a construction shack on the parade ground and converted it to fuel. Later on, the blacksmith shop went the same way.

There was plenty of powder, but cartridges were short. The charges for the guns were made up in flannel cylinders sewed by the soldiers. The fort's ability to defend itself depended on a good supply. There were just six needles available. The soldiers plied them busily and took elaborate pains to prevent one from going astray.

There was no shortage of energy or ingenuity. While some of the soldiers heaved and sweated the big guns

into position in a few selected embrasures on the barbette tier, others contrived imaginative defenses against assault.

Overhanging galleries were built outside the walls. From them the soldiers could fire down on the heads of enemies.

Large barrels filled with rocks — each with an 8-inch shell in the center — were placed along the parapet. In an emergency, the barrels would be rolled over the parapet to explode like giant hand grenades.

The engineers dug holes in the paved walkway along the south wall of the fort. Into each hole they placed an explosive charge. Then they tamped the holes full of rocks and debris. If an enemy passed that way, these "fougasses" would be touched off.

The gates which opened out onto the wharf on the Morris Island side of the fort were narrowed and reinforced. Small guns were located where they could sweep the approaches of the fort with canister.

A forgetful gun crew exercising with one of these pieces forgot about the windows which opened through this wall into the quarters inside the fort. The blast from the gun shattered every pane of glass. After that, the chill winds blew through this wall into the quarters making life even more miserable than it had been.

With the fort ready to reply to an artillery bombardment or beat off an attack by boat, the garrison had a right to feel that it had accomplished a great deal.

Would it be enough?

The soldiers hoped so, but even as they surveyed their accomplishments, a new worry began to nag at them. The Charleston newspapers reported that rifled guns had been ordered for the Southern batteries. Fort Sumter's bricks were hard but they were not intended to withstand the impact of rifle shells.

Maj. Anderson speculated on the possibilities of this new kind of weapon and wrote his worries to Washington. There they received his confidences as information and did nothing to reassure him. As late as April 1, nobody in the U.S. capital was ready to tell the major how much longer he would be expected to stay in Sumter.

The only thing Maj. Anderson knew for certain was that he was expected to fight back if he was attacked. He was ready to fight if necessary. He didn't think it would be necessary because, he told Washington, he would be starved out first.

On April 3, there was sickness and hunger in Fort Sumter and food for a few days.

"Unless we receive supplies, I shall be compelled to stay here without food or to abandon this post very early next week," the major wrote on April 5.

Next week?

Washington had hoped he might stay there comfortably a bit longer while it debated the problem with itself. But Anderson's message forced the government's hand.

Now Fort Sumter had to be relieved.

The chance of war had to be taken.

A.M.W.

Main battery of Fort Sumter bearing on Moultrie and the channel.

Who Fired First Shot Of The War

A hand jerks a lanyard.

A 10-inch mortar belches flame, smoke — and a round shell that arches across the water leaving a fiery train from its fuse.

It explodes over Fort Sumter, briefly illuminating the brick fortification in the darkness.

The time is 4:30 a.m. The date, April 12, 1861. The shell has launched four years of war — and a 100-year controversy over who fired it.

Chief contenders for the honor were three men, a captain, a lieutenant and a civilian.

The civilian was Edmund Ruffin of Virginia. His name was preceded so often in contemporary reports by the word "venerable" that the word almost has become a part of it. Through the years, Ruffin's name has kept cropping up as that of the man who pulled the lanyard, but he is one who may definitely be eliminated. The first shot was fired from Fort Johnson. Ruffin was at Cummings Point, the last, not the first, location to go into action.

That leaves the captain, George S. James, and the lieutenant, Henry S. Farley. Both were at Fort Johnson.

James was in overall charge of the two mortar batteries as well as other troops at the fort and Farley in command of the East, or Beach, Mortar Battery which fired the first shot.

Col. Alfred Roman's book on Gen. P.G.T. Beauregard's military operations quotes the general: "...From Ft. Johnson's mortar battery at 4:30 a.m. issued the first shell of the war. It was fired, not by Mr. Ruffin of Virginia as has been erroneously supposed, but by Capt. George S. James of South Carolina to whom Lt. Stephen D. Lee issued the order...."

Unfortunately, Gen. Beauregard, who was in command of Confederate troops in the Charleston area, was not present at the firing of the first shot. He wrote, presumably, from official reports. Did he mean that James actually pulled the lanyard, or that James' battery fired on Lee's order?

Some years later, Lee backed up Roman's quotation of Beauregard, or perhaps the quotation backs up Lee since he, no doubt, was one of Beauregard's sources for a report on the firing.

At any rate, in the 1896 issue of the Southern

Historical Society Papers is an article with this statement by Lee: "...Capt. James offered the honor of firing the first shot to Roger A. Pryor of Virginia. He declined saying he could not fire the first gun. Another officer then offered to take Pryor's place. James replied: 'No. I will fire it myself,' and he did fire it...."

Another attempt to identify the man who pulled the lanyard was made by Dr. Robert Lebby who also witnessed the firing, but from a distance too far to determine who fired the weapon. Dr. Lebby gathered as much material as possible and his article ran in the News and Courier of 1906 and the S.C. Historical and Genealogical Magazine of July 1911.

He quoted an eyewitness, Dr. W.H. Prioleau, surgeon at Fort Johnson who was present at the East Battery when the first shot was fired. Prioleau stated that he did not know who actually pulled the lanyard, but he recalled that the weapon was sighted by Farley and that James gave the order to fire. Presumably, Dr. Lebby commented, James would not have given the order to himself.

Dr. Lebby also quoted a letter from Farley written

(Continued On Page 16)

Fort Johnson signal shell bursts over Fort Sumter. Scene was sketched from Cummings Point.

(Continued From Page 15)

WHO FIRED FIRST SHOT

many years after the war: "...That the circumstances attending firing of the first gun at Sumter are quite fresh in my memory. Capt. James stood on my right with his watch in his hand and gave me the order to fire. I pulled the lanyard, having already carefully inserted a friction tube, and discharged a 13-inch mortar shell...." (Farley's memory was in error here. The first shot was from a 10-inch mortar. The South had no 13-inch mortars at Charleston.)

If Farley's memory tricked him as to the caliber of the weapon, did it also play him false in other parts of his statement?

It's a puzzling question and one which no one has been able to solve conclusively. However, it seems fairly certain that the initial shot was fired by either James or Farley — and from there on you can take your pick with the odds about even.

W.R.

Opposing Leaders Were Once Friends

By comparing the two men who were chief actors on the war stage at Charleston April 12, 1861, we get a miniature view of the tragedy of the Civil War.

Robert Anderson and Pierre Gustave Tutant Beauregard were military officers of the United States who had served her all their adult lives. Each had received honors at her hands. Each had ancestral roots which went deep into her history. They knew and respected one another. Beauregard had been Anderson's pupil and friend.

Yet here they were as dedicated enemies in Charleston Harbor.

Both Maj. Anderson and Gen. Beauregard were "Southern men," but they did not by any means place the same values upon Southern connections.

Beauregard was a Louisianan, eager, ambitious and proud. Most important, he was the inheritor of a belief in states rights deeper and more comprehensive than anything most U.S. citizens can imagine today.

Anderson, sober, sensitive and deeply religious, was a native of Kentucky, a border state. He was southern in his politics and certain instincts, but otherwise his feelings were for the Union. It did not occur to Anderson to put state above country when sorting out his patriotic inclinations.

The attitudes of the two men as they faced each other in Charleston Harbor clearly reflect this fundamental difference in their thinking. From Beauregard's letters and dispatches, we get the picture of anger and determination. In Maj. Anderson's we find determination, too, but touched by sadness.

Of the two men, Anderson was the more closely connected with Charleston. His father, also a U.S. soldier, had served at Fort Moultrie against the British in 1780. When Charleston was surrendered to the Redcoats, this earlier Maj. Anderson had been packed off to the city to a British jail. He lay there nine months.

His son was just the kind of man to take a sentimental view of this connection with Charleston.

Five feet nine inches in height, Maj. Anderson in 1861 was a well set up man of soldierly figure.

"A stranger would read in his air and appearance determination and an exaction of what was due him," said Harper's Weekly in January of that year.

His painfully slow progress up the list of commissioned officers since his graduation from West Point in 1825 had been marked by praise and by commendations for gallantry. In Mexico, he had served with skill and had been wounded as well as praised.

"A True soldier and a man of the finest sense of honor," said his friend and fellow West Pointer, Jefferson Davis. And a patriot in a broad sense of the term.

P.G.T. Beauregard — Old Bory or "Peter" the soldiers called him — was a patriot, too, but of a different kind. He was a son of an aristocratic family of South Louisiana. When he announced he wanted to attend West Point, his parents were shocked. They had no objections to soldiers as such but they had no use for the U.S. Army. As good creoles, his father and mother thought that joining the Army was carrying cooperation with Americans too far.

Still, they let him have his way because they knew from experience it was impossible to move him once he had made up his mind.

Beauregard, short, swarthy and dour, was a good officer, but where soldiers like Maj. Anderson extended their loyalties to the country, Beauregard reserved his for the Army alone.

Like Anderson, Beauregard starred in the war with Mexico. Unlike Anderson, who was content to accept honors modestly, Beauregard sought to insure himself a place in history. He wrote a book about his experiences and gave it the grand title: "Personal Reminiscences of an Engineer Officer During the Campaign in Mexico Under General Winfield Scott in 1847-48."

By 1856, 18 years after graduation from West Point, Beauregard was only a captain. He was disgusted with slow promotion and low pay. He decided to resign. Superior officers, who were aware of his talents, flattered him into changing his mind.

Instead, he went to New Orleans in charge of Army engineering works there. It was an important post but it did not use up all his time and talent. He dabbled in politics, ran for mayor of New Orleans — strange occupation for an Army officer on active duty. He was

Gen. P.G.T. Beauregard

defeated, took it philosophically and began to sound off on the subject of national affairs.

Secession was being talked all over the South, and Beauregard wrote and spoke in favor of it. At the same time, he was writing letters recommending himself for the choice position of superintendent of West Point.

Incredibly, he landed the post. He lasted one day. His superiors in Washington suddenly recognized that they had placed an avowed secessionist in charge of training the officers who might have to fight to save the Union. The day after he became superintendent, his orders were revoked.

Beauregard protested. He could not understand what led his government to remove him, a faithful soldier of the Army, from a position where he might do great harm to its interests.

"So long as I keep my opinions of the present unfortunate condition of our country to myself," he wrote, "I must respectfully protest any act which might cast...reflection upon my reputation...."

Then he packed up and left. On his way home to New Orleans, a telegram reached him. Louisiana had seceded. Beauregard resigned.

A more perceptive man than Maj. Anderson, Beauregard knew that war was coming. He set out to insure himself a high position in any army formed to fight it. Jefferson Davis made him a brigadier general and sent him to Charleston.

The situation there was made to order for Beauregard's talents. A splendid engineer, he set about refining the crude preparations the unskilled Carolinians had made to capture Fort Sumter.

When Beauregard arrived in Charleston on March 3, 1861, the Southern soldiers were a long way from being ready to capture Maj. Anderson despite months of preparation. A little more than a month later, they were completely ready.

While Maj. Anderson prepared with a heavy heart to fire on his countrymen, Beauregard went about the same task with zest and vigor.

This was the measure of the two men — each of whom knew and loved the phrase "our country" but who applied it in different ways to different things, as millions of men were about to do.

A.M.W.

Maj. Robert Anderson

Confederate Col. L.T. Wigfall (standing) and U.S. Maj. Robert Anderson discuss terms for surrender of Fort Sumter.

(Northern artist, not present at Fort Sumter, drew on his imagination for this scene. Actually, the meeting occurred inside the fort.)

Fort Sumter Surrenders

The small boat nudged against the wharf of Fort Sumter.

A visitor stepped ashore, but he was in no mood for sight-seeing. It was Saturday afternoon, April 13, 1861, and shot and shell were knocking pieces from the brick walls of the fort with an unhealthy regularity.

The visitor glanced at the flames from the burning officers' quarters near the gateway and decided on a safer entrance. He headed for an embrasure through which, after waving a white flag tied to his sword tip, he was permitted to crawl into the casemate.

The visitor was Col. L.T. Wigfall, aide-de-camp to Gen. P.G.T. Beauregard.

Stationed at Cummings Point on Morris Island, Wigfall had watched the pounding of Fort Sumter from the ring of Southern batteries around the harbor.

He had seen fires start aboard the besieged fort, die down, then flare anew as shell and hot shot found their marks. Finally, one gained too much headway for the defenders to knock it down.

Flames shot above the walls, smoke poured into the casemates and oozed out of the embrasures.

The fire from the fort's cannon slowed to an occasional round, then died entirely. The flagstaff, weakened by several hits during the morning, fell.

Thinking the fort had struck, Wigfall obtained a small boat and with Pvt. H. Gourdin Young of the Palmetto Guard and Negro oarsmen started for the fort.

The Cummings Point batteries had ceased fire but, unseen by the colonel, the flag of Fort Sumter had been replaced and Fort Moultrie continued firing.

Having entered the fort, Wigfall asked to see the commanding officer, Maj. Robert Anderson. While Anderson was being notified, Wigfall pointed out to officers and men in the casemate that the fort was in sad straits and urged that they raise the white flag.

Told that Sumter's flag was again flying and that none but the commanding officer could hoist a white one, Wigfall asked that his own flag be waved to stop the fire from Fort Moultrie.

This also the defenders refused to do but told the colonel he could wave his flag if he wished. Climbing into an embrasure, Wigfall waved the flag for a few moments, then a Fort Sumter officer permitted a corporal to relieve him.

The corporal's tenure at flag-waving was short-lived, however. Soon after he had started, a shot struck near the embrasure and the corporal jumped back inside the casemate declaring to Wigfall that "he would not hold his flag, for it was not respected."

About this time, Maj. Anderson arrived. He had been delayed by a trip outside the fort where he mistakingly believed Wigfall awaited him.

Wigfall commended Anderson on his defense of the fort and renewed his request that hostilities be suspended pending arrangement of terms of evacuation.

Asked what terms, Wigfall replied: "Any terms that you may desire — your own terms — the precise nature of which Gen. Beauregard will arrange with you."

Anderson accepted the offer saying that the terms he accepted were those proposed by Beauregard on April 11. These were that he evacuate the fort with his command taking small arms and all private and company property, saluting the United States flag as it was lowered and being conveyed, if he desired it, to any Northern port.

Having reached this agreement, Wigfall left and the white flag was raised.

A short time later, a boat arrived from the city bearing three other aides of Gen. Beauregard. Informed of Wigfall's visit, they acknowledged that he was an aide of the general but said he had not been near Beauregard for two days.

Thereupon, Anderson said he would run up his flag again and continue the battle. The aides prevailed upon him, however, to let hostilities remain suspended until they could check with Beauregard.

They returned later in the day with word that the conditions were accepted with exception of the salute to the flag, an exception which later was removed.

Anderson remained in charge of the fort until the following day when he lowered the United States flag and left for New York.

W.R.

Exterior view of Fort Sumter the day after surrender.

Artillery fire snapped flagstaff.

War's First Death Accidental

The white flag flies over Fort Sumter. The first battle of the Civil War has ended — a clear-cut victory for the Confederacy.

The guns fell silent shortly after 1:30 p.m., April 13, 1861, but negotiations between Maj. Robert Anderson, commander of the fort, and Brig. Gen. P.G.T. Beauregard, commander of Confederate troops, took up the rest of the afternoon.

About 7 o'clock that night, Anderson accepted Beauregard's surrender terms. They were the same ones offered two days before the bombardment started and provided for the removal of the Fort Sumter defenders to the United States port of their choice, that they retain small arms as well as company and private property and that they salute their flag upon lowering it.

Anderson agreed to protect the fort during the night. Consequently, no Confederate troops were stationed at Sumter until after its evacuation. This was arranged for 11 a.m. of the 14th with a Confederate steamer to convey the Union troops to vessels of the Federal fleet lying off the Charleston bar.

However, an accident delayed the departure and not all of Anderson's men were embarked until after sundown. By then it was too late to cross the bar. The Union troops were placed aboard a steamer where they remained during the night and were taken across the bar the next morning and transferred to the steamer Baltic for the trip to New York.

The accident occurred during the saluting of the United States flag.

Anderson had decided upon a salute of 100 guns upon lowering the flag, and, because it flew from the ramparts, decided to use such barbette guns as were still serviceable.

There was a stiff breeze blowing off the sea that morning into the muzzles of the guns as they fired.

About midway through the salute, a smouldering piece of cartridge was blown back toward one gun by the wind. It landed on one of the piles of cartridges which had been placed near each weapon amid the debris of broken masonry.

The cartridges exploded sending bits of broken masonry whirring across the parapets like shell fragments.

The blast instantly killed a gunner, Pvt. Daniel Hough, fatally injured another private, who died soon after reaching a Charleston hospital, and injured four others. One of the injured was taken to a hospital in the city from which he later was sent north without exchange. The remainder were treated and permitted to accompany the other troops.

Funeral services for Pvt. Hough were held by the Confederates at the fort and he apparently was buried on the grounds. Hough was the first man killed in the war, the bombardment having produced few casualties and no deaths.

State troops under the command of Col. Roswell S. Ripley took over the fort after the evacuation and raised the Stars and Bars and the Palmetto flags from the ramparts.

The new tenants began at once to clean up the debris of battle and to strengthen the defenses, weakened by the bombardment, in preparation for the years of siege that would see the fort pounded into rubble but never again surrendered.

W.R.

Sallyport and burned officers' quarters (left)

Southern officers inspect columbiad emplaced in Sumter as a mortar (right)

War Ended Privateering

Privateering, lucrative sideline of many of the world's wars, met its end during the Civil War.

It was tried by the South and considered by the North, but a combination of circumstances soon lowered it to a very minor status.

Hardly had the guns ceased firing at Fort Sumter when President Jefferson Davis announced that he would issue letters of marque to privateers to prey on Northern shipping.

Remembering the tales of former wars when privateers became patriotic, and generally rich, heroes. Southerners leaped at the chance to harry Yankee shipping and make a quick buck on the side.

New Orleans privateers were the first under way with those from Charleston a close second. But the green crews had hardly gotten over the first taste of seasickness when they found that privateering in the 1860s was a far cry from that of the early part of the century and before.

Several factors had combined to virtually end privateering in this "modern" age although few Southerners were sufficiently farsighted to see it.

The first, and perhaps the foremost, was an occurence in Europe several years before with which no Americans were even concerned, yet it effectively knelled the death of privateering by a nation that didn't even exist at the time.

In 1856, the major nations of Europe had signed the Declaration of Paris which outlawed privateering. The United States, however, refused to sign the declaration, so the Confederate States felt perfectly free, legally and morally, to engage in this age-old form of warfare.

Confederate privateers, however, soon discovered that the nations which had signed the declaration, and this took in the major countries of the world, closed their ports to both privateers and prizes.

Consequently, once a privateer took a prize, it had to be sent to a Confederate port. This was simple enough in the beginning, for the Union blockade amounted to virtually nothing.

However, before long the blockade was enforced and merchant ships slow enough to be caught by privateers, were too slow to run the blockade.

This considerably dampened enthusiasm for privateering since it removed the profit. After all, a prize was no good on the high seas — it only became valuable after it had arrived in port and been sold.

Another problem for the privateers was a lack of sufficiently good ships in the South to outrun or outfight the better vessels in the United States Navy.

In addition, the North, although it had refused to sign the Declaration of Paris, conveniently forgot its privateer heroes of the Revolution and the War of 1812, and, with the shoe on the other foot, promptly branded privateersmen pirates.

The first privateer to capture a ship in the Atlantic, for instance, was the Savannah. She was a former pilot boat that slipped out of Charleston harbor June 2 to go a-roving.

The following day, the Savannah overhauled the brig

U.S frigate St. Lawrence sinks Confederate privateer Petrel Aug. 1, 1861.

Joseph and sent her into Georgetown.

That afternoon, however, the cruise of the Savannah came to an end. She tangled with the United States brig Perry and, because the Savannah had lost a bit of her top rigging in a blow the previous night, was unable to outrun the man-of-war. She surrendered after a 20-minute fight.

The crew of the Savannah was taken to New York where the men were paraded through the streets in chains and thrown into cells reserved for felons. They were accused of piracy and faced a hangman's noose at the end of what their captors hoped would be a speedy trial.

The case, in view of its legal aspects and because it would establish precedents, took on international importance, but the actual trial was delayed several times.

In October, the privateersmen finally faced a jury, but the case ended in a mistrial. A new trial was scheduled for the next term of court.

Other privateersmen were not so lucky. During the delays of the Savannah trial, members of the crew of the Jefferson Davis, captured taking a prize into port, were convicted of piracy.

Conviction of piracy carried the death penalty, and the Confederacy set out to save its privateersmen. President Davis set in motion a previously announced plan of retaliation. Captured Union Army officers were designated as hostages for the condemned men. They were selected by lot and were treated in all respects as their counterparts in the Northern prisons with their ultimate fate to die on the gibbet if the privateersmen were hanged.

This apparently tied Lincoln's hands. There were no more piracy trials and the entire matter was quietly dropped. Both those convicted and those awaiting trial

within a year or so were returned home in the normal exchange of prisoners, several to again man privateers.

About two months after the Savannah tangled with the U.S. brig Perry, another Charleston privateer, the Petrel, also had the misfortune to flirt with a man-of-war.

The Petrel was the former U.S. revenue cutter Aiken which had been taken over by South Carolina at the time of secession. She was later sold and her new owners, a group of Charleston gentlemen, fitted her out as a privateer with a commission dated July 10, 1861.

She slipped out of Charleston harbor during the night of July 27 and at dawn bumped into the U.S. frigate St. Lawrence. The Petrel made a run for it, but by 10 a.m. the frigate was in range.

The captain of the Petrel ran up the Confederate flag and went into action, more as a matter of honor than with any hope of success — he had two guns, the frigate mounted 52, almost all of far heavier caliber.

The Petrel got off one good shot. It went through the enemy's mainsail and nicked a yard. Then the frigate brought her forcastle battery to bear and an 8-inch shell slammed into the Petrel's bow.

The Petrel filled rapidly and her crew surrendered, four of them drowning before they could be rescued. The others were taken to Philadelphia for trial, but were later exchanged.

The little Petrel was not the first, nor the last privateer to discover too late that the privateering era was gone. A few took several prizes and proved highly profitable, but the majority sooner or later wound up flying a white flag under the guns of a Union man-of-war.

W.R.

The privateer Savannah *(left)*

Rig advised for ships chasing privateers *(right)*

Contemporary sketch of Confederate steamer Nashville destroying Federal vessel.

Nashville Slips Through Blockade

Left behind when Mason and Slidell slipped over Charleston Bar on their way to England, the CSS Nashville did not linger long in port.

Perhaps encouraged by the success of the Theodora in breaking through the blockade with her two distinguished passengers, Lieut. R.B. Pegram, commanding the Nashville, promptly laid plans to get his own ship out.

The prescription for success remained unchanged: a dark night and a high tide at the bar. The principal passages to sea were guarded by Federal ships. Fighting clear was out of the question — the Nashville carried but two feeble brass 12-pounders for armament.

Lieut. Pegram had to accept the risks of trying to creep unseen past the blockaders through the dangerous rips and shallows beyond Fort Sumter.

At best it was a chancy business and Pegram sought to reduce the risks.

Selecting a likely point for passage over the bar, he buoyed it with two small boats a few hundred feet apart.

On the night of Oct. 26, 1861, the Nashville made her break, steaming past Fort Sumter in the darkness, hoping to be over the horizon and gone before the moon should rise.

Feeling his way out toward the bar, Capt. Pegram found bad luck. A gale was blowing. One of his marker boats had been swept away.

As the Nashville groped for deep water over the bar, her keel grated on sand. She suddered to a stop.

Pegram backed off, tried again, hit again, kept going, pushing his ship bodily over the bar with her straining paddle wheels. Meanwhile he kept an anxious eye on the lights of the blockaders. They showed no signs of action.

The moon camp up, lighting the surface of the sea. The blockaders stood out in clear relif. Still they showed no signs of excitement.

With a final thrash of her wheels, the Nashville slid over the bar. The blockaders slumbered on.

Of the Confederate ship, the Federal lookout saw never a sign. Long after the Nashville had gained the high seas and was threatening Federal shipping, the commander of the blockading squadron refused to believe she had escaped him. Angry dispatches rolling in from his superiors finally prompted him to send a quartermaster aloft to study the harbor with a long glass.

But the Nashville was long gone. After a brief stop at Bermuda, she headed for England. Pausing briefly at the entrance to the English Channel, she captured and burned the Yankee ship Harvey Birch.

On Nov. 21, 1861, while correspondence was still flying between those responsible for the blockade off Charleston, the Nashville was safe in Southhampton, the first Confederate warship to show the Stars and Bars in English waters.

A.M.W.

Trent Affair Irked British

The escape of the Confederate commissioners Mason and Slidell from Charleston Harbor aboard the steamer Theodora in October 1861, started a train of events which brought the Southern states briefly and tantalizingly close to independence.

Having arrived safely in Cuba on the first leg of their journey, the two envoys caught the British steamer Trent for Southhampton.

In the Old Bahama Channel, north of Cuba, the Trent was overhauled and captured by the Union cruiser San Jacinto. Mason and Slidell were marched off the British steamer at bayonet point and carried away to prison in New York.

When the San Jacinto made port there, her captain found a storm of angry protest breaking around his ears. The British government had fought a war with the United States 50 years earlier to establish her own right to make seizures on American ships. Now the British lion yelped in outrage at the same treatment.

For a time it looked as if England might recognize the Confederacy and give armed aid to boot. British troops boarded transports bound for Canada. The South rang with sardonic praise for the overzealous captain of the San Jacinto whose ill-considered action promised to accomplish for the Confederacy what diplomacy could not.

But the promise was not fulfilled. In London, sober appraisal of Yankee power soon restored calm. The lion ceased to roar. The Washington government released the prisoners.

Ironically, release from prison marked the failure of the mission of Mason and Slidell. In London, they were never able to arouse a tiny fraction of the interest they had stirred all over Europe by languishing in jail on the other side of the Atlantic.

A.M.W.

Warships and transports of the "Great Expedition" on their way to Port Royal Sound, Oct. 31, 1861.

Fleet Sails For Port Royal

In no engagement of the Civil War was the inability of the Confederacy to protect its extensive coastline so clearly demonstrated as at Hilton Head in 1861.

The strategic designs of the Union against the South Carolina coast were well conceived. Only the total poverty of the South in resources for coastal defense permitted them to be executed in decisive fashion, however. The Federal expedition to Hilton Head is notable not entirely for overwhelming victory but also for singular good fortune in reaching the objective area at all.

It is doubtful whether so clumsily contrived an armada as the fleet which gathered in Hampton Roads in the fall of 1861 had ever in history set out upon so important a mission. Certainly, no harbor in the United States had ever looked upon as heterogeneous an array of ships as that preparing for the voyage south.

There were, as one witness put it, all kinds of war vessels at Hampton Roads, "regular, irregular and defective." There was the big, modern steam frigate Wabash, flying the blue flag of Flag Officer DuPont, and carrying a battery of 46 guns. A broad white stripe broken by black ports marked her as a "regular."

There was the ancient sailing sloop Vandalia — vintage 1830 — as innocent of steam power as the Santa Maria. She was a genuine warship, too, but a holdover from a vanishing era, a "defective" because of her inability to maneuver independently of the wind.

There was a small flock of "90-day gunboats," rushed to completion in the marvelously short time of three months — and suffering accordingly from defects of crude conception and hasty birth.

There were the "irregulars," sidewheelers, converted merchantmen of different kinds, hastily armed and fitted out for war.

One of the fleet which defied precise classification was USS Pocahontas, a screw sloop lately arrived from the Washington Navy Yard. She partook to some degree of the faults of all categories of her sisters.

Though a regular warship, incorporating all the usual eccentricities of U.S. naval vessels of the period, she had been purchased from merchant service and therefore possessed peculiarities of design all her own.

Nominally a steam vessel, she had a ridiculously small coal capacity — 63 tons. Her battery was of the kind which even sailors in a transition period of weaponry looked askance. She carried a 10-inch gun — maximum effective elevation, two degrees — and four 32-pounders, all smoothbores. There was also a small rifled piece. Its projectiles, her officers testified, were quite as apt to go end over end as to fly true. It was rarely used.

The Pocahontas' skipper was Cmdr. Percival Drayton, an officer well thought of in the service but one over whom a cloud lay. He was from South Carolina. There was suspicion in Washington that Drayton, a Southerner, and the Pocahontas, small and slow, might prove to be liabilities to the fleet bound for Port Royal.

In addition to the men-of-war, such as they were, the Navy was employing 20 colliers and six supply vessels. The Army, which was going to have to make landings, had its own fleet of 25 transports. Aboard were 16,297 soldiers under the command of Gen. T.W. Sherman (Thomas W., not "War is Hell" Billy). Six hundred of these troops were U.S. Marines, crowded aboard the old coastal passenger steamer Governor.

The fleet, largest ever commanded by an American officer, sortied from Hampton Roads Oct. 29 in a symmetrical V-formation led by the Wabash.

Coming around Cape Hatteras, the ships encountered a rising wind and a dull, leaden sky. The sea worked up. In the afternoon watch, Friday, Nov. 1, station keeping became impossible. The flagship signalled "disregard the order of sailing." Fleet formation vanished in the teeth of the rising gale.

Mist and rain shut in. Watch officers took shelter under the lee of the weather bulwarks. There they could be within shouting distance of the helm and at the same time keep a lookout to windward, ready to bear away if another ship should be sighted coming down upon them.

Some captains, fearful of a lee shore, bucked mounting seas to gain an offing. Others, fearing collision more, allowed their ships to lie to under close-reefed canvas, engines barely turning over.

Rain swept like stinging sleet across the decks as the storm approached hurricane fury. Phosphorescent spray broke high in the rigging.

Forty-eight hours of this punishment might have been enough to scatter any fleet in the world. DuPont's force, manned partly by amateurs, was literally blown to the winds. By Saturday morning, with the storm still raging, but one vessel remained in sight of the flagship.

Some of them the flag officer never saw again.

The ancient Governor, whose element was the placid waters of New England sounds, began to break up. The sea smashed her frames, crippled her engine, shattered her rudder, chopped down her funnel and left her a hulk.

The frigate Sabine stumbled upon her in the darkness and ordered her to anchor. Then the Sabine's captain, in a spectacular display of seamanship, snatched the Governor's crew and all but seven of the 600 Marines to safety.

Afterwards, the storm took over again. It rolled the Governor on her beam ends and swept her under.

The supply ships Peerless, Belvedere, Union and Osceola, either sank or never reached their destination. The big transport Winfield Scott jettisoned her cargo to save the regiments aboard and made it all the way. She was so badly damaged that she never left Port Royal.

The Isaac Smith, one of the extemporized ships of war carrying eight heavy guns, threw them overboard to save herself.

While confusion reigned for miles across the tumultuous ocean, the Pocahontas rode out the storm with serene ease.

She might have been feeble and cranky, said her first lieutenant, but she was a veritable sea-bird for wind and wave. Under the sure hand of Capt. Drayton, the little ship found herself still in fighting trim as the storm began to abate — even if her skipper and her navigator, their reckoning blasted by the gale, had to admit they had temporarily lost their way.

There was nobody around to ask directions of, either.

The Pocahontas found herself alone as Sunday, Nov.

(Continued On Page 24)

Union fleet bombards Confederate forts defending Port Royal Sound.

(Continued From Page 23)

FLEET SAILS

3, dawned bright and clear. She completed the rest of the voyage alone, too.

Full speed for the Pocahontas was not much to boast about. "Economical speed" — enforced by scanty coal supply — left her nothing at all with which to catch up.

While DuPont was rounding up a nucleus of his scattered forces, the Pocahontas, out of touch, plugged slowly southward by herself. Her captain fretted about his inability to rejoin and found additional cause for gloom as he contemplated his fuel reports from below.

Coal was vanishing fast. Drayton thought he might not make Port Royal at all. If he did, he would probably not have enough fuel on hand to risk going into battle.

What would the country say about a naval officer from South Carolina who missed a fight on his own doorstep?

Day broke, Nov. 7. The Pocahontas lookouts raised Tybee light, Savannah River entrance, a few miles away. Tybee was just down the coast from Hilton Head. The chief engineer reported coal on hand for less than 24 hours.

Then, "Sail Ho."

Dead ahead there loomed up through the haze one of the fleet colliers, a schooner loaded with coal. She had proceeded down the coast. Now, blessedly, she was at hand! Drayton, unwilling to lose a minute, took her in tow and steamed as fast as he could for Hilton Head, coaling as he went, feeding his hungry furnaces to the limit.

As the Pocahontas and her grimy consort drew near the entrance to Port Royal Sound, a breeze brought a rumble of gunfire to the ears of the watch on deck.

Too late, Drayton thought.

But not quite.

The coal schooner was cut loose. The Pocahontas hurried on.

The fight was still raging when she hove in sight of the fleet. Drayton and the Pocahontas plunged into action. Left out of the fiery circle, DuPont was tracing in the Wabash, the Pocahontas took station on the flank of Fort Walker. There she poured in a cross fire.

Though already punished half to death by the broadsides from the main fleet, Fort Walker was goaded into fresh life by the galling fire of the Pocahontas.

"Good line but high," commented her executive officer as Confederate salvoes whizzed overhead. A projectile shattered the mainmast but the Pocahontas' hull and crew escaped unharmed.

Presently the fort was silent. The fire of the fleet tapered off and died. From beyond the harbor entrance, where the transports lay, there came the sound of band music and troops hurrahing.

Amid general jubilation, the Pocahontas steamed through the fleet in search of the flagship. Perhaps Capt. Drayton was looking for a chance to explain why he happened to be late. If so, he never got the chance — or needed it.

As the Pocahontas swung by the Wabash, Flag Officer DuPont's voice boomed reassuringly across the interval between the ships affirming for all to hear his confidence in the naval officer from South Carolina.

"Capt. Drayton, I KNEW you would be here."

A.M.W.

Imaginative sketch of the bombardment of Forts Walker and Beauregard.

Union Fleet Defeats Forts

In a blazing ring of gunfire traced by Union warships upon the placid face of Port Royal Sound late in 1861, it was possible to read promise of ultimate triumph of Northern seapower over a landbound Confederacy.

The capture of Port Royal Sound confirmed the apparent helplessness of the South against descents from the sea.

It became perfectly clear to Northerners — and discerning Southerners as well — that the Navy was to be a decisive weapon.

Steaming in sweeping, lazy circles under the muzzles of the Confederate guns, presenting first one broadside then another to hapless Southern gunners, 15 U.S. warships smothered the two forts which protected Port Royal Sound.

When the last gunner, except the dead and wounded, had fled in shock and despair before the iron hail, the fleet moved quietly in. It landed the force of soldiers it had brought with it and hoisted the Stars and Stripes. From this vital stronghold thus secured, Union ships and soldiers would range freely up and down the coast for the rest of the war.

"The Battle of Port Royal, occurring a little less than seven months after the fall of Fort Sumter, was of surpassing value in its moral and political effect, both at home and abroad," wrote Lieutenant Commander Daniel Ammen of the gunboat Seneca, one of the captains of the fleet.

"It gave us one of the finest harbors on the Atlantic Seaboard, affording an admirable base for future operations; and, by the establishment of coaling stations, shops and supply depots, made it possible to maintain an effective blockade within the entrances of the whole coast from Charleston to Cape Florida...."

This was, if anything, an understatement of the case.

The Battle of Port Royal offered to the Confederates positive proof of the power of the fleet and its heavy batteries. It compelled them to reorganize all their strategic thinking with regard to the defense of the coast.

On the advice and orders of no less an engineer than Gen. Robert E. Lee, new commander of the Department of South Carolina, Georgia and East Florida, the Confederates promptly abandoned all minor points of defense along the coast not protected by difficult water approaches. They moved their troops and batteries out of the range of naval gunfire. Thereafter, they placed their chief reliance in the obstruction of channels as the principal element of defense.

The strategy which brought the United States Navy and its attendant Army to Port Royal was clear and to the point: The Navy needed a base upon which to anchor its tenuous line of blockaders stretching up and down the coast. On the map, Port Royal, located midway down the line, looked good and orders went out to capture it.

The battle plan of Flag Officer (that's what they called admirals then) Samuel F. DuPont was equally straightforward. On Nov. 5, 1861, DuPont called his captains to his cabin in the frigate Wabash, at anchor off the entrance to Port Royal Sound.

DuPont told his captains to form their ships into two parallel columns. The columns would push right between the Confederate forts on Hilton Head and Bay Point, shooting as they went.

Inside the sound, the western column, composed of nine heavy ships led by the Wabash, would turn to port and swing in a giant circle between the two forts, pouring in broadsides as it passed them at close range.

The eastern column, composed of light gunboats, could make sure that the feeble squadron of Confederate river craft stationed in the sound did not cause trouble. When they had disposed of the Confederate ships, the gunboats could lend a hand with the forts, taking stations from which they could lay down a crossfire.

The heavies would maintain the circle of fire until the forts were silenced.

This arrangement permitted DuPont to bring to bear in rapid succession the firepower of more than 50 heavy guns, first upon Fort Walker on Hilton Head and then upon Fort Beauregard on Bay Point as his ships swung in their circle.

Returning to their vessels after getting their orders, the captains were anxious for an early start. They were pleased to see the flagship Wabash weigh anchor almost immediately. Before she was in range of the forts, however, the Wabash reported herself aground on Fishing Rip shoal. The Union sailors had to resign themselves to another night of idleness while the Wabash was worked off the shoal.

The next day, the 6th, the wind blew hard from the west, in the teeth of the fleet, whipping up the calm waters of the sound and threatening to make maneuvering and gun laying difficult. All morning, DuPont seemed on the point of giving orders to move to the attack. At last, discretion got the better of his impatience. He ordered the battle deferred.

His reward for waiting out the gale was a bright,

(Continued On Page 25)

(Continued From Page 24)

UNION FLEET

serene dawn on the 7th. The lookouts reported scarcely a ripple on the expanse of the sound. In the first light of morning, the fleet began to prepare for action, but hours passed before the signal came. While the crew of the Wabash struggled under the stern of their ship to clear a rope which had fouled the propeller, DuPont fumed on the quarterdeck over their heads. Finally, at 9 a.m., the ships were underway.

Driving the tiny Confederate naval squadron before them, the ships moved with precision between the forts. At 9:26 the Confederates opened on the Wabash. A few minutes later, the broadsides of the Federal fleet began to flash.

Presently, the noise of the battle had reached a deafening peak. Seventy miles away, at Fernandina, Fla., people heard the roar and wondered at its meaning. Great clouds of dust and smoke overhung the sound. Giant plumes of sand raised by exploding shells sprouted like tall trees along the shores. The vessels, shrouded in the smoke from their own guns, could scarcely be seen in the haze which clung close to the surface of the great water.

On the main decks of the big ships, the sights and sounds of battle were weird and impressive. With hatches battened down, only faint light crept through the ports. The flashes of the guns gave fitful illumination by which hundreds of men worked to load their guns, run them out and fire.

Within a few minutes, the fleet had run the gauntlet of Confederate fire. The Wabash put her rudder to port and turned back past her consorts. In her wake, the squadron moved slowly past Fort Walker. Once more it dropped its shells with precision into the little earthwork.

The flank squadron, having chased Commodore

Landing of U.S. troops at Fort Walker after bombardment.

Tatnall's river boats into the shelter of Skull Creek, took up enfilading positions.

Again and again, from ranges as close as 600 yards, the fleet delivered its smashing fire. The Confederate gunners began to desert their guns.

At 1:15 p.m., the Ottawa signaled that the enemy was leaving. The Wabash, just commencing another run, held her broadside, moved in close, and fired two inquiring rounds at the silent work. No response. At 2:30, the Federals, landing in small boats, raised the Stars and Stripes above Fort Walker.

Across the sound, the Confederates in Fort Beauregard, where the Stars and Bars still flew, heard the sounds of cheering. Diagnosing the battle as lost, they slipped quietly out of their works, leaving Port Royal Sound in Federal Hands.

A.M.W.

South's Forts Outgunned By Fleet

Sentries on the Confederate forts guarding Port Royal Sound watched Nov. 7, 1861, dawn bright and still — and knew they'd be ducking Yankee shells before darkness came again.

Four mornings ago they had seen the first elements of Flag Officer Samuel F. DuPont's fleet drop anchor off the bar. More vessels straggled in during the day, and the following morning several of the warships bombarded the forts for about 45 minutes causing little damage. The attack probably would have been resumed on the following day had not stormy weather intervened.

The seventh, however, was perfect for the fleet. Hardly a ripple rocked the heavy decks to disturb the accuracy of Union gunners.

Slowly the warships weighed anchor and started their grim advance upon Fort Walker on Hilton Head Island and its companion work, Fort Beauregard, at Bay Point across some 2½ miles of water. Fort Walker mounted 21 guns, of which 13 bore on the fleet.

Beauregard had 18 guns of which seven could be fired at the fleet. The remaining guns in each case were sited for land defense.

The forts had been started only a few months ago and delays and shortages had plagued construction.

Walker, for instance, originally had been designed to mount on the sea face seven of the Confederacy's heaviest cannon, 10-inch columbiads.

But when the engineers were ready for the guns, only one 10-inch had been found and in place of the other six, a dozen lighter weapons were emplaced.

This was a serious mistake for the lighter guns could do little damage to the fleet and the additional number had prohibited the installation of traverses, or mounds of sand between guns, to protect both the weapons and their crews from flanking fire.

Fort Walker opened the battle with a shot at the lead vessel, the Wabash, about 9:25 a.m. Firing soon became general as the ships started into the first of what would be three elliptical courses from which each fort was pounded in turn by broadsides from the fleet's heavest guns.

Although the Confederate gunners obtained hits, they were few because the moving ships, which continually varied the range, presented difficult targets and the bare mention of a breeze served to remove the smoke from the Union guns and push it into the eyes of the defenders of Fort Walker.

The Confederates also had tough luck with their weapons — their best pieces were unusable during most of the engagement. Ammunition for Fort Walker's only two rifled guns was the wrong size and they became unserviceable after two or three rounds had been fired. The fort's largest weapon, the 10-inch columbiad, due to an accident in firing, also was put of action after four or five rounds. Other guns were damaged by enemy fire.

The lack of traverses between Fort Walker's guns became dangerously apparent soon after the battle opened when two or three gunboats took position on the north flank and another, later in the battle, began firing from the south.

The single gun in the south bastion of the fort had been shattered early in the fight by a round shot and no gun had been mounted on the north due to lack of a suitable carriage. This enabled the gunboats, with complete impunity, to pour a flanking fire on the Confederate gunners who had virtually no protection.

Despite the vast discrepancy in number and size of weapons, the experience of broadsides at close range, and the lack of flank protection, the fort's garrison stood to their guns like veterans.

Hilton Head Island was garrisoned by some 1,800 men, but only 220 manned Fort Walker when the battle opened. The remainder were mainly infantry reserves designed to stop a landing from the fleet.

The Confederate commander, Brig. Gen. Thomas F. Drayton, about 10:30 a.m. noticed that the gunners were fatigued from combat and from traversing the heavy guns in sand. He left the fort for a time and brought back 35 men from a light artillery battery, thus swelling the fort's complement to 255.

Shells burst in Fort Walker during bombardment by Union fleet.

(Continued On Page 26)

Photograph of Fort Walker made about 1865.

Fort Beauregard after capture by Federal forces.

(Continued From Page 25)

SOUTH'S FORTS

By 2 p.m., with only three of the fort's guns still in action and powder down to 500 pounds, the fort was abandoned.

Leaving a small rear guard to keep up a slow fire from the three guns still serviceable, the garrison filed out. They crossed a field in rear of the fort which was swept by fire from the fleet and, joined by the rear guard and the infantry reserves, started the retreat to Ferry Point, about six miles away, from which they were transferred to the mainland by steamers and flatboats.

Although the Confederates defended Fort Walker with considerable bravery, there apparently was a certain amount of panic during the retreat which was conducted to a large extent in darkness and with the vivid fear, groundless as it turned out, that at any moment enemy gunboats would appear and cut off their escape.

As evidence of this panic, Gen. Drayton, in his official report, goes to some length to explain how certain rifles happened to be left behind. Union reports show the retreat route was strewn with haversacks, knapsacks, cartridge boxes, canteens and other personal equipment abandoned by the men in their haste.

While the evacuation was under way on Hilton Head, Fort Beauregard was still in action, although by this time ignored by the fleet which was concentrating on Walker.

Beauregard, manned by 149 men, mounted 13 guns in the main work, flanked by three in a hot shot battery and two in a sand battery. The infantry reserve on Bay Point numbered slightly less than 50 men.

Beauregard bore the brunt of the opening shots as the fleet started its first circle and, like Walker, was plagued by faulty ammunition. Fuses did not work properly, some of the hot shot guns were too exposed and others found the range too great throughout most

Northern artist's conception of Confederate retreat from Fort Walker.

of the battle. Ammunition for the single rifled gun had been found to be of the wrong size during the engagement of Nov. 5 and had been refitted. Consequently, the rifled gun did good service until it exploded at the 32nd discharge.

The last gun from Fort Beauregard was fired at 3:35 p.m., the eighth to which the enemy had not replied. Shortly before this, the defenders had realized that

Walker had ceased firing and, when they heard cheers from the Yankee fleet, knew the fort had fallen.

Further resistance being useless, the defenders of Beauregard spiked their guns, destroyed the majority of the powder and started an orderly retreat to Eddings's Island, leaving the Union in possession of one of the finest harbors on the South Atlantic Coast.

W.R.

Union Occupies Hilton Head

The guns that battered Forts Walker and Beauregard into submission were hardly stilled when the triumphant Federal troops set out to take the rest of Hilton Head Island.

The two Confederate forts guarding the seaward approach to Beaufort fell during the afternoon of Nov. 7, 1861.

Shortly after 11 o'clock the following morning, Capt. Q.A. Gillmore of the U.S. Corps of Engineers, set out on reconnaissance across the island — his objective, Seabrook Landing at Skull Creek about six miles from Fort Walker.

Neither Gillmore nor anyone else in the Union Army had the slightest conception whether the Confederates were one or a dozen miles away, so the captain took along a regimental escort of some 900 men.

They started from camp with skirmishers out to protect the main body against attack and apparently made fair time while the route lay through relatively open land. However, much of the way was through

"impenetrable jungle," according to Gillmore, which slowed progress to a crawl and delayed their arrival at Seabrook Landing until 2 p.m.

They encountered not a single Confederate, but found considerable evidence of their passing — in haste if not in panic.

The Southerners retreating from Fort Walker had gone this way and the road was littered with knapsacks, haversacks, canteens, cartridge boxes and other accoutrements thrown away by the men in their hurry to escape an imagined pursuit.

The wharf at Seabrook also held its share of abandoned property including a number of rifled muskets, bayonets and 15 or 18 wagonloads of food.

Gillmore also located an excellent site for a battery which could cut Skull Creek as a waterway between Savannah and Charleston.

He reported that five or six heavy guns could effectively close the creek, but advocated a strong work of 15 guns and 1,000 men to secure the area

against surprise attack.

Returning that afternoon, Gillmore was off again on the night of the 10th to reconnoiter the opposite end of the island. With an escort of five companies, he arrived at daylight at Braddocks Point at the extreme southern tip of Hilton Head.

Again no enemy was met, but a number of abandoned Confederate cannon were found. Gillmore reported that three 24-pounders and a 10-inch columbiad were in an abandoned Confederate work. A quantity of ammunition was found in magazines and a number of rounds of ball, grape and canister were scattered on the beach marking the haste with which the work had been abandoned.

Although the two expeditions accomplished little of great or lasting value, they did prove that the Confederates had completely abandoned Hilton Head — comforting knowledge for Union leaders starting to build an important naval base for serving the blockading fleet.

W.R.

Much Of City Is Consumed By Flames

In the winter of 1861, there died the last echoes of the shouts of triumph with which South Carolinians had received news of the fall of Sumter and victory at Manassas.

Neither of these conquests had achieved what South Carolinians had confidently expected — independence and the end of fighting.

A feeling of elation had persisted — despite some sobering setbacks — but it was finally swept away by defeat at Hilton Head and a general retreat of Southern troops from the guns of the Federal Navy.

From Savannah River to Winyah, the Yankee fleet now ruled the coast. Except at Charleston, where the defenses were numerous and strong, gunboats ranged the inland waters wherever they could find water deep enough to float them.

At the entrance of Charleston Harbor, the garrisons kept the Federals at a respectful distance. While the soldiers were facing east, however, watching the enemy, another struck behind their backs, leveling a quarter of the city they were set to guard.

It was fire.

Throughout the night of Dec. 11, 1861, the troops in the fortifications watched in helpless anguish as flames swept across Charleston from the Cooper River to the Ashley.

By daylight, many of the finest landmarks of the Confederacy, including those nearest and dearest to the hearts of secessionists, lay in ashes. From that time on, Charleston wore the look of a ruined city.

How the fire began nobody could say with assurance.

The first building to go up was the woodworking shop of William P. Russell at the foot of Hassell Street. There, all had been secure a few hours before the alarm sounded. Mr. Russell had checked to see that the fire under the plant boiler was out after the workmen had left at 5:30 p.m.

Then, about 7 o'clock, Mr. Russell himself stepped into the cloudy, windy night and headed home. Just one hour later, the first bells began to sound.

Fires were frequent in the city. Charleston had long ago developed an efficient system to spread the alarm. Unfortunately, for reasons of pride and prejudice, the methods of fighting the fire were not so efficient.

Firemen were all volunteers. There was great competition between the different companies. Sometimes, it seemed, the firemen looked upon a fire as a challenge to prove their physical prowess rather than a menace that might engulf ther crowded, flimsy city.

In other cities, steam engines were beginning to replace muscular firemen swinging on the brakes of hand pumpers. Charleston had a steam pumper, but it was an outcast. It stood ignored in the shed it had occupied since its purchase in 1860. The firemen looked upon its ways with distaste. The firemasters, swinging the gold-headed canes which were their badges of office, kept it at a distance.

When the hand trucks rolled out of their houses toward the crimson glow playing on the clouds above Mr. Russell's sash and blind factory, the steam pumper remained in its shed.

Long before the engines jouncing over the cobbled streets could reach the scene, the blaze had swelled to

Path of fire. Unitarian Church (left) and St. John's Lutheran Church.

monstrous proportions. The brisk wind from the northeast had chilled Mr. Russell on his way home. Now it was breathing hotly upon ranges of tindery wooden buildings. Presently, they burst into flame.

The firemen pumped for all they were worth, but the fire coursed on down to Market and State Streets. There it paused to consume a block of frame dwellings and shops. Afterwards, it ranged up toward Meeting Street. Crossing Cumberland, it narrowly missed St. Philip's Church and closed in on Institute Hall — Secession Hall.

In the Mills House, across Meeting Street from Institute Hall, Gen. R.E. Lee, the military department commander, was relaxing in a parlor. He was not prepared for the swift approach of the fire. Choking fumes filled the hotel corridors. Gasping, carrying a baby which belonged to another guest, Lee beat a retreat, leaving his belongings behind.

The Mills House lay directly in the path of the flames. Its determined proprietor mustered friends and servants, armed with water buckets and wet blankets and fought off the blaze. The fire swept on by, continuing its mad career across the peninsula.

By now it was evident that all that man could do would not be enough to stop it. Even the military engineers, touching off demolition charges, trying to blast out fire lanes with gunpowder, seemed helpless.

The Daily Courier, going to press in the middle of the

roaring night, moaned: "There is no telling where it will end."

Far outside the city, on John's Island, 14 miles away, lay the First Regiment of Rifles. Many of its soldiers were Charleston men. They saw the high towers of flame and begged their commander for permission to go to the city.

When he was slow in giving leave, the soldiers began to break out of camp, legging it through the woods and over the fields toward home until they reached the new bridge across the Ashley.

"The river flowed like a molten tide," wrote one horrified private. "The horrible swath, out of which jetted leaping tongues of flame and curling masses of smoke, was plainly outlined by the tall buildings left on either side, from which the windows, like great, startled, fiery eyes, gazed down on the ruin below."

Six miles at sea, the crew of the Federal transport Illinois, bound from Port Royal to New York, saw the fire and marveled at it. To them it seemed as if the whole city was on fire.

The fire did not touch everything, but what it touched, it all but obliterated. Down went Institute Hall where the Secession Ordinance had been discussed. Down went five churches, 500 residences and many commercial buildings.

St. Michael's and St. Philip's, white as specters against the flames, were spared. The lovely Circular

(Continued On Page 28)

Charleston, after fire of 1861, looking north in Meeting Street. Circular Church is right of center.

(Continued From Page 27)

MUCH OF CITY

Church was destroyed. Its unique, glass-roofed auditorium collapsed about 3 a.m. Its bell tumbled from the high steeple shortly afterwards and fell with a doleful clang into the ruins.

Down Broad Street, the Cathedral of St. John and St. Finbar, next to St. Andrew's Hall, was swallowed up. As the bells of St. Michael's were striking 5:15, the gilt cross atop the steeple of St. Finbar toppled into the furnace below and disappeared.

In the last extremity, the routed firemen, exhausted from hauling heavy machines, scorched, drenched, worn out and weary, beaten and baffled, thought of the steam pumper waiting in its shed. Someone gave the word to bring it out. Its boiler was stoked and in a few moments with a preliminary shriek and much rattling of wheels and valves and cranks, it went to work.

"It remained at work," wrote one fireman, "never getting tired, never wearying but always sending a steady stream of water. The foreman did not have to shout: 'Down with her my hearties,' to get up steam. He simply put his hands upon the valve, blew a blast on his steam whistle to warn the pipemen that he was about to 'shake her up,' and there she was."

There she was, all right, but far, far too late. The fire which had defeated hundreds of men, dozens of hoses and many pounds of gunpowder, could not be checked by this contraption, no matter how wonderfully untiring it might be. The fire kept right on down Broad Street through Logan, New, Mazyck and Savage Streets, making a clean sweep of the private residences in the city.

At last it stood at the river bank, out of fuel. In one last burst of energy, it engulfed the home of W. Izard Bull at Tradd and Council Streets, then it guttered out.

With the great fire, the old life of Charleston ceased to be. Staggered by uncountable losses, the people settled down to endure the war with grim determination. Reconstruction was beyond their resources in the midst of siege. The swath of the fire remained like a dreadful scar across the city until the end of the war.

A.M.W.

Ruins of Institute Hall.

Blockade Strangled The South

The dreariest chore performed by the Union Navy in the Civil War — and its greatest single contribution to victory — was blockade.

Charlestonians had inaugurated the shooting. They also possessed the finest harbor on the east coast of the Confederacy. Therefore, it was not surprising that they should be the first to feel the blockade.

To begin with, the grip was feeble. It grew stronger as time went on. At last, it strangled the Confederacy. Long after other ports had been closed tight, a few blockade runners continued to filter through the Yankee squadron anchored off Charleston Bar, but they brought little more than feeble hope. They were too few to keep the Southern cause alive.

The war was less than a month old when the Federal sloop Niagara hove in sight off the bar and commenced serving notice on passing merchantmen that the U.S. government meant to seal off the city from the sea.

The Niagara, a deepwater fighting ship, was badly suited to this kind of work, like most of the rest of the feeble U.S. Navy. But she accomplished her mission.

Before departing on other business in the Gulf, she put eight foreign merchantmen on notice that Confederate ports were to be off limits. She established the blockade on a respectable, practical and legal footing.

Charlestonians greeted this meddling with their commerce with cries of anger and hoots of derision. They were familiar with the weaknesses of the Federal Navy, particularly its shortage of ships. They were confident the Union could not make the blockade stick.

Besides, they said, England depended on Southern cotton. The British lion would not suffer interference with vital trade.

Across the Atlantic, the lion was consulting lawyers on this very question. The lawyers remembered that in the war of 1812, the U.S. had stoutly opposed "paper blockades" — proclaimed without men and ships to enforce them. Then it had been British blockading Americans.

Now the British, inclined by self-interest to the Confederate cause, were poking exploratory fingers into the fabric of President Lincoln's Blockade Proclamation, seeking holes which might give excuse to tear the whole affair to shreds.

The lawyers pointed with amazement to the tough language of the Blockade Act, much tougher than anyone really intended, thrown together in a panic following Virginia's secession by a cabinet which knew nothing of maritime law.

It provided for absolute blockade. No traffic in or out, period.

The lawyers, digging through their legal tomes, announced that such a blockade was not legal unless it was effective from the very start. In other words, there must be ships to back up the fancy language. If the blockade could not hold water, then it ceased to exist. It must be proclaimed again — and, most important, a probationary period instituted during which ships could be warned but not captured.

"Do you really intend to blockade the WHOLE coast," the royal government asked pointedly. "Yes," said Washington, not at all sure it could be done, but willing to bluff it out.

Such hearty talk by diplomats caused king-sized headaches in the Navy Department. Secretary of the Navy Welles set about scraping up for blockade duty ships of whatever kind. At first there were times — weeks — when the blockade was of the paper kind the lawyers talked about.

Then, late in 1862, the blockade stations began to fill up. Down the coast came the ships, a few at a time,

(Continued On Page 29)

Blockaders off Charleston. Vandalia (left), Arthur Middleton, a prize (center) and Roanoke.

(Continued From Page 28)

BLOCKADERS

then in numbers. Converted ferry boats some of them were. Ex-merchant packets, too. A few regular warships. Later on, some fine, handy, well-armed gunboats.

Some of the improvised watercraft were good, some bad. They rejoiced in names ranging from prosaic — like "Isaac Smith" — to ridiculous — like "Hunchback." But they were ships.

In eight months, the strength of the "soapbox navy" was up to 79. The Confederates had laughed at blockade instead of making serious plans to break it wide open. Now they woke up to trouble too late.

The fleet had come to stay. It brought with it blockade tactics new to naval war with small gunboats operating inside the coast line and ocean cruisers off the deep water ports like Charleston.

The blockaders never succeeded in choking off the flow of cargo in and out of Charleston, but they quickly reduced commerce to the barest trickle.

The trickle, however, included just enough vital military stores to permit the Confederacy to continue to operate on a day-to-day basis. Every ship that slipped through carried a promise that the war would last a little longer.

For most of the officers and men of the fleet, no matter how long they had been on duty off Charleston, the war had already lasted too long.

"Blockading was desperately tedious work," wrote Alfred Thayer Mahan, a lieutenant on the USS Pocahontas.

"The largest reservoir of anecdotes was sure to be run dry, the deepest vein of original humor to be worked out.

"I remember hearing of two notorious tellers of stories being pitted against each other for an evening's amusement when one was driven as a last resource to recounting that 'Mary had a Little Lamb.'"

Compared to those on other stations, however, the blockaders off Charleston were exceedingly fortunate. They were not very far from bases in the Chesapeake and Delaware and, later, at Port Royal.

Supply vessels from the North came regularly at short intervals. They brought food and newspapers, both of which were still fresh when they reached Charleston. By the time the store ships worked around

Preparing merchant vessels in the North for blockade duty.

Florida into the Gulf, to Galveston or Sabine Pass, the news was stale and the ships there got the bottom tiers of beef.

"Charleston," remarked Mahan, "was a blooming garden of social refreshment compared with the wilderness of the Texas coast."

Usually, the weather off Charleston was pleasant enough, too. Many Northerners got their first enjoyable experience with the winter climate of South Carolina.

In daytime, when the seas were smooth, the ships would weigh anchor and move into close quarters to permit officers and men to exchange visits. In these moments of relaxation, old friendships were renewed, former cruises discussed, yarns exchanged.

But this was not enough to take up idle time entirely.

"The dead monotony of the blockade was neither sea nor port," complained Mahan. "It supplied nothing. The crew, once drilled, needed but a few moments each day to keep up the level of proficiency and there was practically nothing to do, because nothing happened that required either doing or undoing."

Under such circumstances, even a storm was a

welcomed change. After a short time, however, it became the rule among blockaders to ride out gales at anchor. So the crews were denied even the departure from routine involved in getting under way in a hurry.

If boredom was the blockaders' worst enemy, the energetic Confederates were a hazard, too, particularly at Charleston. There the Southerners had a fleet of sorts and were experimenting with torpedo boats capable of escaping the eyes of ever vigilant lookouts.

Off Charleston, one dark night, the fleet dozed. A pair of Confederate ironclads fell upon it, scattering the squadron for miles and severely damaging two of its ships. The triumphant Southerners then raised a cry of "the blockade is ended."

It was not ended, of course. The ironclads went home on the next tide and the Federal ships took up stations again, chastised, but resolved to be everlastingly alert from then on.

And they were — when torpedo boats sneaked out, headed for the New Ironsides and the Housatonic, it was good fortune, not carelessness, which permitted the Confederates to score hits each time, sinking the Housatonic and damaging the Ironsides.

A.M.W.

Contemporary sketch of the Stone Fleet under sail on its way south.

Stone Fleet Sunk Off Charleston

Bluff-bowed whaling ships forging their way through the harbor waters were no novelty in New Bedford in 1861, but the fleet of whalers that left port Nov. 2 brought cannon salutes and cheers from citizens thronging the waterfront.

It was a strange fleet with a strange mission which would have repercussions throughout much of the civilized world before it was done.

Known as "The Stone Fleet," the 25 whalers were destined for Charleston where they were to be sunk off the bar in an effort to prevent blockade runners from slipping past the Union fleet guarding the harbor entrance.

About two months before, the government secretly began buying up old vessels in various ports along the North Atlantic seaboard. These were primarily whalers that had seen better days and were destined for the scrap heap before long. They averaged about 300 tons and cost about $10 a ton.

Before the fleet got under way, purchasing agents already were trying to obtain additional vessels for a second fleet. Ultimately, some 45 bottoms were obtained for the two fleets.

The first fleet consisted of 11 barks and 14 ships. Each had been stripped of non-essential gear and

loaded with New England granite blocks until the fleet took on many aspects of a floating quarry.

A captain, two mates and a cook were assigned each vessel as well as nine men for each bark and 10 for the ships.

Before sailing, each of the 25 had one important alteration — five-inch holes were bored in the bottom. Surrounding each hole was a lead pipe and a plug arrangement. When the plugs were removed, the vessel was expected to fill and sink within 15 or 20 minutes.

(Continued On Page 30)

(Continued From Page 29)

STONE FLEET

Although the commodore of the first fleet wanted to follow the coast, he was dealing with a bunch of whaling captains who were strictly individualists. As soon as the fleet cleared port, each captain simply set a bee-line course for Savannah and the cruise took on the aspects of a fatman's race as the ancient whalers lumbered south.

Apparently, the first to arrive was the Rebecca Simms. She made port Dec. 5 with the pack strung out behind and the commodore, who stuck to his plan of following the coast, bringing up the rear.

Their arrival proved a decided shock to the senior naval officer at Savannah who had been left in ignorance of their coming — or their purpose.

Helpless to stop the ragged procession, he watched in horror as ship after ship of this lunatic fleet blundered into his well-run anchorage.

In desperation, he fired off a letter to his superior, Flag Officer S.F. DuPont, commander of the blockading squadron, that "...seventeen ships and barks (had arrived)...but few good vessels among them and all badly found in every respect especially in ground tackle, few having more than one chain and anchor and one of the others no anchor...several ...had arrived in a sinking condition...."

He reported that one parted her chain and ran ashore, another was ashore and bilged. The Phoenix had struck bottom in trying to enter the harbor. She had lost her rudder and was leaking. To prevent her sinking at an undesirable spot, he had her towed to a point where she would make a good breakwater and bridge for landing on Tybee Island at the mouth of the Savannah River. The Archer, he said, had struck three times entering the anchorage and was leaking badly, but was still afloat. He also mentioned that the nightmare was far from ended, more vessels were expected hourly.

Originally, it had been planned to block Savannah with the first fleet, but this plan was abandoned when it was found that the Confederates had already done the job — they had sunk three steamers in the river channel approach of the Yankees.

Consequently, the fleet, which had been towed to nearby Port Royal, set sail Dec. 17 for Charleston. It was now down to 16 vessels. DuPont reported that one put back to New England shortly after her departure from New Bedford and eight had, he said, been put to "very useful purposes," such as store and coal ships at Port Royal.

The departure for Charleston was not exactly awe-inspiring. The airs were too light for the whalers to make headway, so one after another was towed across the bar by escorting vessels.

They spent the night off the bar, then, some under sail, others under tow, set out early the next morning for Charleston where they began to straggle in during the afternoon of the 18th.

Small boats were sent out to buoy the channel and the first whaler was taken under tow for her final run

Sailors
leave
sinking
ships
of the
Stone Fleet.

about 4:30 p.m., Dec. 19. She dropped the hawser near one of the buoys marking the edge of the channel and with headway still on her, moved slowly to the channel edge and grounded.

Sailors let go the anchor as soon as she touched and knocked out the plugs in her hold. Immediately she began to settle as water flowed around her granite cargo while crewmen swung out her two whaleboats, loaded them with personal gear and the ship's instruments and pulled over to one of the escorts.

The Rebecca Simms, which won the race south, was anchored at the other edge of the channel. She sank slowly and in a dignified manner, going down, as one witness put it, "...with every rope and spar in place as a brave man falls in battle with his harness on."

Work continued during the night as each of the old vessels was towed to its designated spot. By morning, only a few remained. These were sunk during the day with one exception, the Robin Hood, aboard which all sails and cordage not worth returning north was deposited. Masts were cut away from all but the Robbin Hood and during the early evening of the 20th, she was burned.

The hulks were sunk in two groups, the first of seven ships in two lines and the second of nine ships in three lines, the lines in each overlapped to prevent

even the most enterprising skipper from weaving his way through.

The dismasted vessels presented a chaotic picture. Some were down by the head, others by the stern, some heeled to the starboard, others to port while a few remained upright. Some were well above water, others almost out of sight, their positions betrayed by sudden geysers of spray as waves slammed into them.

Although the first stone fleet temporarily blocked the main channel off Morris Island, blockade runners were still slipping through Maffitt's Channel near Sullivan's Island.

To block this, a second fleet of roughly 20 vessels left Port Royal Jan. 20, 1862. It was plagued with heavy gales which caused several vessels to part their chains, blew one out to sea for a number of days and drove another close ashore where she sank well away from her designated spot.

Despite the gales, DuPont was able to report that by Jan. 26 the second fleet had been sunk, blocking Maffitt's Channel between Rattlesnake Shoals and the shore. This left only the Swash Channel and a small portion of Maffitt's for Confederate blockade runners to slip into port and these entrances were constantly guarded by at least three vessels of the blockading squadron which stayed on post riding out good weather and bad at anchor.

The sinking of the stone fleets stirred the maritime powers of Europe as probably no other event of the war.

Cries of "vindictive vandalism" and "outrage on civilization" were heard far and wide in Europe, while the Northern press in this country gleefully recalled incidents in history when European ports were similarly blocked.

But shouts failed to raise the sunken vessels and eventually the clamor was stilled to a mere mutter when the Federal government, although admitting no wrong, tacitly informed Europe that no more stone fleets would be sunk.

The storm of protest no doubt had something to do with stopping the sinkings, but probably more important was the fact that they were not particularly successful.

Even in the beginning, Northern officers were under little illusion as to the value of the stone fleets. They knew the wrecks would soon go to pieces under pounding of the seas and the granite would work its way into the sand.

But they needed a breathing spell in which to build sufficient vessels to mount an efficient blockade and this the stone fleet did — a trade of a few ancient vessels for a few precious months.

W.R.

Loaded with New England granite, vessels are sunk off Charleston.

Slaves Steal Confederate Ship

A straw hat and a chance remark led to one of the most courageous exploits of the Civil War and may have changed the history of Charleston.

The hat belonged to C.J. Relyea, captain of the Confederate inland steamer Planter and apparently was sufficiently distinctive to be well known along the Charleston waterfront. It probably, however, was neither new nor in particularly good condition since the captain left it in the vessel's pilot house when he went home for the night.

To him it was just a hat. To the Negro slaves who served as deckhands and firemen aboard the Planter, it was the symbol of authority.

Consequently, one day when Relyea was not aboard and the Negro "hands" were loafing, one of them playfully clapped the hat onto another's head..."Boy, you look jus' like the cap'un," he said.

The incident was immediately forgotten by most of the men, but not by the one who had worn the hat.

This Negro, Robert Smalls, although a slave, was a decidedly unusual man. Owned by Henry McKee, he had been brought up in the Beaufort area and, in accordance with custom, had been permitted to work for various tradesmen, his pay going to Mr. McKee.

Smalls quickly gained the reputation of being a bright lad and after various jobs wound up working for Capt. Relyea aboard the Planter where he rapidly became a first-class pilot for South Carolina waters.

He also had been permitted to marry during this period and he and his wife were saving pennies to buy their freedom although, since most of Smalls' wages still went to Mr. McKee, the attainment of the goal appeared to be many years in the future.

Consequently, the casual remark about the hat started Smalls thinking. If his friends thought he resembled the captain, maybe guards, at a distance, would make the same mistake. If so, there was a chance of stealing the Planter and a quick dash to freedom — or a quicker death at the end of a rope if the attempt failed.

Considered one of the top steamers in the area, the Planter was 147 feet long, a twin-engine, wood-burner of 300 tons. Shallow draft made her valuable in navigation of coastal streams and she also was reported to be the fastest vessel in the harbor.

In addition, the Planter was dispatch boat for Brig. Gen. Roswell S. Ripley, district Confederate Army commander at Charleston. As such, her berth at Southern Wharf (near the present day Shrine Temple) was only a hundred yards or so from the general's headquarters, an area well-patrolled by sentries.

None the less, the night of May 12, 1862, saw seven men, including Smalls, walk openly one at a time past the sentry and quietly gather aboard the Planter.

There they waited until about 3 a.m. when Smalls finally gave the order to fire up.

Smoke from the fire drifted slowly over the city, an added worry for the slaves who feared Charlestonians might smell it and think a house was on fire.

However, no alarm was sounded and at 3:30 the lines were cast off.

Slowly, the Planter eased from the wharf in the bright moonlight — past the sentry who thought she was on routine business.

She went upriver first, and slid gently alongside another steamer, the Etowah, aboard which another of Smalls' men and the wives and children of the company were hiding.

After picking them up, the Planter turned and headed seaward. She moved slowly because Smalls did not want to run past Fort Sumter in the darkness when he might be challenged.

Timing the trip, he passed Fort Sumter about 4:15 a.m.

This was the crucial moment. Any one of the fort's guns could sink the frail steamer and a broadside would smash her to bits.

Now, Smalls donned Capt. Relyea's hat and, as he

The Confederate steamer Planter.

later said: "...stood so that the sentinel could not see my color...."

He also gave the correct signal with the steamer's whistle.

The fort remained silent. Maj. Alfred Rhett, in command, later stated: "...the sentinel on the parapet called for the corporal of the guard and reported the guard boat going out. It was so reported to the officer of the day, and, as it is by no means unusual for the guard boat to run out at that hour, no further notice was taken of the occurrence...."

Normally, the Planter would run out past the fort quite a distance, then turn for the landing at Morris Island.

This time, when near the point to turn, Smalls opened her up and went straight — heading for the Federal blockading fleet lying off the bar a few miles away. On the way, he hauled down the Stars and Bars and hoisted a white sheet.

Seeing the Planter approach, the nearest blockader beat to quarters and was about to fire when the white flag was noticed.

She sent over a boarding crew and Smalls surrendered his vessel.

The Planter's monetary value was not great — she was appraised at $9,000. Nor was her cargo, valued at $168. With one exception, her passengers and crew (eight men, five women and three children) were a liability rather than an asset.

But the monetary value is deceiving. The vessel, since she drew only 3 feet 9 inches, proved invaluable to the North for operating among the shallow South

Carolina creeks and the Planter later participated in a number of engagements including the skirmish at Coosawhatchie in October. She served the Union Army throughout the war and in 1866 was taken to Baltimore by Smalls and sold to private interests. She reportedly was wrecked near Cape Romain in 1876.

Her cargo, although valued low, consisted of four fairly heavy guns, which had been removed from Cole's Island at the mouth of Stono River and were being taken to Fort Ripley in the harbor for installation, and a carriage for another weapon located at Fort Sumter.

The main value of these weapons, along with a 32-pounder and a 24-pounder howitzer with which the planter was armed, lay in their removal from the South which was desperately short of heavy ordnance.

Smalls also was a valuable addition to the Union force, first for the Navy and later the Army. He was an experienced and courageous pilot who later won promotion to captain of the Planter, an unheard of attainment for a man who was only a few months removed from slavery.

But the main prize was the information Smalls brought with him.

He reported that the South was abandoning Cole's and Battery Islands guarding the Stono.

The information enabled the North to land forces on the southeastern tip of James Island and resulted in the disastrous attack against Secessionville.

The Union defeat led the Yankees to abandon their foothold on James Island and to give up plans for attacking Charleston across James Island — a campaign which held considerable promise for success.

W.R.

Ex-Slave Became A Politician

Many war heroes fade into obscurity after the fighting stops, but a former slave who became a hero to the North also made a mark in politics.

Robert Smalls, who abducted the Confederate steamer Planter from her wharf in Charleston and ran her past the forts to the blockading fleet in 1862, was destined for state and national offices after the war.

His rise in politics was inevitable. The Planter episode had made him the darling of the Northern conquerors. His moderate views and kindness toward the family of his former master made him, to the Southern whites, the least objectionable of the freedmen entering politics. Moreover, the fact that he was the pet of the Yankees, led other former slaves to believe he was the smartest Negro in the state. These were an unbeatable combination during the Reconstruction era.

Smalls was named a delegate to the State Constitutional Convention of 1868 and that year was elected to a two-year term in the South Carolina House of Representatives. At its end, he was sent to the Senate, where he served through the session of 1874.

After this apprenticeship in Columbia, Smalls was elected a representative to Congress where he served from 1875 to 1887, with exception of the years 1880-81.

Smalls' career in Congress was not particularly notable. His most important speeches were attacks on the election tactics of South Carolina Democrats and in support of a bill to provide equal accomodations for the races on interstate public conveyances. He also made an unsuccessful attempt to have $30,000 voted to him as additional compensation for the Planter abduction.

Toward the end of 1889, he was appointed collector of customs for the port of Beaufort, a post he held until 1913 except during Grover Cleveland's term.

He was a conspicious figure at Republican National Conventions of 1872 and 1876 and served in the State Militia from 1865 until 1877, rising to the rank of major general.

His last important activity was as one of six Negro members of the State Constitutional Convention of 1895 at which he made a vain effort to prevent the practical disenfranchisement of members of his race.

The last 20 years of his life were spent quietly at Beaufort where he apparently enjoyed the confidence of both races. He died in February 1915 at the age of 76.

W.R.

Robert Smalls

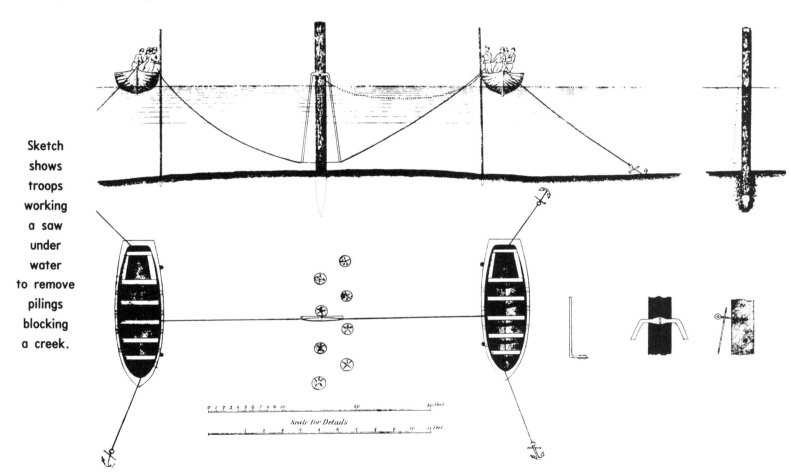

Sketch shows troops working a saw under water to remove pilings blocking a creek.

Federal Device Removed Pilings

Yankee engineers became underwater timber cutters during Civil War operations around Charleston.

Faced with the necessity of removing pilings with which Confederates had blocked shallow creeks, the engineers came up with an ingenious solution.

They devised an underwater saw to cut the 10 or 12-inch diameter poles which studded creek channels like picket fences. It removed them at the rate of one every 10 minutes — probably considerably faster than the Confederates had been able to put them down in the first place.

The device consisted of pieces of iron fastened together in a rough "V" shape. Across the arms of the "V" was bolted a crosscut saw while at the point, which was flattened a bit, was inserted an iron pin.

In operation, the pin was stuck into a hole bored in the piling. The "V" hung inverted with the saw blade underwater against the piling only a few inches clear of the channel bottom.

Boats were stationed on each side of the piling anchored bow and stern. Poles were pushed against the bottom to check lateral drift. A line ran from each boat to the saw blade and by alternately pulling one rope, then the other, the saw was worked across the piling.

The saw was always positioned with tide working against the back of the blade to force the cutting edge into the wood and to tilt the piling as the cut deepened to keep the saw from binding.

When the piling started to fall, a lanyard pulled the pin and retrieved the saw. This enabled a quick repetition of the operation.

The worth of the device was proved during the July 1863 assault on Morris Island when in one night Yankee engineers cleared pilings from a 22-foot wide channel, enabling the scows and launches of the assault force to utilize Folly River for the approach.

W.R.

Secessionville in 1865. The two houses at left are still standing. Fort Lamar is in the distance at right of center.

Secessionville — Hard-Fought Battle

A half-forgotten fort on James Island was the scene of one of the sharpest local engagements of the Civil War.

No marker commemorates the Battle of Secessionville, or Fort Lamar. No plaque names the almost 900 men who were killed, wounded or captured there in the space of a few hours.

Several Secessionville houses which heard the roar of gunfire are still standing. But Fort Lamar, which saw bitter hand-to-hand fighting, is today no more than a few mounds of earth. A road cuts through one side and the remainder is so overgrown with trees and shrubs that it is difficult even to follow its outline.

Its appearance was far different June 16, 1862. Then, Fort Lamar dominated the flat landscape, its yellowish-brown sides of raw earth sloping to parapets on which were mounted four cannon. Inside was

another weapon, a mortar.

The fort was in the shape of a rough "M" with the top, about 130 yards wide, pointed toward the enemy encamped on the southwest tip of James Island. Its sides extended toward Secessionville. Rising above it was a wooden observation, or signal, tower which led the Yankees to refer to Fort Lamar as "The Tower Battery."

The fort had been built at the instigation and insistence of Col. Lewis M. Hatch who had it thrown up by his own troops despite considerable criticism and derision from both civilian and military sources who maintained that it was unnecessary.

Located at the narrow neck of the Secessionville peninsula, Lamar served as the eastern anchor of the Confederates' James Island Defense Line. Its guns could drop shells within the Yankee encampments on the southwestern tip of the island.

At the time of the battle, the fort was commanded by its namesake, Col. T.G. Lamar, who had fewer than 500 men — the smaller part artillerymen in the fort, the rest infantry encamped in fields stretching behind it toward Secessionville a short distance away.

The artillerymen had worked all night of the 15th and into the following morning on the fort's defenses and had been asleep only a short time when about 4:30 or 5 a.m. Lamar was awakened by his pickets who had been overrun by the advancing Yankees.

He ran to the parapet and spotted the enemy less than 700 yards away. They were coming at the double quick, bayonets fixed.

While his junior officers awakened men sleeping near the cannon, Lamar dispatched couriers to notify his commanding officer, Brig. Gen. N.G. Evans, who was

(Continued On Page 34)

Drawing shows battlefield of Secessionville engagement.

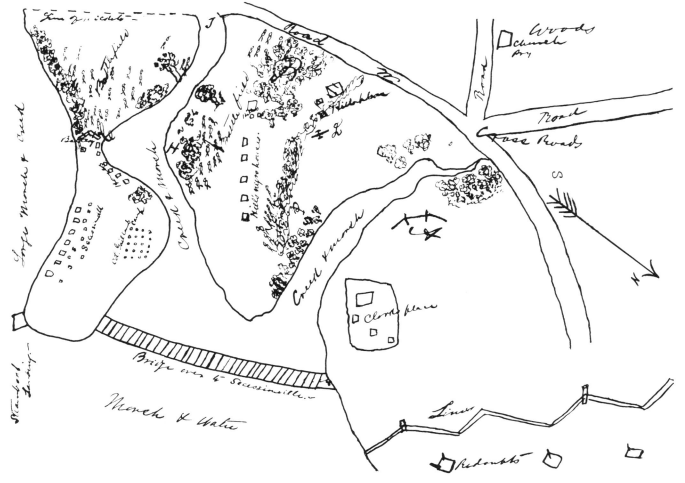

(Continued From Page 33)

SECESSIONVILLE

encamped near Fort Johnson some five miles away, and to summon the infantry.

The footsoldiers had been hauled out of bed at 3 a.m. and set to work dragging cannon to the fort from a floating battery moored to the wharf at Secessionville. Unfortunately, they had stacked their rifles near the dock and when the battle opened, were forced to run almost half a mile for their weapons then return to the fort. This delay left the artillery bearing the brunt of the initial Federal wave.

Watching the approaching Federal lines, Lamar personally trained his heaviest gun, an 8-inch columbiad, but just before it fired its charge of grapeshot into the advancing enemy, he heard the roar of a 24-pounder, the opening gun of the battle.

Then the firing became general. The enemy advance was a blue tide that suddenly, terrifyingly became a line of running, yelling men who swept to the base of the fort and struggled up its sloping sides to the parapet.

There they were met by the defenders — with bayonets, clubbed rifles and even empty whisky bottles, the aftermath of more convivial hours.

For a moment it was touch and go. Then the enemy, those still alive, were pushed back down the slope and were withdrawn a short distance to reorganize.

The Confederates watched them go, glad for a moment's rest. Cannoneers slumped down by the guns. Infantrymen leaned against their rifles while officers moved quietly among them, occasionally moving a man or two to plug holes in the defenses. One, a lieutenant colonel, discovered a quick method of requisitioning new guns to replace those in his unit which would not fire. He simply strolled down the slope at the front of the fort and struggled back with an armload of rifles picked up from dead Yankees.

The Confederate rest was short, however. Within minutes a second, and then a third charge brought Federal troops to the parapets.

Both times they were thrown back. But the Yankees were far from beaten. They took cover amid trees on the flanks and in the furrows between rows in a cotton field that ran in front of the fort perpendicular to the direction of fire. From here, they continued to shoot until the signal for withdrawal several hours later.

About the time of the failure of the main assault, a Federal flanking column began pouring in a hot fire from across the marsh to the right of the fort. This fire drove the Confederate cannoneers from their guns and had it occurred during the main assault, might well have caused the fall of the fort.

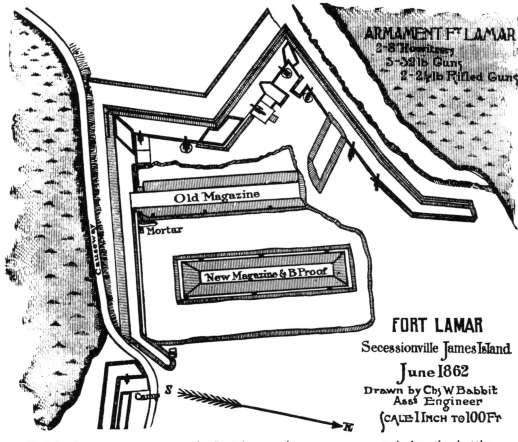

Sketch shows more weapons in Fort Lamar than were present during the battle.

It was finally silenced by the 4th Louisiana Battalion. This unit, encamped some 2½ miles away, rushed toward the fort via a footbridge which connected the tip of the Secessionville peninsula with the adjacent James Island shore.

Arriving at Secessionville, the battalion, about 250 strong, went into action from the cover of trees lining the banks of the peninsula and fired across the marsh into the Federal flanking column.

Although heavy fire was poured into the fort by both assault and flanking forces until the retreat about 9 a.m., the primary assault was over within half an hour and the majority of casualties in the assault force were sustained during this period.

Confederate losses in Lamar and on the Secessionville peninsula were 32 killed, 92 wounded and three captured or missing — one of the latter was grabbed

by the Yankees retreating from the first fight on the parapets. The South also lost 20 killed, 52 wounded and 8 missing from units operating outside the peninsula against the Federal flanking column.

Federal casualties were listed in official records as 529 in the assault force and more than 160 on the flank. Of the total, 107 were killed, almost 500 wounded and the remainder missing or captured. The Confederates, however, recorded a much higher figure. Gen. Evans placed the dead in front of the fort at 168 and Lamar said 341 Federal soldiers were buried in front of his works.

Regardless of which figures are used, it adds up to an extremely bitter fight — and a major Confederate victory.

W.R.

Confederates Stop Union Attack

Pluff mud and a bit of luck helped Confederates whip Federal forces attacking Fort Lamar at Secessionville.

The attack, ordered by Brig. Gen. Henry W. Benham, commander of Union troops holding the southwestern tip of James Island, consisted of two divisions.

One, under command of Brig. Gen. Horatio G. Wright, provided flanking support. It consisted of three brigades, two of them fairly small, and totaled some 3,100 men.

The other, which made the main assault, was commanded by Brig. Gen. Isaac I. Stevens and had two brigades with a total strength of 3,200.

The assault division moved out of camp at 2 a.m. June 16, 1862. Most of the men carried unloaded guns and all were under strict orders to remain silent and to carry the fort with the bayonet.

The division passed the picket line about 3:30 a.m., capturing the four-man Confederate outpost, and marched on until it reached an open field extending roughly half a mile.

As each regiment of the assault division's first brigade entered the field, the formation was changed to line of battle instead of column and the brigade

continued forward at the double quick. The three regiments of the brigade were in echelon, the leading unit on the right.

They were seen by the Confederates shortly after entering the field, but the leading elements were within 100 yards of the fort before the first blasts of grape from the fortification's cannon began tearing holes in the lines.

Despite the fire, members of the leading regiment charged into the fort where they locked with the defenders in bitter hand-to-hand combat.

However, while these men were in the fort, the other two regiments were in trouble.

Approaching the fort, they found that the ground narrowed between the marsh and pluff mud on either side until, directly in front of the earthwork, there was less than 200 yards — too little room for even one regiment to deploy, much less three.

Consequently, the second regiment in the echelon lost part of its line in the mud on the left and the third, even though it moved toward the right, also wound up with many of its men floundering in the marsh.

Without support from the main portion of the brigade, the elements of the first regiment which had gained the fort were soon forced to withdraw.

The second brigade, attacking in a similar formation, met a like fate. The right, or leading, regiment made it to the fort and so did portions of the second, but the third was held up by the marsh and broken by retreating elements from the first brigade.

Less than half an hour had passed from the first shot until the last Yankee was driven from the fort. But the battle was far from over. The regiments were pulled back and reorganized, but many of their men failed to heed the order and remained close to the fort keeping up a hot fire from the shelter of the trees lining the banks of the marsh and from furrows in the plowed field over which they had attacked. They did not retire until the general retreat about three hours later.

While the main assault was going on, the flanking division was moving into position.

These units had left camp about 3 a.m. and marched quietly to the left of the assaulting column, the leading elements moving down a narrow finger of land which parallels the Secessionville peninsula.

One regiment, the 3rd New Hampshire, soon found that the finger brought it to within only a few yards of the flank of Fort Lamar, but separated by water and

(Continued On Page 35)

Union troops brave artillery and rifle fire in attack on Fort Lamar at Secessionville June 16, 1862.

(Continued From Page 34)

CONFEDERATES

pluff mud which could not be crossed.

A hot fire was quickly opened on the fort and Southern cannoneers were driven from the guns firing on the assault force which by this time, however, had been thrown back.

But the fire was not all one-sided. As the Federal riflemen shot into the western flank of Fort Lamar, a Confederate force peppered them from behind or farther to the west. The Southern force consisted of a small group of skirmishers backed up by a single cannon which was firing grapeshot.

The New Hampshire unit also came under fire from another gun located about a mile to the north under the command of Lt. Col., later bishop, Ellison Capers.

This gun, which was out of sight of the Yankee artillery, continued to play on both the flanking column and the assault force throughout the remainder of the battle.

The cannon to the west could be approached, however, so a second unit of the flanking column, the 3rd Rhode Island, faced left and attacked the skirmishers, driving them back until the gun was in sight.

The Rhode Islanders did not press home the attack, however, since at this point it was seen that the 3rd New Hampshire was beginning to withdraw.

This outfit, mauled by the skirmishers on the west and Capers' gun to the north, were now under intense fire from a new source — Southern reinforcements had arrived on the Secessionville peninsula and had taken position among trees along the banks behind the fort. From this relatively secure position, they were sniping across the marsh at any Yankee foolish enough to show his head.

The 3rd New Hampshire stuck it out for awhile, then, realizing that the main assault was not going to be renewed, it started an orderly retreat.

Although the leading elements of the flanking column received heavy casualties, the majority of units were not engaged and received no more than respectful notice from the fort's artillery.

About 9 a.m. action was broken off and the Federals withdrew to camp to lick their wounds.

The Confederates celebrated THEIR victory, but the real salvation of Fort Lamar lay in mud — gooey, bottomless pluff mud — and luck.

The mud trapped the assaulting regiments so that the units hit piecemeal instead of together and prevented more than a relatively few men from reaching the fort at any one time.

It also prevented the flanking column from crossing and entering the fort from the side.

Finally, Lady Luck favored the Confederates in delaying the arrival of the flanking column until after the main assault had failed.

Had the 3rd. New Hampshire been in position a few minutes earlier, the Confederates would have been between two fires and doubtless the fort would have fallen.

W.R.

Units of flanking division attack Confederate sharpshooters during Battle of Secessionville.

Confederate rams in Charleston Harbor. Probably Chicora (left) and Charleston.

Ironclad fever

Gunboats Raised Southern Hopes

At the beginning of the War Between the States, Southerners did not foresee as clearly as their enemies in the North the important part that sea power was about to play in the new struggle for independence.

When Union blockaders appeared off the coast soon after the fall of Fort Sumter, the Confederates laughed and thought about their gallant armies.

Presently, however, concern replaced the jests of the ignorant. Within a few months, as the grip of the blockade began to tighten, it became painfully clear that victories would have to be won at sea as well as on land if secession were to be made permanent.

Southerners began to look seriously about them for the means with which to build a navy. Mostly they were lacking. The South was pitifully short of everything that was needed to build, equip and man warships except ingenuity and the ability to improvise.

Mainly on the strength of these two qualities, Southern shipwrights at the old Portsmouth Navy Yard in Virginia were soon fashioning a new and distinctive profile for the former U.S. sloop of war Merrimack.

The Merrimack had been a high-sparred sailing ship with steam power as an auxiliary. She had been burned by her former owners as they cleared out of Norfolk in the first days of the war. The tall spars were gone forever from her, but in their place, on what was left of the Merrimack's hull, there was rising an ugly iron house which represented a revolution in naval architecture.

Though it would be months before she took the water under a new flag and a new name — CSS Virginia — the Merrimack had by late in 1861 begun to set the fashion for Confederate warships.

Soon a similar ship was taking shape in Charleston Harbor. She was to be much smaller than the Virginia — perhaps half as long and correspondingly less formidable — but to admiring Charlestonians, who included a large percentage of landlubbers, she appeared an incomparable fighting machine.

Capt. D.N. Ingraham, the naval commander at Charleston, was ordered to gratify the city's pride in the ship by assigning the name "Charleston." An outburst of patriotism among women in all parts of South Carolina, however, caused that name to be abandoned in favor of one less parochial in flavor.

In March 1862, the Virginia steamed into Hampton Roads and fired the imagination of the Confederacy by a single-handed punishing attack on the Federal squadron there. Perhaps no other occurrence of the war so stimulated the hopes of the South as did this battle. Seemingly, it confirmed the hopes of all those who saw in iron warships the potential downfall of the

Yankee Navy. Within 24 hours, there came the USS Monitor upon the scene. She fought the Virginia to a standstill but she cast no damper upon the celebrating Confederacy.

Everywhere the new contagion of ironclad fever spread. It traveled down to Charleston where a halting progress was being made on the new ship on the stocks of Marsh and Son on the bank of the Cooper River.

Even before the news of Hampton Roads arrived, Charleston was enjoying a home-made excitement over the possibilities of iron warships. The Charleston Daily Courier had touched it off late in February by publishing a story telling how Confederate women in New Orleans had subscribed to a fund to pay for the building there of a "gunboat."

It is impossible to tell what kind of visions the word "gunboat" aroused in the minds of South Carolina women, but they wanted one, too. On March 1, 1862, Miss Sue L. Gelzer, a resident of Orangeburg, sent the Courier a check for $5 to be spent helping build a "gunboat." Soon there were other letters coming in with contributions and in a few days people began to talk about a "ladies' gunboat," the gift from keel to truck of South Carolina women.

Capt. Ingraham had some cold water for this idea. Ironclads, he pointed out, cost upwards of $200,000. Such a sum was far beyond the capacities of the women. But Capt. Ingraham could not quench Southern enthusiasm any more than could the Monitor and her crew.

Stimulated by the conquests of the Virginia in Hampton Roads, the trickle of letters became a flood. They came from all directions. They included, besides cash, donations of jewelry, silverware, household linen, china, cooking utensils, paintings, bales of cotton — anything that might in one way or another be converted into money to pay for the ladies' gunboat.

In truth, however, there was no ladies' gunboat. Nor did it appear to authorities that there could ever be one unless the capacity of the women for giving vastly exceeded expectations or the price of gunboats came down.

Then the Navy Department at Richmond stepped into the picture. Impressed by the determination of the women, the authorities offered to accept their gifts for the new ironclad under construction at Charleston. The Navy Department said it would be pleased to accept the name the ladies had in mind — Palmetto State — and apply it to the new ship in place of "Charleston." As for plans to build a second vessel and name it the "Lovely Sue" — well, the seadogs in Richmond

tactfully let the matter lie, hoping perhaps it would never come up again.

So now the ladies had their "gunboat" and under the impetus of their constant interest, spurred on by the fund-raising activities which continued on all sides, the mechanics and carpenters at Marsh and Sons began to work faster and faster.

"The recent success of the Merrimack places it in the power of South Carolina to raise the blockade and whip the Yankees," wrote a correspondent of the Daily Courier, reflecting fairly accurately the sentiments of his fellow South Carolinians.

In the "iron-plated monsters" in the shipyards, every loyal South Carolinian saw the means to put the blockaders at the bottom of the sea. That was the only portion of Southern soil, said the Courier, which they should be permitted to occupy.

This was all very well, but the truth was that the "monsters" were not quite as formidable as they appeared to the unsophisticated eyes of the people of Charleston.

Both the Palmetto State and her consort, the Chicora, laid down two months later at the shipyard of James M. Eason behind the Charleston Post Office, were doomed by the poverty of the Confederacy to be of meager fighting quality.

In their design, basically akin to that of the Virginia, were reflected the shortages and crude skills of the South. They were of casemated construction, iron houses set on wooden hulls. The walls of the houses were pierced for guns like the sides of old-fashioned frigates. This made them weak compared to the stout monitors under construction in the North.

The circular steam-driven "pill boxes" could train right around from beam to beam, permitting one or two guns to do the work of many in the casemated ships. To bring their broadsides to bear the great floating houses of the Confederacy had to be maneuvered slowly into position. Nearly all of them, like the Palmetto State and the Chicora, were propelled by improvised engines borrowed from tugboats or merchant vessels or worse, and they were anything but handy.

A monitor could jab and thrust while keeping her bow — her least vulnerable point — toward the enemy. The Confederate ironclads were compelled to expose their whole towering sides to punishment.

As a matter of fact, the "squadron" building at Charleston did not even compare favorably with the best of the Confederate warships.

The Palmetto State, for example, was somewhat

(Continued On Page 37)

Photograph of Confederate ram, probably the Chicora.

(Continued From Page 36)

GUNBOATS RAISED

more than half the length of the Virginia although her armor was equally as thick. The Virginia carried 10 guns, the Palmetto State but four — one forward, one aft and one on each broadside.

The Chicora, 150 feet long, would have a more powerful battery, somewhat less protection. Her plating would be two inches thick, laid on a wooden backing 22 inches thick and would extend deep below the water line. Carried forward to a stout spur, this would give the Chicora a powerful ram, but there was a

serious question whether her creaky engine could develop enough power to permit her to throw herself bodily upon an opponent.

Their low speeds, particularly in the face of the swift currents of Charleston Harbor, would limit these vessels when they were completed to the inner confines of the harbor. And there was another factor which would tend to localize their operations — this was their deep draft.

Drawing 12 or 13 feet of water because of the heavy weight of their armor, both Palmetto State and Chicora would be incapable of crossing the bar except under the most favorable conditions. The blockaders habitually lay outside the bar. Opportunities to come to close quarters with them would occur but seldom.

But these problems were not much on the minds of eager Charlestonians, chafing to possess a navy. In their eyes, the new "gunboats," into whose timbers went the hopes of the people of a whole state, meant an opportunity for deliverance.

When they were finished, if the people of Charleston could bring it to pass, they would carry the Stars and Bars to a glory which armies could not hope to achieve no matter how brave and skillful the generals and soldiers might be.

They could, thought Charlestonians, open the door to the world which the Yankees and their armada of blockaders had so rudely slammed shut.

A.M.W.

Gunboats Disperse Blockading Fleet

As the year 1862 drew to a close, Charlestonians contemplated two developments which suggested that their city might yet be delivered from the strangling grip of the Union blockade.

First, Gen. P.G.T. Beauregard, the hero of Fort Sumter, returned to take command of his old stamping grounds around Charleston.

Second, the Navy, undernourished stepchild of the Confederate services, was finally able to put together in Charleston Harbor what would pass for a squadron of warships.

The coincidence of Beauregard's return from the West, and the commissioning of the Chicora and Palmetto State opened many possibilities for rewarding operations against the Yankee fleet.

Better than some admirals on both sides, Beauregard had a keen appreciation of the possibilities of sea power. He was intensely interested in how the new rams might be used to relieve the pressure on the coast. Though his official position demanded attention chiefly to land operations, his eye never strayed very far from the sea. The availability of the gunboat "fleet" gave Old Bory a splendid opportunity for one of those glamorous tactical enterprises of which he was so fond, whether the stage was set on land or sea.

Beauregard cast his eye over the two warships lying at anchor in the harbor.

There were good reasons, particularly from a sailor's point of view, why the Chicora and Palmetto State should remain at anchor. In spite of the confidence which Charlestonians professed to place in the "armored monsters," neither of the two ships was very impressive.

Both were small and cramped, even by Confederate standards, which were generally low. They were amateurishly designed, built of inferior material and armed with second-rate ordnance.

They were heavily armored but the armor was a handicap as well as an asset. Its great weight made the ships lie deep in the water. There were not many places in Charleston Harbor where they could move with freedom. Getting across the bar into the open sea was out of the question except under the most favorable circumstances.

The machinery of both ships was in parlous condition. Their engines were second hand. Breakdowns were frequent. In the strong currents of the harbor, the Palmetto State and the Chicora were lucky to make four knots against the tide.

Capt. Ingraham, the flag officer in command, was 61 years old and he seemed to lack the offensive spirit needed to overcome the handicaps imposed upon his ships by the Confederacy's lack of resources.

Not so Old Bory. He saw reasons why action was at

least worth contemplating. The Charleston ships were exceptionally well manned in comparison with other Confederate vessels. Each had a fair proportion of professional seamen among the landsmen and soldiers who constituted the bulk of their crews of about 120 men. The crews were comparatively well disciplined. These factors might go a long way to make up for deficiencies in materiel if the ships could be once gotten into battle.

Most important of the considerations before Beauregard, however, was the valuelessness of the rams in a purely defensive role.

Confined to the harbor, there was little they could do to stop the Yankees from breaking in. Both Beauregard and Ingraham knew this and had consigned them to the role of last ditch defenders to be run aground and scuttled rather than captured if the enemy should pass Fort Sumter.

After balancing the possible rewards of action against those of continued inaction, Beauregard brought pressure against Capt. Ingraham to take the initiative. Once the proposal was made to him, Ingraham, who was no coward, proved cooperative enough.

Near midnight on Jan. 30, 1863, the Palmetto State

(Continued On Page 38)

Palmetto State rams USS Mercedita during attack on blockading squadron. Chicora is at right.

(Continued From Page 37)

GUNBOATS DISPERSE

and the Chicora weighed anchor and started for the bar. Across it at 4:30 a.m. the ships found the sea outside smooth and dark. The moon had set. A light haze now shrouded them as they steamed toward the blockaders.

Aboard the anchored Federal ships, many men were asleep but the watches were generally wide awake.

At 4 a.m. the USS Mercedita was settling down to her anchor after returning from a wild goose chase. Capt. H.S. Stellwagon, half-dressed, was dozing in his bunk, but the executive officer, Lt. Comdr. Abbott, was about the ship giving routine orders.

"Man the guns," Capt. Stellwagon heard someone shout. Snapped to his feet by the alarm, Stellwagon raced to his battle station on the quarterdeck. Out of the mist, under a plume of smoke, a strange, low craft materialized. She was headed straight for Mercedita. Observing protocol, Stellwagon held his fire and hailed.

"What ship is that?"

"Halloo," replied a muffled voice from the bowels of the approaching vessel.

Then clearly enough, "This is the Confederate States steam ram..."

"Fire," shouted Stellwagon.

Too late. The Confederate was so close the Mercedita's guns could not be brought to bear.

The ram crashed into the Union vessel's starboard side, heaving her far over to port. Simultaneously, a heavy shell passed through her port boiler and blew a hole in the port side.

Holed from one side to the other, with scalded men screaming on her decks and her captain's resolution shaken, the Mercedita hauled down her flag.

The Confederate ship lay close enough so that her name "Palmetto State" could be clearly seen. Over to her in a small boat went Lt. Comdr. Abbott, the dejected bearer of surrender. The Confederates, however, saw other business before them that prevented their taking possession of their trophy. They preferred to accept Capt. Stellwagon's parole for his ship and her crew. The pledge was given and the Palmetto State steamed away in search of fresh prey.

Soon her guns were firing again. Trading salvoes left and right she steamed through the stunned blockading fleet until she drew up with the Chicora and joined in a running battle with the USS Keystone State, another big converted merchant steamer.

The Keystone State was slow in getting up steam and for a time the Chicora had the speed advantage of her. Instead of using his ram, however, Lt. Comdr. John R. Tucker stood off and engaged in a gun battle with the Keystone State.

The Union vessel replied stubbornly to the fire of the two Confederates. Presently a blaze broke out aboard her. She sought to break away. A shell cut steam lines deep below her main deck and she limped nearly to a halt. Then she hauled down her flag.

The Chicora, her decrepit engines exceeding all expectations, steamed up to take possession. But the Keystone State was not yet finished. One paddle wheel began to work. It turned faster and faster. She began to draw away from the rams. Soon she was beyond their reach.

Now day was breaking and the aroused blockaders were flying in every direction. Two big men of war wearing the Stars and Stripes came pounding down from the north. As they drew near the two rams, they boldly opened fire. There was a brief exchange. Then the steamers swung past at a fast clip. The slow rams could not follow.

The Confederates looked around for more enemies but there were none to be had. Those that were in sight were taking pains to stay out of range. It was a victory, but as far as the Confederates could tell, an empty one.

Not only had the undamaged blockaders cleared the scene, but the injured ones as well. The prizes the Confederates coveted had all escaped.

The baffled rams crept back toward Charleston. Outside the bar they anchored. It was late in the afternoon before the tide rose high enough to take them over. In the meantime, their crews scanned the ocean for a sign of the enemy returning. There was none.

For the Confederate sailors the day had been one of military success. Gen. Beauregard, however, sought something more. He wanted political success as well.

At the beginning of the war, lawyers on both sides of the Atlantic had been deeply imbued with the legalities of blockading. Under the quaint procedures which encumbered warfare of the period, it was held to be a rule that one could not seal off an enemy harbor without giving exhaustive notice of his designs. This was intended to protect innocent merchantmen who might stumble on a blockade without even knowing it existed.

Depending on who happened to be blockading whom, the "rules" were variously interpreted. In their own interest, the Confederate lawyers construed them as narrowly as possible.

Force away the blockaders for even a few hours for any reason, said the Southern sea lawyers, and you have a perfect right to insist the enemy start all over again. He will have to give notice of his intention for a long time and while he is doing this, we can sneak some ships in.

Gen. Beauregard grasped at this legalism. He packed a number of foreign diplomatic officials off in a steamer to look for themselves beyond the bar and see if there were any ships there.

Then he and Capt. Ingraham got together and drafted an impressive proclamation declaring the blockade at an end, lifted by a "superior force" of the Confederate States.

In Richmond, the State Department enthusiastically endorsed this move and got off copies of a similar document to the agents of foreign powers in the capital and to Confederate agents overseas.

Then the Confederates settled back and waited hopefully for favorable reactions from abroad.

In the chancelleries of Europe, however, there was fault to be found with this line of reasoning.

The British government, declared crusty old Lord Russell, minister of foreign affairs, could not accept the notion that the rules meant that a port must be closely blockaded under all conceivable conditions. How about a storm that drove the blockaders away? Were the Confederates about to argue that the gods of the winds were on their side, too?

Also, if the blockade actually had been raised, what about all those ships at anchor off Charleston again?

Alas, it was true. As soon as their fright had died down, the Union vessels had returned to station.

The blockade was being clamped down tighter than ever.

A.M.W.

Battery Beauregard on Sullivan's Island with Battery Rutledge and Fort Moultrie in the background.

East Cooper Guns Guarded Channel

East Cooper batteries, by the end of the Civil War, could force any vessel entering the harbor to run through a gauntlet of steel.

Chances are they wouldn't have stopped a determined attack on the city, but they could have made it a distinctly unpleasant voyage for the invader.

These defenses were built gradually during the war as need arose and materials were obtained.

In the beginning, the Confederates had only Fort Moultrie, acquired when Maj. Robert Anderson skipped to Fort Sumter during the latter part of 1860.

The fort played a part in the defeat of Fort Sumter, then switched to a defensive role with its cannon bearing solely on the channel while the Confederates awaited attack by the North.

With Moultrie on one side of the channel leading to Charleston and Fort Sumter on the other, the Southerners, for the time being, felt reasonably secure against attack from the sea.

Then they plugged the route from the south by a series of defenses across James Island and St. Andrew's Parish, and corked the opening at the narrow neck of the Charleston Peninsula with a line of breastworks.

This still left Charleston vulnerable to a landing farther up the coast, say in the Bull's Bay area, and attack southwest against the city.

To guard against this, the Confederates threw a line across Christ Church Parish. It extended from Elliott's

(Continued On Page 40)

Battery Bee looking toward Fort Moultrie.

Battery Marshall, a Sullivan's Island fortification, guarded Breach Inlet.

One of four two-gun batteries on Sullivan's Island.

(Continued From Page 39)

EAST COOPER GUNS

Creek, a branch of the Wando River, to Copahee Sound. Advantage was taken of a deep drainage ditch cut for agricultural purposes and it was proposed to fell timber in advance of this line in case of necessity.

After the loss of Hilton Head Island to the Union fleet in November 1861, the defenders of Charleston realized that it was just a question of time before the city would be under attack.

Consequently, extensive building of defenses got under way throughout the area early in 1862 with the East Cooper section coming in for its share of construction.

Because the channel was the major source of danger to the city, Sullivan's Island, which lay parallel to it, received the majority of attention. Several works were started and by October, although still unfinished, Batteries Bee (west of Moultrie), Beauregard (east of Moultrie), and Marshall (at Breach Inlet) were within a few weeks of completion and already mounting part, or all, of their armament. These fortifications were all built of sand, well sodded, and contained excellent magazines and bombproofs.

The wisdom of reinforcing Moultrie with additional firepower was soon proved when Adm. Samuel F. DuPont threw his monitors against Fort Sumter and the Sullivan's Island forts in the "Ironclad Attack" of April 7, 1863.

The engagement saw Batteries Bee and Beauregard and Fort Moultrie playing a major part and encouraged the Confederates to further reinforce the Sullivan's Island defenses.

They extended Battery Bee to Fort Moultrie by lines and an intermediate work which became known as Battery Marion. A similar connection of Moultrie and Beauregard resulted in Battery Rutledge.

In addition, four 2-gun batteries were placed between Beauregard and Marshall. These were separate works with no connecting lines.

A final battery was added later at Cove Inlet. This was referred to as the Cove, or New, Battery.

These were the major defenses of Sullivan's Island toward the end of the war and although the Confederacy was deficient in heavy ordnance, this defensive network packed a sizeable punch. At the evacuation of Charleston in February 1865, Union engineers reported the forts held five mortars and 77 guns of which the majority were of heavy caliber.

Backing up the Sullivan's Island defenses were several relatively small works.

On the mainland, almost immediately behind Battery Marshall, two single-gun batteries were constructed to guard the creeks leading to Breach Inlet.

Mount Pleasant had two fortifications, Battery Gary, a two-gun work, guarded the bridge leading to Sullivan's Island. The other battery was located on the site of an older fort between Hibben and Venning Streets. The latter fortification apparently was not armed and is listed on only a few charts of the area.

Two small works rounded out the East Cooper defenses. One, the Hog Island Battery, was located in marsh of that island. The other, the Hobcaw Point Battery, was at the site of Riverside Beach not far from the Cooper River Bridge. Neither was ever armed.

W.R.

Inner Defense Ring Guarded City

Two rings of forts guarded Charleston during the Civil War.

The first, or outer ring, included the James and Morris Island defenses, Fort Sumter, and the Sullivan's Island complex.

These were designed to prevent the enemy from coming within artillery range of the city. If they failed, Confederate troops were prepared to fight within the harbor and inside the city itself.

This inner circle of defenses included batteries east of the Cooper and west of the Ashley Rivers, across the Charleston "Neck" and along the city's waterfront.

By the end of the war, they were quite extensive although their effectiveness against a determined attack by the Union fleet may be subject to question.

The inner ring started with Battery Gary at the southeastern tip of Mount Pleasant and not far from the old Cove Inlet Bridge. Continuing toward the city, it included three forts that apparently were never armed. These were a work between Hibben and Venning Streets, a battery in the marsh of Hog Island, and a fortification at the site of Riverside Beach Park on Remley's Point.

Across the Cooper River near the city, was the main Charleston line which Brig. Gen. P.G.T. Beauregard in September 1862 described as a "...line of works on the Neck to defend the City of Charleston from land attack from the north. It is a continuous bastion line of strong profile and elaborately constructed, but badly located, I believe, not being well adapted to the

(Continued On Page 41)

1865 photograph of Frazier's Wharf Battery shows Custom House in background.

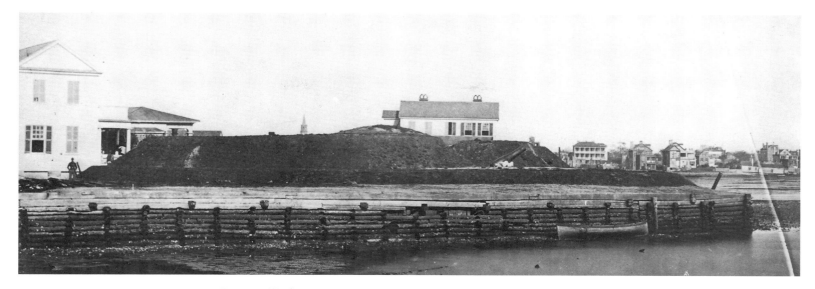

Battery Waring was constructed at the west end of Tradd Street.

(Continued From Page 40)

INNER DEFENSE RING

ground...it can be taken in reverse by gunboats on the Cooper and Ashley Rivers, particularly the last. No traverses have been constructed. They are absolutely required. Even then, this line could hardly be held successfully against a fleet of gunboats in each of the said rivers....''

Although no traces remain, the line apparently started just outside the northern boundary of Magnolia Cemetery and zig-zagged across the Neck to the Ashley River between Mechanic and Monravia Streets.

It picked up again across the Ashley River at Battery Avenue in Maryville as an extension of the western section of the James Island Line and continued across Highways 61 and 17 to the Coburg Dairy area on Wappoo Creek across which it joined the Western James Island Line.

On the eastern side of the Charleston Peninsula, the Confederates erected the Half Moon Batteries. They fronted on East Bay Street and were designed to deny the enemy use of Town Creek.

The northern battery, Half Moon No. 2, was later called Battery James. It was located at East Bay and Cooper Streets. South of it was Half Moon No. 1, between Columbus and Amherst. This battery was variously known as Battery Aiken or Battery Augustus Smith.

Concord Street held three bastions, the Calhoun and Laurens Street Batteries at the foot of those thoroughfares, and the Frazier's Wharf Battery between Gaillard and Cone Streets.

Two other batteries also bore on the Cooper River from the city. The Vanderhorst Wharf Battery, roughly at the site of the present East Bay Playground, and

Battery Ramsey, at the eastern end of White Point Garden.

Turning to follow the shore of the Ashley River, the next battery also was located in White Point Garden, the King Street Battery established at the foot of that street.

Chisolm's Mill, site of the Coast Guard Station on Tradd Street, was the location of Battery Waring. The final city fortification, Battery Gadberry, was constructed between Spring and Cannon streets near Courtenay Drive. It protected the bridge across the Ashley River.

On the other side of the Ashley, the bridge was defended by two works located near the intersection of Highways 17 and 171. The bastion south of Highway 17 was named Fort Gladden and that north of the roadway, Fort Barnes.

Furnishing further protection to the bridge was Battery Means atop which the Country Club of Charleston now stands. Between Means, which also guarded Wappoo Creek and the Ashley River, and Fort Johnson were three works — Batteries Glover, Wampler and Harleston.

These fortifications all bore on the harbor. Glover, initially called the Battery at Lawton, was located approximately opposite White Point Garden. Wampler, which has been leveled, was a few hundred yards east of the James Island Yacht Club. Harleston, which masqueraded under the name of Hallsted on some charts, adjoined Fort Johnson.

Although it, too, bore on the harbor, Fort Johnson was not considered particularly important defensively should the Union fleet enter the harbor. However, it was deemed necessary to retain the fort to prevent its capture and subsequent utilization by Federal forces as a site for breaching batteries against Fort Sumter.

With this end in view, it was strengthened intermit-

tently as the war progressed until by the time it was evacuated during the night of Feb. 17, 1865, it had become a strong, entrenched encampment capable of putting up a good fight.

Two additional forts, Ripley and Castle Pinckney, were part of the inner circle, but their worth in battle against the Union fleet was of doubtful value.

Gen. Beauregard, in his report of September 1862, said that although Pinckney was armed at the time with 10 cannon, he considered it ''...nearly worthless, capable of exerting but little influence on the defense of Charleston.''

Pinckney is a brick fortification, but during the latter years of the war it was turned into an earthwork by the simple expedient of piling sand against the outside of its walls.

Ripley, variously called Middle Ground or Fort Timber, was located about 1,300 yards from Pinckney and roughly midway between it and Fort Johnson.

The fort was started during the early part of 1862 and was constructed by sinking wooden cribs, ballasted with rubble from the 1861 Charleston fire, into some eight feet of water atop a shoal known as Middle Ground.

Using the cribs as a foundation, the fort was constructed of palmetto logs and was designed for five cannon mounted en barbette. Although it was later armed, its original armament never arrived. These were the guns aboard the steamer Planter when she was abducted and run past the Charleston forts to the Federal fleet.

These batteries and forts constituted the inner ring of Charleston defenses. Their armament differed from time to time depending on the defensive situation, but a rough idea of their strength may be obtained from the ordnance figures of Oct. 4, 1865, which list some 50 guns and mortars for the inner defense network.

W.R.

King Street Battery in White Point Garden.

Union ironclads advance in column to attack Fort Sumter (center). Left to right are: (A) Keokuk, (B) Nahan

(1. Morris Island Sand Battery. 2. Battery Wagner. 3. Battery Gregg. 4. Fort Johnson. 5. Fort Ripley. 6. Fort Sumter. 7. City Of Charleston. 8. Castle Pinckney.

Union Ironclads A

In the spring of 1863, the most powerful naval squadron ever assembled under the Stars and Stripes gathered at Port Royal to attack the Confederate citadel at Charleston.

To the landlubber's eye, the squadron was not impressive. It consisted of seven ugly Passaic class monitors, the "tin-clad" experimental vessel Keokuk and the bulky, clumsy, armored frigate New Ironsides, flagship of Rear Adm. Samuel F. DuPont, U.S. Navy.

Looks were deceiving. The vessels under Rear Adm. DuPont's flag were the best protected, heaviest gunned the country could supply. Their captains were handpicked for bravery and competence. Their commander, who had planned and executed the capture of Port Royal late in 1861, was judged one of the most enterprising in the Navy. In addition, to a unique degree, the squadron enjoyed the full support of its military superiors, the blessings of the politicians and the wholehearted good wishes of the ordinary people back home.

The war was now two years old but hotly patriotic Northerners had not forgotten hatred of Charleston conceived at the first firing on Fort Sumter. To many of them, the forthcoming assault appeared a crusade. Radical politicians particularly looked with anger upon Charleston, the "Cradle of Secession," and hungered for its capture. "A morbid appetite," said Adm. DuPont, with a shudder, "prevailed in the land."

From the highest levels, where the influence of the radicals was acutely felt at this period, came the instructions for attack.

"This department has determined to capture Charleston as soon as Richmond falls," Secretary of the Navy Gideon Welles had informed Adm. DuPont as early as May 1862.

Richmond had not fallen on schedule, but the mind of the "department" firmed with respect to Charleston.

In January 1863, a directive from Secretary Welles outlined DuPont's mission.

"The New Ironsides, Passaic, Montauk, Patapsco and Weehawken have been ordered to and are now on the way to join your command to enable you to enter the harbor of Charleston and demand the surrender of all its defenses, or suffer the consequences of a refusal."

This communication would not qualify under modern staff procedures as a model directive, but it should have left no doubt what was in Mr. Welles' mind.

On the assumption that Adm. DuPont understood his orders and was planning with enthusiasm for the capture of Charleston, the people of the North waited in hopeful suspense. No event since the first great battle of the war had so caught hold of popular imagination.

There was corresponding suspense in Charleston. Southerners looked upon the city where the war was born as the birthplace of independence, symbol of Southern will to resist tyranny. Also, it was one of the few remaining ports open to blockade runners which still filtered with regularity through the screen of Union warships. The fall of Charleston might have disastrous effects upon both the morale and economy of the Confederacy.

Carefully, with precision, the Confederate commanders assessed the possibilities of successful defense. In the winter of 1862, Gen. P.G.T. Beauregard, military commander at Charleston, sat in conference with Commodore D.N. Ingraham, the naval commander. They reviewed the courses of action open to the enemy if he should attack from the sea.

They came to this conclusion: "The plan of naval attack apparently best for the enemy would be to dash with as many ironclads as he can command, say 15 or 20, past the batteries and forts without halting to engage or reduce them.

"Commodore Ingraham thinks they will make an attack in that way by daylight."

This evaluation of Federal capabilities was based upon realistic appraisal of Confederate resources and a careful comparison of strengths and weaknesses.

"Dashing" was technically beyond the capacity of the sluggish monitors, but the Confederates recognized that even at low speeds they would present difficult targets for the clumsy ordnance of the forts at th harbor entrance.

While the Confederates were thus competent analyzing their situation, Adm. DuPont was permittir his mind to stray from his own legitimate aims.

Obsessed perhaps with the brooding presence of Fo Sumter — the so-called cork in the bottle at th entrance of Charleston Harbor, clearly visible from o the bar — DuPont failed to put his finger upon th essential nature of his assignment: "...Enter th harbor of Charleston," Secretary Welles had ordere "and demand the surrender of all its defenses."

As the spring wore on, DuPont gathered intelligence, formed no estimate, prepared no positi plan to carry out this directive. Instead, the fir conviction grew upon him that he could not captur Charleston.

While the Confederates were gloomily discussir their estimate that Charleston lay at the mercy c Yankee ironclads under a vigorous commander, th admiral whose squadron they feared so much wo writing his friends that the forts could not be passed

The squadron began to join up at Port Royal i January 1863. Three or four of the monitors wer ordered to conduct "experiments" in action wit Confederate Fort McAlister, a few miles away on th coast of Georgia.

In January, February and March, four trials wer made under fire to test the defensive and offensiv qualities of the Patapsco, Passaic and Nahant.

The results were not encouraging to Adm. DuPont He had made up his mind in advance that the monitor could not fight forts. The engagements with For McAlister confirmed this distrust.

"The injuries to the monitors were extensive ano their offensive powers found to be feeble in dealing with forts," DuPont wrote the Navy Department. Th kind of talk, DuPont said later, was intended to conve to the department the admiral's fear that too muc was being asked of his ironclads. The department di not take the hint. Unaware that DuPont did not hav

antucket, (D) Catskill, (E) New Ironsides, (F) Patapsco, (G) Montauk, (H) Passaic, and (K) Weehawken.

n'' (Probably Battery Bee). 10. Fort Moultrie. 11. Moultrie House. 12. Battery Beauregard. 13. Harbor Obstructions. 14. Cooper River. 15. Ashley River.

tack Fort Sumter

his heart in his assignment, Welles and President Lincoln pressed for action.

As confidence in Charleston's doom continued to run high in Washington and public excitement rose all over the North, sullen despair prevailed in the cabin of the flagship at Port Royal.

Rumors of Confederate activities inside the harbor ended to deepen the listlessness of the planners in the fleet outside. Gen. Beauregard, deserters said, was aking energetic steps to improve his position.

"Old Bory," a genius when it came to defending places, needed all his genius at Charleston. The Confederates were faced with irremediable shortages n coast artillery and ammunition.

Beauregard was a first-class military innovator and he had a clear eye for the value of naval weapons. He devised ingenious methods to make up for his shortages. He developed elaborate new obstructions, plunged enthusiastically into the new field of mine warfare and spurred the construction of fast, semisubmersible orpedo craft.

In the inner reaches of the harbor, the Confederates sowed mines. The problem of effectively mining the harbor entrance was too much for them at this time. In and around the channels past Fort Sumter, the currents an swift and deep. There was no holding ground for mines. Even the sturdy booms the Confederates constructed at great expense of labor and precious material were carried away.

In the end, they had to compromise on token defenses. Instead of mines and booms, a frail barrier of rope netting supported by empty barrels stretched art way across the harbor entrance.

To the Union sailors beyond the bar, these barrels bobbing at their moorings took on frightful aspect. Reports that they marked impassable obstructions filtered out to the fleet and were discussed in wardrooms and messes.

DuPont heard the gossip. He came to believe firmly hat the presence of mines made the harbor entrance mpassable. He did not bother to investigate the yarns

told around the fleet. He accepted them at face value.

His neglect to collect reliable intelligence later was the subject of bitter comment by Secretary Welles.

After the battle was over, the secretary wrote DuPont that although the defenses of Charleston were "like a sealed book" to the Navy Department, "we had hoped that you, during the blockade and months of preparation, had become possessed of their true character."

DuPont let this criticism pass — testimony perhaps that he recognized his neglect. He defended himself vigorously and angrily against implications that other phases of the operation against Charleston had been improperly handled.

While DuPont was seing "ghosts" — a word unkindly applied by some of his brother officers later on — other observers were at the same time skeptical of the existence of the mine fields.

One of the skeptics was Capt. Thomas H. Ross, RN, commander of HBMS Cadmus. Capt. Ross, openly sympathetic with the Union cause, arrived at Charleston Bar in February to communicate with the city on behalf of his government. Exchanging calls with the U.S. ships, Capt. Ross heard the stories of the minefields and took note of the number of blockade runners lying inside the harbor, waiting to steam out when a dark night should come.

Well, said Ross, he thought it strange that if all those difficulties were in the way of the American squadron that several large vessels should now be lying inside ready to run the blockade.

Ross's remarks were discussed with the admiral, but DuPont did not attempt to iron out the inconsistency. He had already made up his mind the torpedoes were there. Now, on the basis of this conviction, he was formulating his plans — unassisted and unadvised.

"Indeed," said the admiral proudly a few weeks afterwards, as he faced up to the wrath of the politicians, "I never held a council of war in all my life."

Adm. DuPont, mistaking the clear language of his directive from Secretary Welles, had misinterpreted

his problem — how to get safely past the defenses of Charleston and in position to capture the city.

Instead of providing for the capture of Charleston, the operations plan he was preparing to issue called for the reduction of the outer forts, four miles away.

"The vessels," read the order, "will on signal being made, form in the prescribed order ahead at intervals of one cable length.

"The squadron will pass up the main ship channel without returning the fire of the batteries on Morris Island...

"The ships will open fire on Fort Sumter when within easy range and will take up a position to the northward and westward of that fortification, engaging its left and northwest face at a distance of from 600 to 800 yards.

"After the reduction of Fort Sumter, it is probable that the next point of attack will be the batteries on Morris Island."

This was no order to "capture Charleston."

To the captains of the fleet, it meant that an effort would be made to work around to a vulnerable side of Fort Sumter and remain there until the fort could be shelled into silence. Then the fleet would return outside the harbor.

If DuPont felt a sense of urgency — such as the pressure from Washington would have justified — he did not convey the feeling to his captains. Accordingly, when the battle began, they behaved as if there were no pressure upon them at all.

This was a tragedy.

The skippers of the ironclads were chosen for gallantry and professional accomplishment. They were just the men DuPont needed to crash through or run right around the defenses of Charleston, just the men to have taken huge delight in a forthright challenge to drive past the forts, as the Confederates believed they would, and bring their guns to bear upon a helpless rebel city.

(Continued On Page 44)

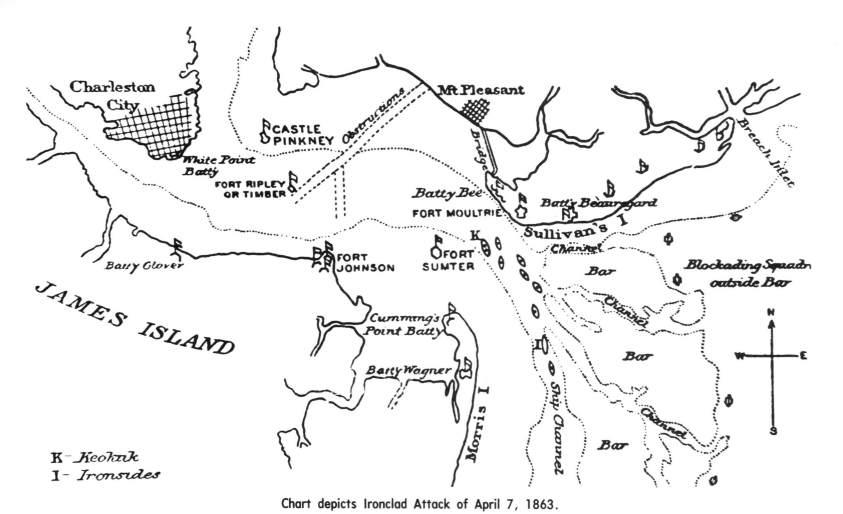

K - Keokuk
I - Ironsides

Chart depicts Ironclad Attack of April 7, 1863.

(Continued From Page 43)

UNION IRONCLADS

DuPont recognized these qualities in some of his captains, but his battle orders were not designed to bring out the best in brave men.

Capt. John Rodgers, U.S. Navy, selected to lead the advance toward Fort Sumter in the Weehawken, was a superb choice for a dangerous task, but he was fatally handicapped on the day of the battle by his admiral's fears and lack of forcefulness.

As the Weehawken advanced under heavy fire, the squadron strung out behind her, Rodgers peered through the narrow slit of his conning tower. Directly ahead there came into view the line of barrels.

Into Rodgers' mind leapt the admiral's concern for mines. In his imagination (he swore afterwards he had not been deceived) he felt his ship shudder under the impact of an underwater explosion. He stopped his engines, backed and filled.

Astern, the straggling column of ships fell into disarray. Formation was lost. The battle became a slugging match, ships against fort at impossibly close range, outside the harbor entrance.

DuPont was in no position to rectify matters. Sheltered behind the iron walls of the New Ironsides, he could not make effective signals to the monitors. He had depended upon Rodgers to lead the way and Rodgers had lost the path.

After neglecting to estimate the situation correctly and failing to issue uncompromising orders for the assault, DuPont was now trapped in a third error: He could not control the action he had planned.

The battle started about 2:30 p.m., April 7. At 5:30, the admiral got word to his monitors to withdraw. The squadron crawled southward along the shore of Morris Island.

As the New Ironsides moved past the Keokuk, Capt. A.C. Rhind limped to the deck of the riddled "tin-clad," reported her in danger of sinking. She sank the next morning and the Confederates, putting the final touch of ruin to DuPont's reputation, came out and stole her guns from where she lay.

The other ships were not sinking, but most were severely damaged. Between them, they reported 439 hits. The New Ironsides alone had received 93.

Astonishingly enough, only one man was killed and 22 hurt — a casualty list that started the politicians on DuPont's trail with a vengeance. They never did understand how it was that the death of one sailor and the wounding of a score could add up to defeat.

Looking his ships over with a lonely eye ("for I never hold councils of war") Adm. DuPont saw defeat clearly enough. Despite all that Lincoln and the Navy Department could do to hinder him, he retreated over the bar and dispersed his fleet beyond recall.

A.M.W.

Spectators line Charleston's Battery to watch attack of ironclads on Fort Sumter.

Confederates Salvage Guns Of Keokuk

Federal ironclad Keokuk sinking on the morning after attack on Fort Sumter.

A ponderous cannon on Charleston's Battery today is the sole reminder of one of the most incredible salvage jobs of the Civil War.

The weapon, an 11-inch Dahlgren smoothbore, was recovered from the wreck of the Keokuk in an exploit of courage and ingenuity which has few equals.

The Keokuk, one of Adm. S.F. DuPont's ironclads, was riddled with shot holes during the April 7, 1863, attack on Fort Sumter.

After the battle, she crept to her anchorage off Morris Island where hard work at the pumps kept her afloat until morning. Then a rising sea sent her to the bottom only minutes after the last of her crew stepped aboard a rescue vessel.

She settled gently in an upright position, her stack jutting above the waves at high water and her twin turrets barely awash at low tide.

During the next few days, to judge from contemporary records, she was a leading "tourist attraction" with the Confederates visiting her at night to pick up such souvenirs as rifles, clothing and flags, and the Yankees prowling around during the day trying to figure out how to destroy her.

Finally, after deciding this was impractical, the vessel was given up to the sea with the Northern public informed that she was filling with sand and would be of no use to the Confederates.

Southerners thought differently.

Confederate Army leaders believed salvage of the Keokuk's two guns was feasible, and the town's top civilian shiprigger, Adolphus W. LaCoste, was called in to do the job.

LaCoste, an Ordnance Department employe skilled in the mounting of heavy cannon, gathered a nucleous of experienced civilians to be augmented as needed by Army personnel.

His next job was to obtain equipment for recovering the 15,700 pound guns. A suitable vessel, the hull of a former lightship, was found and heavy timbers erected at her bow as a derrick.

While this work was under way, LaCoste and his men started the difficult job of preparing the guns for removal.

Their problems were many. The wreck lay roughly 1,300 yards from Morris Island which could be reached if danger threatened only by a quick pull for the shore. Danger, in the presence of the Union blockading fleet, was only about two miles away — if the vessels were on station. But there was no guarantee the Yankees would stay on station. They could cross the bar day or night and at any moment an ironclad might wander over to check on the Keokuk.

Silence was imperative and obviously no lights could be used.

The turrets were conical in shape, about 20 feet in diameter at the bottom and 14 at top which provided scant working space. Moreover, since they were awash at low water, tide prevented work except for about two hours a night — during the last of the ebb and first of the flood. Even then, breaking waves kept the workmen continuously drenched.

But water and danger failed to dampen their enthusiasm as each night with crowbar and wrench they attacked the heavy fastenings of the iron-plated turrets while guard boats stood nearby to put up a rear-guard fight if the Yankees attacked.

Night after night, muttered orders and muted curses came from the turrets as men strained and slid on the slippery iron for their two-hour stint, then climbed wearily into the boats for the long row back to the harbor. They were bruised, cut, cold and miserable, but the work went on with each night showing a little more progress — the signs carefully concealed in case the Yankees investigated the wreck during the day.

At last they had removed enough of the tops of the turrets to pass the huge guns, about 13½ feet long and roughly four feet in diameter at the trunnions.

Now, holding their breath, men slipped beneath the water inside the turrets to work for a few seconds on the heavy brass trunnion caps which held the guns in their carriages. They came up, lungs aching, to perch for a time on the top of the turret, then drop below again for another moment's work.

It was slow going, but finally the guns were free — yet still in the turrets and a long way from Charleston.

Now came the ticklish part. Derrick and lifting tackle were already aboard the old lightship. Piled on her deck at the bow were 1,500 sandbags to make her ride low and shorten the height of the lift.

The steamer Etiwan was ordered to tow the expedition to the wreck and, in view of the amount at stake, the Navy sent along its ironclad rams Palmetto State and Chicora to put up a fight in case the Yankees interfered.

The expedition silently made its way to the Keokuk. The lightship was made fast to the wreck and the lifting tackles rove through the cascabel at the breech of one gun.

Men strained at the tackle. The gun lifted, the breech eased through the turret and broke water. Slowly it rose, the long tube inching out of the turret. Then movment stopped — the blocks of the tackle had met. It could lift no farther, yet the tube was still well inside the turret.

"Belay — move the bags...." LaCoste was gambling that a shift in weight of 1,500 sandbags would raise the bow sufficiently to free the gun.

Snubbing the tackle, the crew formed a line to the stern and began passing the bags. LaCoste saw the bow rise.

Then the last bag dropped on the stern. The last man moved aft.

The bow was high, but not high enough. The gun still stayed in the turret — caught by the last few inches of its muzzle.

Men could do no more. Dawn was beginning to show dim silhouettes. The Etiwan was signaling frantically that it was time to leave. LaCoste faced the decision — drop the gun back down into the turret and give up, or face loss of the expedition when light revealed it to the Yankees.

Then nature took a hand.

While the operation was under way, the sea had been building until now the old lightship was rolling sedately, grinding the cannon muzzle against the sides of the hole in the turret.

Then, as if an answer to a prayer, came a wave a little larger than the rest. Ship and cannon lifted, dropped as the wave passed. Again the cannon slammed against the turret — now on the outside, free.

Lines to the Keokuk were cast off. The Etiwan took the lightship in tow and the procession sailed quietly back into the harbor as day lighted the lonely scene of the Keokuk wreck.

Three nights later, the expedition again moved to the scene of the wreck, this time without LaCoste who was temporarily ill due to exposure during the first operation.

His brother, James, was in command and the entire maneuver was accomplished without a hitch.

The second gun was lifted from its turret and later in the day joined its fellow in Charleston where both were made ready for future action.

The operation, from start to finish, had taken about three weeks and the labor and risk of several hundred men, not to mention three ships, a hulk and numerous small boats.

Yet the prize was worth it. The Dahlgrens, with exception of two English weapons which didn't work, were the heaviest guns in the area and as such were an extremely valuable addition to Confederate defenses.

One went to Fort Sumter where it remained until the latter part of August and at one point was the only serviceable gun in the fort. It subsequently was returned to the city and mounted in Battery Ramsay. Apparently, it was destroyed at the evacuation of the city in February 1865 or was later sold as scrap.

The other Dahlgren was mounted at Battery Bee on Sullivan's Island and helped guard the harbor until the evacuation. Abandoned then by the Confederates and ignored by the victors, the gun and carriage eventually overturned and were buried by the shifting sands.

In 1898, it was discovered, identified beyond all doubt and dug out by troops stationed on the island. It was lent to the city and in August 1899 was mounted on The Battery.

It stands there today, at the corner of East Bay and South Battery, a monument to a group of Americans who proved that courage, ingenuity and hard work can accomplish what many believe impossible.

W.R.

Dahlgren cannon, salvaged from USS Keokuk, is now mounted at White Point Garden.

Land Forces Capture Ship

The gunboat Isaac P. Smith in the Stono River — from a sketch by a naval officer.

During the fall of 1862, the officers of the USS Isaac P. Smith liked to relieve the monotony of the Stono River patrol with pistol practice.

One afternoon, while the gunboat lay at anchor in the river, some of the officers landed at an abandoned plantation house on John's Island. On the gable end of a carriage house they drew for a target the crude charcoal figure of a man.

Often after that, parties of officers got permission from Lt. F.S. Conover, USN, the captain of the Isaac P. Smith, to take their revolvers ashore. They spent many afternoons banging away at the charcoal man on the wall of the carriage house.

Confederate pickets, sheltering themselves in the woods a half mile away, watched with curiosity. When the officers returned to their ship, the pickets sometimes crept down to the carriage house to mark the results of the shooting.

Confederate headquarters was not much interested in the target practice. But just the same, the staff officers read carefully the pickets' reports. The Isaac P. Smith and her sisters prowling the Stono were a nuisance. They made life miserable for gray soldiers on both sides of the Stono. An infantry picket or cavalry vidette who showed himself as a gunboat passed could count on being hustled on his way by a shell. Much more serious was their role in preventing the Confederates from fortifying the banks of the river to bar landings by the enemy at the back door of Charleston.

The staff officers noted that the Isaac P. Smith was the boldest of all the gunboats. Her captain pushed her upriver almost to within range of the Confederate forts near Elliott's Cut before turning back. They told Gen. P.G.T. Beauregard, the commanding general at Charleston.

Gen. Beauregard was an enterprising officer, partial to unconventional techniques of warfare. He ordered a trap.

On the 28th of January, 1863, the Confederates hauled big guns to the Stono shore of James Island. Two were rolled into position near an old Confederate post at Battery Island, lately evacuated because of the Yankee gunboats. Two more heavy guns were placed in position at Thomas Grimball's place on James Island, higher up the river.

That night, field batteries rolled out of their camp near what is now Hampton Park, were taken across the Ashley and over the Stono to John's Island. The teams dragged them down the country roads to Paul Grimball's plantation on the western shore of the Stono. The Grimball house stood on high land just north of the mouth of Abbapoola Creek.

Under a big live oak at the water's edge, a howitzer of the Palmetto Light Artillery was placed. The gunners had a clear view south down the river.

In the same carriage house used by the Federal officers as a target went two more guns. The doors were shut. The officer in command was told that when shooting started he was to throw open the doors, run his pieces into the yard and fire over the garden fence.

Behind the carriage house, the artillerymen parked two big caissons full of ammunition.

At the right of the carriage house, pointing downriver, its muzzle showing over the garden fence, was placed another gun.

More guns were concealed on a line southward from the carriage house. Down the bank of the river went a detachment of signal corps troops with orders to keep watch for advancing gunboats.

By late afternoon, the trap was fully set.

Maj. Charles Alston, the commander of the batteries at Paul Grimball's looked over his arrangements carefully. The Confederates planned to let the Isaac P. Smith steam past the guns near Battery Island on the James Island shore. As the Yankees drew near to Paul Grimball's, they would come under fire from guns on both sides of the river. The guns at Grimball's would discharge their shells "down the throat."

Maj. Alston pointed out to his gunners a bend in the river about 800 yards downstream. There the Isaac P. Smith would come into view. At the bend some timbers from the abandoned fort at Battery Island had drifted ashore.

When the gunboat reached that point, said Maj. Alston, the shooting was to start. He hoped that in the confusion of the unexpected attack, the gunboat might run aground.

At any rate, he said, the guns at Grimball's would halt her and the guns farther down the river could settle with her.

Satisfied that the cannon in the carriage house, behind the garden wall and under the live oak tree were well concealed from view downriver, Maj. Alston ordered his men to bivouac in the woods.

The next morning there was an alarm. The gunners sprinted across the fields to their pieces. The alarm was false. Maj. Alston, however, was pleased with the way his men had responded. He kept them at the guns for a while, making sure the pieces were carefully sighted and ranged. Then he ordered them back to the woods.

The gunners spent the rest of the morning smoking, gossiping and waiting for another warning from the signalmen. Dinner was prepared and eaten. The gunners lolled in the pine straw.

About 4:30 p.m. there was a clatter of hooves. The gunners saw Lt. Gardner, the adjutant, riding full speed down the road which led through the woods to the camp.

When he got close, they heard him yelling, "Get to your guns! Get to your guns!"

The artillerymen rushed toward the edge of the field. They halted in amazement. Within plain view, gliding past the guns at the water's edge was the Isaac P. Smith. Her upper works loomed over the trees that lined the edge of the river. At each of her three mastheads was a sailor, stationed as a lookout.

Where, asked the angry gunners of their excited adjutant, were the signal corpsmen who were to have given the warning signal!

"I don't know, I don't know," said the adjutant, repeating the order to man the guns.

But in order to reach the river bank, the Confederate artillerymen had to cross the field in plain view of the lookouts hanging in the hoops at the mastheads of the Isaac P. Smith. They knew that would be an invitation for a salvo from the four heavy guns the Yankee steamer carried on each broadside.

Yet, unless something was done soon, the gunboat would be safely by and an opportunity lost.

While his men gaped in anger and astonishment at the sight of the Isaac P. Smith slipping out of the trap, Maj. Alston looked about for a way to reach the guns.

A cassina hedge ran from the woods across the field to the yard of the Grimball house. On either side was a ditch. Into the ditch went the major and his men.

Sheltered by the hedge, the gunners crept cautiously toward the plantation yard. At that point, another ditch crossed at right angles. Into this ditch they filed and along it until they reached a gate. Here they halted. The gunboat was now abreast of the house.

Huddling in the ditch at the gate, the detachments waited for a blast which would signal the discovery of their guns.

How could the Isaac P. Smith's lookouts fail to see the howitzer parked under the tree at the water's edge? How could they fail to see the gun looking over the garden fence? How could they miss the caissons parked in the field behind the carriage house?

The Isaac P. Smith passed everything. She disappeared around a bend upstream. The gunners ran toward their pieces.

They were hardly out of the ditch when the boom of shots from James Island told them the gunboat had been fired on by the two guns farther upstream.

The crew of the gun parked beneath the live oak tree were at their stations within a few seconds. Their piece pointed downstream. They stood with their backs to the gunboat. Coming downriver, she would pass less than a hundred yards to their left.

The crews of the two guns in the carriage house piled through the doors and waited impatiently for the gunboat to pass and get far enough ahead to permit them to open the doors and commence firing.

The crew of the gun parked by the garden fence reached the open yard. As they passed between the carriage house and the dwelling, a broadside of grapeshot swept the yard.

By sheer luck for the Confederates, the Isaac P. Smith had anchored in the river just after passing Grimball's.

There she was right under the muzzles of the two guns on the James Island shore. They promptly opened fire. The Isaac P. Smith slipped her cable and ran for it. As she headed around the bend above Grimball's, she was fighting desperately. Whether she ever saw the guns parked at the plantation house the Confederates never found out.

As the steamer passed, the gun beneath the branches of the live oak tree fired into her. The gun looking over the garden fence went into action. The carriage house doors flew open and the concealed battery joined the battle.

The charcoal man on the end of the carriage house shivered in the blast of the guns.

The Isaac P. Smith fought stubbornly. She was only a converted river steamer, but she was heavily armed. The Confederates thought for a few minutes she would run the gauntlet. Then a white plume of steam soared from her escape pipes. A white flag rose into her rigging. Hit three times in her boilers, her power gone, the Isaac P. Smith surrendered.

It was the only instance in the history of the war where a regular warship surrendered to soldiers manning field batteries.

The Isaac P. Smith was hauled upriver and anchored near the Confederate forts. Later she became part of the Confederate naval squadron defending Charleston.

The Confederate reports of the action skipped over the blunders that nearly permitted the prize to escape.

As one Confederate officer wrote later, it didn't make any difference, anyway. "Success," he added, "speaks for itself."

A.M.W.

Blockading ships rested at anchor or cruised slowly outside Charleston Harbor.

Museum Of Naval Architecture

Blockading Ships A Varied Lot

To deal with the tactical problems which confronted it along the difficult coast of South Carolina, the Union Navy assembled a bewildering array of vessels.

In the spring of 1863, as plans were being drawn for an all-out naval assault on Charleston, the South Atlantic Blockading Squadron consisted of more than 60 ships of almost as many shapes and sizes.

Not all were on duty before Charleston at once, of course. The squadron's beat extended from North Carolina to Florida. There were many inlets to be guarded and there were always a number of ships under repair in the North. But because of the emphasis placed in Washington upon sealing off or capturing the "Cradle of Secession" a considerable detachment was constantly off the bar.

By day the ships lay at anchor, rolling to the long Atlantic swells sometimes blistering in the hot sun. At night, either in hope of intercepting blockade runners or from fear of attack, many got under way. Only once, except in the worst weather, did the blockaders move out of sight of Fort Sumter. That was when they were surprised and severely shaken up by a sudden sortie of the two Confederate ironclads stationed at Charleston.

Soon after the shooting stopped, the blockaders were back, however, to stay until the city was surrendered.

A photographer has left a record of part of the fleet — tall sailing vessels and handsome steamers, lying in a long line stretching southward. But the picture is not a fair one. To a sailor's eye, at least, the South Atlantic Blockading Squadron was mostly ugly ducklings.

It was a museum of naval architecture as practiced for better or worse for a period of 50 years. At one end of the esthetic scale was the magnificent old line-of-battle-ship Vermont, a holdover from the days of Nelson. She served out her time as a station ship at Port Royal, a reminder to sentimental tars of the days of wooden ships and iron men.

At the other end, the low end as far as beauty was concerned, were old tubs like the old Hudson River steamer Isaac P. Smith. She got herself captured in the Stono River.

In between the Vermont, a tall, high-sided square-rigger and the Isaac P. Smith, squat, top-heavy and smoky, there were a multitude of other types, regular and irregular.

The Navy tried to classify them in several broad groups.

There were propeller-driven frigates like the Wabash, Adm. Samuel F. DuPont's flagship. She, too, was a handsome ship, a grand example of transition naval design with the lines of half a century ago and the guns and steam power of the modern day.

Smaller than the Wabash but of the same general type were the steam sloops, small frigates. The Housatonic, 11 guns (the Wabash carried 40) was one of these. Another of this class was the Pawnee, a ship which Lieut. A.T. Mahan wryly described as "sui generis," one of a kind and not likely to be repeated. She was the only ship in the Navy, it was said, whose bilges curved lower than the keel.

Handsomer than the Pawnee, but not much use in modern fighting, was the paddle steamer Powhatan, big, square-rigged and vulnerable.

The gunboats, small seagoing vessels designed for naval operations, were a third class of "regular" warship. Some were of the group known as "90-day" gunboats, built in haste at the very start of the war. Others were the so-called "double enders," built for service in narrow, shallow waters.

The gunboats might carry five or six guns of various calibers.

In the largest class of all were the "purchased" vessels, ranging from large seagoing steamers, hastily adapted to war duties, to ferry boats borrowed from New York Harbor, closed in at the ends, armed with one or two big guns and put to work in shallow waters like Stono Inlet.

The purchased ships frequently enjoyed names which did not endear them to professional fighting men. It was hard to get enthusiastic about a ship named Dawn, Quaker City or Madgie. One of the converted merchant ships was named South Carolina, an irony the Confederates allowed to pass unnoted.

As a group, despite their unwarlike names, the purchased ships were versatile and useful. They saw as much action as any others. In January, two of them had absorbed the brunt of the attack by the Confederate ironclads from Charleston.

The most powerful of all the classes was, of course, the ironclads. These fell into two or three groups. The most numerous were the Passaic class monitors of 1,875 tons, each carrying an 11-inch and a 15-inch Dahlgren gun in a single, revolving turret. The monitors were under fire regularly and did their jobs well despite their admiral's mistrust of them.

Often confused with the monitors was the Keokuk, the only one of her class. She also carried two guns — in two fixed "towers" — and that was about the extent of her resemblance to the monitors.

(Continued On Page 48)

U.S. monitor Passaic in heavy weather at sea.

The United States steamer Wabash.

Workmen prepare New Ironsides for sea.

(Continued From Page 47)

BLOCKADING SHIPS

The most impressive of the ironclads was the New Ironsides, a stout, seagoing armored ship modeled on traditional lines but heavily protected and heavily armed with 18 modern guns.

The remainder of the squadron was an assortment of sailing vessels, mortar schooners, tugs, tenders and dispatch boats.

Although ironclads were by no means new in 1863, the Union Navy was the first to bring them into action in squadrons. Off Charleston, for the first time in history, armored warships maneuvered in groups under enemy fire.

They did not accomplish all that was expected of them, but this was due more to defects in command than defects in design. The ironclads, particularly the monitors, were awkward, uncomfortable and not particularly seaworthy, but they were maneuverable and — except for the Keokuk — well protected, quite capable of running in safety past Fort Sumter if ordered to do so.

The Passaic class monitors, especially, could absorb punishment. On the afternoon of April 7, 1863, they lay for two hours under the guns of Sumter, trading shells with the fort as fast as their ponderous guns would permit. The Weehawken took 53 hits and survived. The others received similar punishment. Only one life was lost.

Unfortunately, the Keokuk gave the rest of the ironclads a bad name. She was called a monitor but she was not. Those who served aboard her referred to her as "tinclad" — a "flimsy affair," said an officer who inspected her before she came south.

The guns of the monitors were difficult to serve effectively in action. The Keokuk's were all but impossible. Instead of revolving turrets, her designer had given her two fixed towers pierced on three sides with gun ports. To aim the guns, it was necessary to turn the whole ship.

Her captain on April 7 was a fire-eater by the name of A.C. Rhind. He considered the Keokuk a fraud and to prove it, he took her under Sumter's hottest fire. When he finally pulled her out, she was riddled like a colander. Next day, she went down off Morris Island. Exit the Keokuk design forever.

The remaining armored type, the New Ironsides, was a throwback to the War of 1812, or an advance toward a new era, depending on how you looked at her. She was a high-sided, iron steamer with a formidable ram bow. Though she carried modern guns, they were arranged along the sides in gun ports as conventional sailing warships had always carried them and she had the tall spars of sailing days.

For operations off Charleston, her captain struck the heavy spars and stowed the broad sails. He kept only the stubby lower masts for signaling. The Ironsides had the virtue of looking like a ship and she was heavily armed but she was unwieldy in action. She suffered from a congenital defect of ironclads, a cramped and badly located pilot house which made it necessary for her captain, if he wanted to see what was going on, to expose himself on deck.

But for all that, she was considered a marvelous ship. Displacing more than 3,500 tons, she carried fourteen 11-inch smoothbores and two 150-pounder rifles.

Armor plating 3 inches thick extended from 3 feet above the waterline to 4 feet below. Forward, it terminated in an iron ram 4½ feet deep, 9 inches thick and projecting 6 feet forward of the stem. Above this armor belt, her sides fell back at an angle. They were faced with solid armor plate 4½ inches thick compared to the inch of laminated iron which protected the monitors. On the gun deck fore and aft, were two ironclad bulkheads with rolling doors of iron 5 inches thick.

She was not fast and she drew a great deal of water for the area in which she was employed, but she was nearly invulnerable.

With all these ships at his disposal, Adm. DuPont, commander of the South Atlantic Blockading Squadron, enjoyed an advantage that the Confederates could not hope to overcome. He had ships of every type needed for blockade, assault or fire support of troops ashore.

He had everything — except the confidence he needed to utilize them properly.

A.M.W.

Tiny Davids Were Mighty Weapon

In any catalog of the "ifs" and "might-have-beens" of the Civil War, room should be left for an account of the tiny warships the Confederates called "Davids."

Union naval officers entering Charleston in 1865 found the hulks of these little ships scattered like so many worm-wasted logs along the banks of the Ashley River. They looked upon the wreckage with respect. None knew better that if there had been more Davids, the South might have won the war.

The Davids, semi-submersible torpedo boats, conceived, designed and built at Charleston, were a new form of naval weapon which had the virtue of being practical as well as novel.

The technology of a truly successful submarine was beyond the capacity of American engineers — the Hunley notwithstanding. The construction and operation of semi-submarines was well within their grasp. The Davids, unlike the Hunley, were not ahead of their time. Just one thing stood between them and brilliant success — the incapacity of the South To provide materials for construction.

There were six Davids in various stages of construction or disrepair in Charleston Harbor when the Union Navy finally sailed in at the war's end. These were all that were ever built.

(Continued On Page 49)

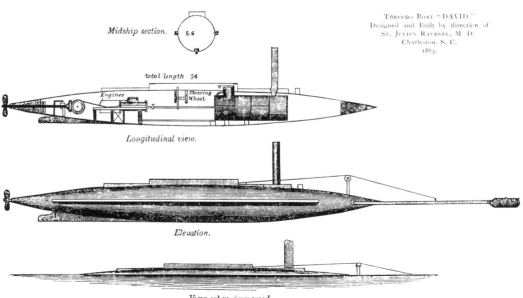

Midship section. 5.6

TORPEDO BOAT "DAVID."
Designed and Built by direction of
St. Julien Ravenel, M. D.
Charleston, S. C.
1863.

total length 54

Engines   Steering Wheel

Longitudinal view.

Elevation.

View when immersed.

Torpedo boat
moored
to dock
in
Charleston
Oct. 25, 1863.

(Continued From Page 48)

TINY DAVIDS

There might have been more if other cities in the Confederacy had been able to muster as many soldiers and civilians with technical ability and imagination as Charleston could.

Some of this talent was native.

Brains and money for creation of the first David came from Theodore D. Stoney and Dr. St. Julian Ravenel, both Charleston men. They teamed up with a young Army officer, named Francis D. Lee, to produce an original naval masterpiece. Stoney paid for her. Dr. Ravenel drew her plans. Capt. Lee provided the torpedo she carried on a long boom at her bow.

One other circumstance helped create a favorable climate at Charleston for the birth of the David. It was the presence here of that remarkable soldier — and practicing naval genius — P.G.T. Beauregard. Gen Beauregard was star-crossed when it came to commanding armies in the field, but he might have flown an admiral's flag with distinction. He had brilliant ideas about naval construction and took a dim view of the lethargic C.S. naval command in the harbor. He was a sharp and continual critic of Confederate shipbuilding at Charleston.

Contemplating the ponderous iron gunboats lying at anchor off The Battery or under construction on the Cooper River, he was displeased. He thought the gunboats expensive, slow, unseaworthy and unfit for long-range fighting, and he told the Navy so.

He was right — so right, in fact, that the Navy Department did not even attempt to refute the charges. If the Palmetto State was too feeble to steam against the tide, if the Chicora could not elevate her guns, if they were all too deep to cross the bar — well, that was the way they were meant to be.

Gen. Beauregard was unconvinced. As far as he was concerned, the ironclads were eating up precious material that might be put to better use elswwhere. Long before the idea of the David came full-blown, Beauregard was writing letters urging the Navy to give up its conventional program of shipbuilding and turn instead to a fast, new type of ship "of perhaps 500 tons" which could carry an explosive charge and place it where it would do the most good against the sides of Federal warships. Work was actually well advanced on this project under the enthusiastic direction of Capt. Lee when it became clear that the iron needed to complete the "torpedo ram" would never be furnished. The wooden hull had to be left to rot.

Capt. Lee, however, still got his chance to try torpedo warfare. He teamed up with Stoney and Ravenel.

The David and her sisters were much of a kind. With one exception, those that the Yankees found at Charleston were 50 feet long and 5½ or 6 feet wide. Each had a boiler and a steam engine which turned a single propeller.

They were equipped with tanks which permitted

Hull of David rests on mud at low tide after end of hostilities.

them to sink low in the water. In fighting trim, only a few inches of freeboard remained. High above, however, was the tall smokestack required to furnish adequate draft for the fires under the boiler.

After the first David had proven itself, the Navy finally saw the light and ordered a number for its own use. None, so far as can be determined, ever saw service. One was to have been 150 feet long, a formidable ship. She was incomplete at the war's end.

But even when they had been thoroughly impressed with the possibilities of the new warcraft, the authorities could not bring themselves to concentrate all their energies upon them. To the end, construction continued in a hit or miss fashion, hampered by the continuing demands of the big ironclads upon the short supply of iron.

By the end of the war, the Navy wanted the Davids badly, but it could not have them. Work went so slowly the worms outstripped the shipwrights. They ate up the Davids at their piers before they could be finished.

The Navy never even got the use of the first David. She was the private property of Messrs. Stoney and Ravenel and they were not taking orders from naval officers.

It took the Federal Navy, finally, to get a second David under way. When the Yankees took over, they put a boiler and an engine in one of the hulks and steamed it around the harbor with great success.

While the Navy was hesitating to experiment with the new medium of torpedo warfare, the Confederate Army in keeping with the example set by Gen. Beauregard, plowed eagerly ahead.

Capt. Lee, the energetic Army torpedoman, was authorized to try to bag the big frigate New Ironsides.

He appropriated the hulk of an unfinished gunboat and put aboard a wheezy old engine. Then he fitted a spar torpedo to the bow and set out across the bar.

With almost incredible carelessness, the watch on the deck of the Ironsides permitted the Confederates to draw right alongside. The Southerners were on the point of firing when the swift running tide took command of their clumsy vessel. She was swept down athwart the ironclad's anchor chain and hung there.

While they struggled desperately to work free, the Confederates invented convincing answers to inquiring hails from the Ironsides. When they finally got clear, it was too late. The sleepy frigate was finally awake, her crew at general quarters. The Confederates returned to port.

Two months passed and it became the turn of the David, now finished and ready for sea, to have a go at the Ironsides.

The Federals were more alert than at the time of the first attack, but the David moved up to the big ship without difficulty. A blast from a shotgun cut down the officer of the deck. Then the David drove home her punch.

The Ironsides was hurt but not sunk. Eventually she had to leave her station and go north for repairs. The David returned safely and the operation was counted a success.

While this attack was not accomplished without difficulties, the David had proved herself. For once, it seemed, the Confederacy had at its disposal a cheap, reliable, formidable weapon with which it might break the blockade.

Still, the Southerners could not bring themselves to abandon their pursuit of seapower through surface ships. Work was commenced on a number of Davids but they were never completed due to scarcity of materials.

A.M.W.

Slaves rush to join raiders who burned plantation homes and buildings along the Combahee River June 2, 1863.

Raiders On The River

Combahee Homes Left In Ruins

A recruiting expedition for Negro units at Hilton Head left charred ruins of plantation homes along the Combahee River.

The Northern raiders, led by Col. James Montgomery, consisted of 300 members of the Second South Carolina Volunteers augmented by a section of artillery. The Second was a Negro regiment composed in the main of former slaves who had escaped their South Carolina masters and made their way to the Union lines where they had been taken to Hilton Head, enlisted as soldiers and whipped into an infantry unit. They were led by white officers. The artillery outfit was entirely white.

The raiders left Hilton Head June 1, 1863, aboard three vessels, the gunboat John Adams and transports Harriet A. Weed and Sentinel. En route, however, the Sentinel ran aground and considerable time was lost transferring her troops to the other vessels.

Resuming the voyage, the two ships arrived off Field's Point (about 20 miles up the Combahee) during the early morning of the 2nd. A small force was landed, and the Confederate six-man picket, which apparently had not been particularly alert, took to its heels after dispatching scouts to warn a Southern unit stationed at Chisolmville about 10 miles away.

The vessels with the main body of troops continued upriver several miles to a group of plantations where the Weed landed many of her troops. The Adams pushed farther upstream to destroy a pontoon bridge.

From start to finish, the raiders had things pretty much their own way. The Southern resistance was disorganized and later a board of investigation rebuked the commanding officer and two of his lieutenants for their failure to prevent much of the loss of property carried off by the invaders or put to the torch.

The investigator's report stated that the Southern commander had little knowledge of the country and had not properly drilled or disciplined his troops. The former resulted in men being improperly stationed to repulse the invaders while the general lack of initiative on the part of the Confederates was attributed to the latter.

From the Northern point of view, the raid was highly successful.

Some 725 slaves were taken aboard the ships as well as five horses. Put to the torch were four plantation mansions, six mills, numerous outbuildings and quantities of cotton and rice.

Southerners, while ruefully admitting the raid was an unqualified success, were scathing in their denunciation of the Yankees. Even normally cold official reports are sprinkled with such words as "fiends," "degraded," and "atrocious conduct."

The newspapers were equally vehement and the Charleston Mercury published an excellent description of the raid as seen by one of the planters who watched his property go up in flames.

The writer, presumably Joshua Nicholls, observed the holocaust from the safety of woods not far from his plantation house.

He saw his residence burn, along with barns and threshing mill, while towers of smoke marked fires consuming similar property on neighboring plantations.

"...The Negroes, men and women, were rushing to the boat (the Yankee vessel) with their children," Mr. Nichols related.

"...The Negroes seemed to be utterly transformed, drunk with excitement and capable of the wildest excesses. The roaring of the flames, the barbarous howls of the Negroes, the blowing of horns, the harsh steam whistle and the towering columns of smoke from every quarter, made an impression on my mind which can never be effaced. Here, I thought to myself, is a repetition of San Domingo...."

After describing the departure of the raiding party, Mr. Nicholls continued:

"...I was left alone to survey with tearful eyes the wide scene of desolation around me. My pleasant and comfortable house was in ashes. My library, containing over 3,500 volumes, in the collection of which I had employed 20 years of my life...which I had treasured up as a consolation for the present and as a refuge against disease and old age. Every memorial I possessed of my past life and every material object to which my heart still clung, not for its intrinsic value, but for the unspeakable associations connected with it...vanished, perished in the flames. And this was not done in a tempest by the lightning of heaven, but sanctioned by the order of the civilized, philanthropic, liberty-loving Yankee...."

Mr. Nicholls went on to say that every slave but one joined the raiders. This was an old woman who was stripped of her clothing by her compatriots and left behind.

On the beach, the slaves left several wagon loads of goods looted from the main house as well as their own pots, kettles and extra clothing which they were not permitted to take aboard ship.

Finally, the writer devoted a few well-chosen words to his opinion of the raiders and closed with these words which, while seemingly mild, leave little doubt to their author's frame of mind:

"They (the Yankees) have laid me under obligations which I hope my brave countrymen will repay with interest."

W.R.

Union troops storm ashore on Morris Island under cover of artillery fire from Folly Island.

Brilliant Maneuver

Yankees Land On Morris Island

Yankee troops stormed ashore on Morris Island July 10, 1863, to launch a long and bitter campaign for the three-and-a-half-mile strip of sand leading to the entrance of Charleston Harbor.

The assault was launched under cover of a vicious artillery bombardment and rolled some two miles before it bogged down from sheer exhaustion of the attackers who had fought their way through heat and sand to accomplish brilliantly one of the toughest maneuvers in warfare — the amphibious assault of a defended beach.

Weeks of preparations and hard work set the stage for the four-hour battle and contributed immeasurably toward its success.

Planning probably had been going on for some time, but actual work at the site started shortly after Brig. Gen. Quincy A. Gillmore assumed command of the Department of the South June 12.

Three days later, the general wrote his superiors in Washington:

''...I have made a reconnaissance of Morris Island and its surroundings next to Folly and James Islands. Gen. (Israel) Vogdes is in command on Folly Island. All arrangements thus far have been defensive. He will openly continue in that attitude, but I have directed him to plant behind the sand hills on the north end of Folly Island (secretly and without being seen by the enemy) batteries that will be able to dismount, in one hour, all the enemy's guns on the south end of Morris Island....''

Vogdes started work immediately and each night saw Yankee infantry and engineers building gun positions on Little Folly Island, adjoining Big Folly, and only a few hundred yards across Lighthouse Inlet from the Confederate positions on Morris.

Men worked quietly within earshot of Southern pickets; then, before dawn, all traces of work were removed and the troops returned to camps on Big Folly to sleep during the day.

After a time, work progressed to a point where at first a few and later a large number could remain in the position and continue to labor during the day despite sentinels on Morris and James Islands who could see across the low sand hills and brush of Little Folly.

A few days before work started on the batteries, a blockade runner, the steamer Ruby, went ashore on a bar just off Little Folly and the Yankees used her to further their scheme.

They brought up field guns to shell the wreck, but quickly retreated when the Confederates lobbed a few shells their way.

Then, to divert interest from the work on Little Folly, the Southerners were permitted to strip the ship although she lay within point-blank range of numerous Yankee cannon.

Work on the position was essentially completed by July 3 and 47 guns and mortars were ready to open fire July 6.

To make up the assault force, some 6,500 additional troops were secretly landed on Big Folly during the

first part of July. The ships carrying them were loaded at Hilton Head, then kept over the horizon until dusk when they moved into the Stono River. They discharged the troops in the dark and were again out of sight before dawn.

In addition to the buildup of troops and construction of the batteries, Gen. Gillmore had devised two more facets to the assault on Morris — two diversionary attacks.

The first involved a demonstration on James Island and the second an attempt to cut the Charleston and Savannah Railroad at Jacksonboro.

The James Island demonstration, designed to draw men from Morris Island, failed in this, but did confuse Confederate commanders and prevented reinforcement of the Morris Island garrison.

The attack on the railroad was a dismal failure with the loss by the Yankees of two pieces of artillery and a small steamer.

Troops making the main effort were loaded into rowboats in Folly River during the night of July 8. They started through creeks behind Folly to Lighthouse Inlet, but were halted en route and the attack postponed because of bad weather.

They embarked again the following night and by dawn were at the entrance to the inlet, but screened initially from Confederate view by marsh.

At 5 a.m., the batteries on Little Folly, concealing brush and sand having been removed during the night,

(Continued On Page 52)

Federals occupy Coles Island, near Folly, in preparation for Morris Island Assault.

(Continued From Page 51)

YANKEES LAND

opened a heavy fire on Confederate positions across the inlet.

Despite the fire, Confederate artillerymen manned their guns and before long, the boats having been spotted, shell fragments were whistling about the ears of the waiting troops.

After two hours, the signal came for the assault. The boats swept across Lighthouse Inlet and bumped the sands of Morris Island while shot and shell poured overhead into Confederate positions just beyond and minie balls from Southern riflemen ricocheted off the water.

Leaving the boats, which immediately went to Folly to pick up reserve forces, the attackers formed ranks on the beach. Some swept forward to overrun infantry in the rifle pits. Others took over single-gun artillery positions driving out, killing or capturing the defenders.

About 9 a.m. the attack ground to a halt within musket range of Fort Wagner. This fortification, located less than a mile from the northern end of Morris Island, served as the outer defense of Fort Sumter and was a strong defensive position.

The Federal attack had been supported by fire from four Navy monitors which during the battle had used their 11 and 15-inch guns to enfilade Confederate artillery positions on the southern end of the island, thus contributing heavily to their downfall.

The assault force numbered some 2,000 men and sustained only 15 dead and 91 wounded. The light casualties were credited mainly to the intense bombardment and to the inability of Confederate guns, due to their location on high sand dunes, to depress sufficiently to hit Northern troops as they landed and formed on the beach for the assault.

Confederate losses were listed at 294 killed, wounded and captured out of a force numbering about 700 infantry and crews for eight guns and three mortars.

Yankee reports claimed the attack came as a complete surprise to the Confederates. The Southerners were careful — perhaps too careful — to emphasize that they knew all about the impending assault.

Probably a little of both is true. Scouts spotted the boats in the Folly River July 8. This obviously presaged an attack. The Confederates also knew that a certain amount of work on gun positions was being done on Little Folly.

However, the Southerners apparently had no idea of the extent of the work and the tremendous weight of metal from 47 weapons that landed on them July 10 proved far more than a surprise — it was a definite shock.

W.R.

July 18, 1863 attack on Battery Wagner. Fighting was hot and casualties heavy.

U.S. Troops Assault Battery Wagner

Yankee invaders found Morris Island real estate a deceptive investment.

They got two-thirds of it for almost nothing when their troops stormed ashore July 10, 1863.

Two months later, they picked up much of the other third free when Confederates abandoned it.

But the remaining few hundred yards went foot by foot at a high price in blood and hardship.

The July 10th attack had swept to within 600 yards or so of Battery Wagner, a formidable Confederate earthwork stretching across a narrow section of the island about three-fourths of a mile from the northern end and three miles from the southern.

This bastion, an outpost of Fort Sumter, bristled with heavy guns which commanded the entire area of Morris taken by the North. It had to be reduced if the Federals wanted to use the island as a base of operations against Charleston.

The first attempt came the following morning when two regiments led by four companies of another jumped off at daybreak.

The four companies, 191 men of the 7th Connecti-cut, started about 500 yards from the fort. They moved quietly, guns loaded, bayonets fixed, until fired on by Confederate pickets. Then, giving a cheer, they rushed forward on the heels of the retreating Southern pickets.

The assault carried across the fort's wet ditch, which held about a foot of water, and to the crest where they lay just below the parapet waiting support.

But aid never came. The first sound of rifle fire had brought Confederate defenders swarming to the parapets and the entire line blazed with rifle and cannon fire over the heads of the 7th Connecticut and into the two regiments advancing in support.

Stunned by the sudden, intense fire at 200 yards, both regiments hit the dirt. The advance stopped cold. Within minutes, the initial shock gone, the attack was rolling again — but too late.

The Southerners had taken advantage of the delay to work over the 7th with rifle and grenade at point-blank range.

The Northerners were forced off the crest and with the foothold lost, a general retreat was sounded, the 7th running a gauntlet of fire which cut their strength to 88 men from the original 191. Total Union casualties were 339. The Confederates lost only a dozen men.

The Yankees fell back to lick their wounds and consider Battery Wagner with new respect. They had failed once with a relatively limited attack. Next time they'd mean business.

They brought up artillery and set the next assault for the following week.

Forty-two guns and mortars opened on Battery Wagner during the morning of July 18. About noon, they were joined by guns of the fleet and a concentrated bombardment was poured into the fortification until nightfall.

The shelling, however, had little effect. The shells simply threw sand into the air to fall back about the same spot and leave the major facilities of the fort relatively undamaged.

The garrison remained hidden in the bastion's bombproof, completely safe from the shelling. Only

(Continued On Page 53)

(Continued From Page 52)

U.S. TROOPS ASSAULT

a few men stayed outside. They occasionally fired a gun to show the fort was still in action and kept an eye on the Federals to sound the alarm as soon as an infantry attack started. These men, despite lack of protection other than the parapets, lost only eight killed and 20 wounded during the day's bombardment.

As night approached, the intensity of the shelling increased until about 7:45 p.m. when the bombardment slackened and the lines of Union troops were seen advancing.

The Yankees, about 6,000 strong, had been assembled in three brigades. The First was composed of five regiments with the 54th Massachusetts, a Negro outfit with white officers, in the lead. The Second and Third Brigades contained four regiments each.

The First Brigade had moved only a short distance when it ran into heavy fire from Confederates who had manned the parapets as soon as the artillery barrage had slackened.

Word was sent back for the Second Brigade to hurry forward, but due to confusion in orders, the Second was slow in starting. The delay, although only about 20 minutes, was long enough in the hectic pace of battle to ruin Yankee chances of taking the fort.

Mauled by artillery and rifle fire during the advance, the leading regiment of the First Brigade broke and its men struggled to the rear disorganizing the following regiments and carrying parts of them along in retreat.

This left the First Brigade a shambles with the mass of its men headed toward the rear, while individuals and small units of all the regiments continued to fight their way toward Wagner. These men battled into one section of the fort where a Southern unit had, in refusing to man the parapets, left a gap in the defenses.

But the attackers in the fort were few and disorganized and, without prompt support could do little but hang on and await reinforcement.

When the Second Brigade swept forward in support, its ranks were disrupted by elements of the First streaming through them and with one of their own

Ditch and southern slope of Battery Wagner after July 18th assault.

regiments breaking under the storm of shot and shell and joining the retreat.

Like the First, parts of the Second Brigade made it into the fort, but also without much semblance of organization.

In the darkness, it was almost impossible to tell friend from foe, yet the battle raged approximately three hours, much of it hand-to-hand.

Finally, when it became apparent the Third Brigade would not be committed, and the Confederates were evidently getting reinforcements and preparing to counterattack, the senior Union officer left alive in Wagner ordered a quiet withdrawal.

He estimated that no more than 500 or 600 men from both brigades had made it into the fort. They were sent to the rear a few at a time while those remaining kept up a hot fire on the Southerners.

Escape of the attackers was attributed to this method of withdrawal for they could have been overwhelmed had the Confederates realized a retreat was in progress.

Failure of the July 18th attack, like the one of the 11th, was blamed on lack of timely reinforcement. However, the second attack was far more costly. Union casualties, including a large number of field-grade officers, totaled more than 1,500. Confederate losses were in the neighborhood of 200.

The attacks ended any hopes of the North for a quick conquest of Wagner and turned their thoughts to siege operations through orthodox approaches. This would be a long, hard process, but one relatively sure of eventual success.

W.R.

Damaged Parrott rifle lies atop parapet of Marsh Battery shortly after gun burst Aug. 23, 1863.

Union Builds Marsh Battery

The whine of artillery shells brought war home to Charleston during the early hours of Aug. 22, 1863.

Dropping out of the darkened skies, the missiles came from a Federal battery in the marsh of Morris Island.

Dubbed officially the ''Marsh Battery,'' the weapon is better known to history as the ''Swamp Angel,'' an affectionate title apparently bestowed by Union soldiers. The gun was a standard 8-inch Parrott rifle which lofted a 150-pound projectile into the city roughly 7,900 yards away.

It opened about 1:30 a.m. of the 22nd, firing some 15 rounds at the sleeping city. The following night, a few minutes before 12, it resumed fire at 15-minute

(Continued On Page 54)

'Swamp Angel' ready to fire on Charleston.

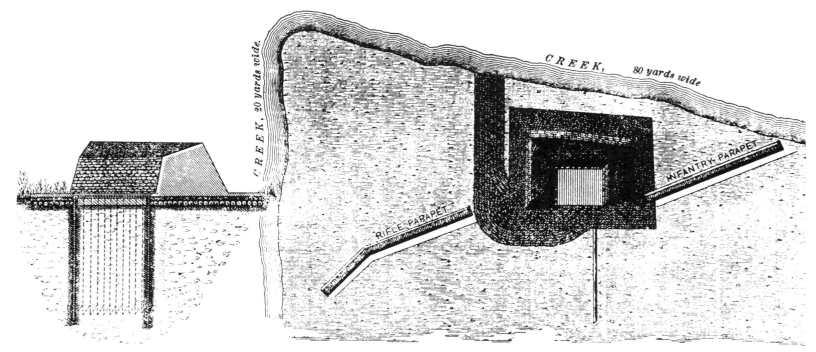

Planks driven into mud (left) formed open-ended box. Parapet and road to creek surrounded platform (right).

(Continued From Page 53)

UNION BUILDS

intervals tossing mainly incendiary shells.

The gun burst at the 36th round, blowing out the breech just behind the vent and hurling the weapon off its carriage and onto the parapet in front.

Its career was short and actual damage inflicted on the city slight, but as a splendid example of Yankee engineering ability, if for nothing else, the Marsh Battery has earned a niche in history.

An 8-inch Parrott weighed roughly 16,500 pounds. Yet Federal engineers and artillerymen managed to transport such a monster into the marsh, fire it from atop 18 to 20 feet of jelly-like pluff mud, and hit a target almost 4½ miles away.

considering that it is difficult even for a man to walk thorugh the mud of Charleston marshlands, the feat must be viewed as a masterful achievement.

July 16, less than a week after the Federals had landed on Morris Island, engineers went on reconnaissance and selected a site about three-quarters of a mile from high ground on Morris in the small bight of land between the junction of two creeks with a third.

During the succeeding days, experiments were conducted to determine the characteristics of pluff mud, particularly its ability to sustain weights. At the same time, plans for the battery were drawn. They were submitted to headquarters Aug. 2 and work on the emplacement was soon under way.

Knowing it would be useless simply to place a gun

Battery was armed with mortars after 'Swamp Angel' burst.

platform on the marsh, the engineers devised a scheme which permitted it to "float" on a column of mud surrounded by, but not attached to, a sandbag parapet which also "floated" on the mud.

Three-by-six inch pine planks, 20 or so feet long, were placed one at a time upright in the mud, then forced downward until their pointed ends struck hard sand and were driven a short distance into it.

Other planks were placed similarly until a rough "box" was formed with the lower edges of the sides driven into the sand and the upper sticking a few inches out of the mud.

On the mud in the center of the "box" was laid

marsh grass, tarpaulins, 15 inches of well-tamped sand, and then three tiers of three-inch thick planks to form a platform or "deck" for the gun.

Surrounding this, but not touching it, were laid logs, spiked together, on a bed of marsh, tarpaulins and sand. Atop the logs were piled thousands of sandbags of which the parapet was built.

The theory of the battery was that weight of the sandbagged parapet would compress the mud and force it upward against the gun platform, holding it at a constant level. If the log foundation of the parapet sank, more sandbags could be added to increase the height of the parapet while displaced mud would exert pressure against the "box" of boards surrounding the gun platform and would also rise around the battery in the form of a gooey glacis, or slope.

Since the battery was located on the edge of a creek, materials, and for awhile workmen, were transported by boat. Later, when a bridge-like causeway was completed, the men walked from Morris Island.

By the night of Aug. 17, the battery was ready for its gun which was brought to the site by boat, installed and ready for operation on the 21st.

Shortly after opening on the 22nd, firing was stopped for a time when it was found the gun had slid backwards 20 inches or so. Engineers inspected the battery and reported that the trouble was easily corrected and that in general the battery worked to perfection.

After the bursting of the 8-incher, no other weapons of such large caliber were placed in the battery, since within about two weeks the North had taken all of Morris Island and guns directed against the city could be fired from easier and closer positions.

However, the Marsh Battery was not abandoned. Sea coast mortars were moved in first, then later a 30-pounder Parrott rifle which directed its fire primarily against Fort Sumter.

W.R.

Civil War photograph of 30-pounder Parrott rifle which replaced mortars.

Bombardment of Charleston came as surprise to its citizens.

City Shelled — Grim New Epoch Of War

Late at night on Aug. 21, 1863, Gen. P.G.T. Beauregard's staff officers in Charleston were aroused to receive an extraordinary message from the direction of Morris Island.

It was an unsigned dispatch, dated that evening at Federal headquarters, to which the name of Gen. Quincy A. Gillmore, the Union commander, was appended.

The note was blunt and to the point: All Confederate troops must be withdrawn from Morris Island and Fort Sumter within four hours or the Yankees would commence a bombardment of Charleston.

The Confederates could scarcely believe their eyes. Would an officer of Gen. Gillmore's reputation consider devastation of a sleeping city filled with women and children? And if he were to authorize such a distasteful procedure, would he be likely to forget to sign a message embodying his threat?

Ordinarily, Gen. Beauregard would have been hastily awakened to pass judgment on such a document. But he was out of the city, inspecting fortifications in the surrounding countryside. Even a fast courier could not reach him before the time allowed by Gen. Gillmore — already half gone — would expire.

The staff officers, still doubtful of the authenticity of the message, but well aware the Northerners could carry out such a threat, decided to stall.

Under a flag of truce, the unsigned message was returned to the Federals with a polite note calling attention to the missing signature.

Then at 1:30 a.m., a little more than two hours after the note had arrived at Confederate headquarters, a gun boomed from the marshes of Morris Island. The first shell of the war deliberately aimed at Charleston crashed into the city. Others followed.

The Federal commander's decision to bombard Charleston marked a grim, new epoch in the struggle for the "Cradle of Secession." From that time forward, the city, already half ruined by the fire of 1861, was given over largely to rats and weeds. The gunfire pushed residents of the lower wards out of their homes into areas above Calhoun Street. Downtown, grass grew in the streets.

All of this served to relieve some of the frustration the Federals felt at failing to capture or subdue Fort Sumter. Otherwise, it helped them little. The Confederates complained bitterly about the bombardment, but they resisted as stoutly as ever.

The first shells during the small hours of Aug. 22 confirmed the authenticity of the warning message, even before it arrived a second time at Confederate headquarters, this time properly signed.

Gen. Beauregard was present to receive it. He sat down and wrote an angry and defiant reply.

"An act of inexcusable barbarity," he termed the bombardment and he predicted that history would take a dim view of Gen. Gillmore's behavior.

After he read this indictment, Gen. Gillmore's confidence in the correctness of his course seemed to waver. He penned a half-hearted justification. Then he called off the bombardment for two days to allow

the Confederates to clear noncombatants out of the city.

Gen. Gillmore's disappointment at his inability to conquer the approaches to the city showed clearly in his message to Gen. Beauregard regarding a temporary suspension in the firing.

If noncombatants suffered as a result of the bombardment, he wrote, the responsibility would rest not with him but with the Confederate authorities who had stubbornly refused to surrender Sumter and Morris Island.

Gillmore conceded that the Confederates had a point when they had asked for a signature to authenticate the surrender demand of the night before, but he did not explain his questionable conduct in opening fire while the message was being passed back and forth through the lines.

That was all that he would yield, however. As far as the Federals were concerned, there was no merit in the Confederate argument that the city should be immune to attack. The bombardment would go on.

Gillmore was as good as his word. Within 48 hours, the city was hearing from the Federal battery again. The shellfire did not continue for long. The heavy gun, especially mounted to command the city, exploded after only a few rounds.

The precedent had been set, however. From now on, the Federals in the operations against Charleston would permit their enemies to draw no distinctions based on age, sex or military status.

A.M.W.

First shots came from notorious 'Swamp Angel' battery in marsh of Morris Island.

Confederates Lived Like Moles

A cycle of events initiated when Southern cannon opened fire on Fort Sumter from Morris Island in April 1861, was completed by Northerners on July 20, 1863.

That day a Union gun, also on Morris Island, fired the first shot from a land battery to be aimed at Sumter since Maj. Robert Anderson's time.

Situations were at last reversed. From now on it would be Federals on the outside of Sumter looking in upon a hapless garrison. And it would be Confederates on the inside looking out — when they were bold enough or foolhardy enough to raise their heads above the parapet.

The shell that brought history full circle caused the Confederates little immediate concern. It was only a nuisance shot, a 30-pounder with little battering power.

A few days passed, however, and the shells from Morris Island, delivered at considered intervals from the new Union batteries under construction there, began to convey a new and disturbing message to the men in the fort: Sumter was doomed to ruin.

For several days ranging shots fell into the fort. As the Federals completed the arrangement of guns in each battery each gun would fire a few times and go silent.

On Aug. 12, one of these shells soared over the wall of Sumter nearest Morris and descended into a casemate on the opposite side of the fort. The explosion shook the fort to its foundations. The baking ovens of the garrison were destroyed. A half-bushel of bricks fell out of the arch of the casemate upon the gun below.

"The effect," the Confederates noted with astonishment, "was not due to penetration but to the shock of the explosion."

Shortly afterwards another shell struck the outside of the wall. The Confederates, probing the scar with a measuring rod, found that the projectile had driven 4 feet 10 inches into the brickwork. The wall at this point was just 5 feet thick.

This preliminary firing, eerily akin to the tuning up of a warlike orchestra, made sufficiently clear to the Confederates what to expect.

The overture to the series of bombardments which was to last for many months finally began on Aug. 17. By this time the engineers in Sumter had taken emergency measures to bolster the brick walls.

The casemates behind the exposed flanks and rear of the fort were closed up and filled with sand and wet cotton. These were the first steps in the transition of Sumter from an old-fashioned brick fort to a modern earthwork.

As the bombardment which began Aug. 17 continued, the brickwork melted away before the iron storm. As fast as they could, working night and day, the Southerners replaced the bricks with earth.

As the earthworks filled up the fort, the Confederates burrowed into them to find places in which to live, work and store their munitions.

Against the rear wall, termed the gorge, and the southeast wall, which also looked toward the enemy on Morris Island, the Southerners erected shellproof shelters to replace the ruined casemates and barracks in which they had once lived.

The rubble of the walls now made a sloping pile facing the Union guns. It served well enough for protection in that direction.

Heavy timbers were erected facing the old parade ground and thick plank roofs were laid over the new rooms thus created. On top was piled sand 6 to 10 feet thick. From bunks in these new underground barracks, the men of the garrison could look out over the parade ground.

For more than 300 feet around the inside of the fort, the underground quarters ran.

On the northwest, the whole lower tier of casemates plus some on the second level were converted into bombproof quarters. On the north face, three casemates were shored up and covered with eight feet of earth. Near this was the main magazine.

On the northeast face, facing Sullivan's Island and the channel, four casemates, not badly damaged, were closed in at the rear and armed with three heavy guns bearing on the entrance to the harbor.

Outside the fort a new dock was built facing the city and a new sallyport cut through the walls.

Soldiers who wanted to pass from one part of the fort to another could use the long, low, narrow passageways which connected the quarters and batteries. On quiet days they could reach the parade ground through one of several doors.

Thus protected from the enemy's guns, the Confederate soldiers, except when they were on duty on the parapets, found life on Sumter fairly safe, but tedious and not especially healthy.

The fort, gloomy when first built, was now gloomier than ever.

"The view by night," wrote Lt. John Johnson, the engineer officer, "was at all times most impressive in

Union shells made short work of brick walls.

its strange, silent grandeur. To a beholder looking down from the rim of the ruin, all within seems alike dark and gloomy, save when a chance shower of sparks, blown out from a smouldering fire left in the parade, lights up for a moment some of the great rugged blocks of brickwork and the pools of stagnant water into which they had tumbled from the battered walls.

"Lanterns here and there glance across the spacious enclosure as, borne by unseen hands, they light the way — some for long files of men toiling with heavy timbers or bags of sand over the roughest footing and up steep, crumbling, dangerous slopes; some to direct the heaping of material over damaged hiding places, repaired for perhaps the fiftieth time since the firing began, or to secure a new and better shelter for the garrison; others, flashing through chance crevices in the ruined casemates, tell of secret galleries of communication burrowing deep and mining their way slowly under hills of rubbish to give unity to the work and confidence to its defenders.

"Halfway up the sloping ruins of the fort, which resemble most the interior of an ancient amphitheatre, the guards are posted in groups, dimly seen wrapped in blankets, sitting around a little fire allowed to warm but to give no light.

"Higher yet are the sentinels, peering into the night over the remains of the old fort's ramparts, while last, though not least, is the solitary lookout, exposed full length to the dangers of the firing at the top of some ladder put up at the most critical breach."

While there was danger in plenty to those exposed in the fort, the soldiers could generally count on escaping the fatigue details which are a soldier's normal lot. Special working forces of Negroes, supervised by white men, did most of the heavy work.

The workmen stayed under cover all day emerging at nightfall to shovel and haul until daylight. The Confederates took care not to expose them to harm more than the occasion required, but they suffered casualties just the same.

Regular reliefs for both soldiers and slaves were provided, although sometimes the boats bringing the relieving forces had to lie hundreds of yards off the dock and send in supplies and men by small boat.

Under these difficult conditions of warfare, the men in Sumter, officers and men, free or slave, preserved a high degree of composure and fighting spirit.

On Christmas Day, 1863, while their comrades on John's Island were engaged in a bloody dispute with Federal gunboats, the garrison of Sumter was enjoying an elegant dinner served on the chassis of a 10-inch columbiad.

For chairs to match this improvised table, the soldiers employed carpetbags, sandbags, stands of grape and round shot from which to open an assault on a plentiful supply of roast turkey, wild duck, oysters and sweet potatoes.

The centerpiece in the headquarters casemate of the "Three Gun Battery" that day perfectly represented the spirit of the garrison.

It was half of a 15-inch shell, delivered presumably by a Yankee cannon, set in a flattened sandbag and serving for a punchbowl.

A.M.W.

Charleston: Battle Of Heavy Guns

The Battle of Charleston was primarily a duel of heavy artillery.

From the opening Confederate shots against Maj. Robert Anderson in Fort Sumter to the final bombardment of that fortification and the city, heavy guns carried the brunt of the work.

There were a few infantry engagements during the years — vicious assaults on Lamar, Wagner, Sumter and Johnson — but by and large, Charleston was a duel between the heaviest cannon both sides could muster.

In the beginning, smoothbore weapons were used on both sides, mainly 24, 32 and 42-pounders. Only one rifled weapon was used in the April 12-13, 1861, bombardment of Fort Sumter. This was a 10-pounder Blakely rifle. It was small, far too light to batter down a fort, but it drilled into Sumter's walls with an effectiveness which showed unequivocally that rifles were the weapons of the future.

The Confederate commander, Gen. P.G.T. Beauregard, recognized this and although he realized the inability of the hard-pressed Confederacy to manufacture sufficient rifles, he immediately did what he could on a local scale. He couldn't make heavy ordnance, but he had a Charleston firm reinforce the existing 24, 32 and 42-pounders with iron bands around the breech, then rifle the tubes. This not only turned a smoothbore into a rifle, but by using an elongated, rather than a spherical, projectile, almost doubled its weight.

The Confederacy did turn out some rifled weapons, primarily the Brooke, several of which were later used here to good effect. It also purchased foreign cannon, notably two huge Blakely rifles.

These were rated as 600-pounders and fired a shell almost 13 inches in diameter. They were brought in through the blockade and eventually mounted in Charleston, but were not particularly satisfactory and were never used against the enemy.

The remaining Confederate heavy ordnance consisted of 8 and 10-inch columbiads and two 11-inch Dahlgrens. The columbiads, orginally smoothbores, were rifled and banded in some cases and were the backbone of the defense against the Union ironclads as well as troops assaulting the various Southern forts.

The Dahlgrens, also fine weapons, were Northern naval pieces salvaged by the Confederates from the sunken Federal ironclad Keokuk in one of the most daring operations of the war.

At the start of the conflict, the Union was little better off than the Confederacy, perhaps even worse since much Federal armament was captured when forts in the South were occupied by the Confederates.

However, Northern industry soon became proficient in turning out arms and its heavy ordnance later in the war was rivaled by none.

Mainstay of Army heavy ordnance was the Parrott. This was a cast iron rifle with wrought iron breech reinforcing. It came in various calibers, the larger being 100, 200, and 300-pounders. These weapons, which fired a cylindrical projectile, were used extensively on Morris Island as breaching batteries against Fort Sumter and later turned their fire against the city.

Battery Stevens mounted two 100-pounder Parrotts. A third lies on the ground.

The site for the first of these batteries, left and rear of the First Parallel, was selected during the night of July 21, 1863. Between that date and Aug. 20, a total of 20 guns and mortars were emplaced in nine batteries. In the main, these weapons were 100 and 200-pounder Parrotts although one battery had two 80-pounder Whitworths and another mounted a single 300-pounder. This huge Parrott rifle — it had a 10-inch diameter bore — was damaged at the 27th round when a shell burst prematurely taking off several inches of the gun's muzzle. However, the ragged edges were chipped true and the gun continued to fire another 371 shells before a crack started and the weapon was declared useless.

The 300-pounder was mounted in Battery Strong, one of the emplacements known as the "Left Batteries" which were located on relatively high ground inland a few hundred yards from the beach and not quite on line with the First Parallel.

Others in this group were Batteries Stevens, mounting two 100-pounder Parrotts; Reno, one 200 and two 100-pounder Parrotts; Hays, one 200-pounder Parrott and Kirby, two 10-inch seacoast mortars. (13-inch mortars, such as those displayed today in White Point Garden, were used later in the war by Union forces on Morris Island).

Batteries nearer the beach were Meade, two 100-pounder Parrotts; Rosecrans, three 100-pounder Parrotts; Brown, two 200-pounder Parrotts, and the Naval Battery which mounted two 200-pounder Parrotts and two 80-pounder Whitworths.

Others, not breaching batteries, held lighter guns and were directed against Wagner. These consisted of the right and left wings of Hays and Batteries Weed, Reynolds, Kearney and O'Rorke. There were also miscellaneous guns and mortars located in the parallels and not designated by any particular name.

Building the breaching batteries was a difficult engineering feat. Confederate guns were within easy range which forced much of the work to be performed at night. In addition, sand, the main building material, proved a constant headache. It drifted into places where it was not wanted and blew away from spots where it was desperately needed.

Sandbags by the thousand were used in an effort to force the sand into some semblance of shape. But the muzzleblast of the guns soon ripped or burned the bags if dry and when wet, the cloth rotted. In either case, the sand spilled out and violent storms arose each time the guns fired, an annoyance to the gunners and a damaging abrasive to the guns.

Various methods of control were tried. Sods of marsh, layers of pluff mud, even rawhide was spread over the sand in an effort to keep it from blowing. All helped, but none, apparently, was entirely successful.

The sand also hindered transportation. All lumber and other materials had to be ferried across to Morris Island from Folly then hauled through the sand to the battery positions.

Bringing in the guns was a particularly tough job. They were transported to Morris by ship from Hilton Head, then hauled down the island in sling carts. Two of these carts were used to carry the huge 300-pounder Parrott. Even so, the tires of the carts sank two inches into the sand on the hard beach and a full 12 inches on the sandy roads above high water line.

In addition to the Army, the Navy on both sides used many heavy weapons. The Confederates, in general, fired the same type of arms as their Army — mainly what was available at the time.

The Federal fleet, however, not only used Parrotts, particularly in the lighter calibers of 10, 20 and 30-pounders, but in the Charleston area the Dahlgren, which was the main heavy weapon of the ironclads.

These were generally 11 and 15-inch smoothbore weapons which fired round shot and shell. The New Ironsides, for instance, carried fourteen 11-inch Dahlgrens as her main battery while most of the monitors were armed with one 11-inch and one 15-inch.

The Dahlgren was not so accurate as the Parrott, which could slam its pointed shell against a relatively small target with amazing regularity. Due to movement of the vessels, however, it was felt that pin-point accuracy was not feasible and, consequently, the smoothbore was sufficient. This was especially the case when the Dahlgren was fired with a ricochet technique that bounced the balls off the water and into the air where they exploded, presumably over the heads of the enemy showering them with bits of iron.

They could, however, fire directly at a target, especially one the size of Fort Sumter, and the shock of 15-inch shot slamming into the brick walls at one time caused Confederates considerable concern for the safety of the bastion.

The heavy ordnance, particularly the rifles, played havoc with brick fortifications, but was relatively ineffective against earthworks, especially those made of sand.

Shells striking these simply blasted the sand into the air, where, being light, it traveled only a short distance and most of it fell back into the same shellhole. What little was dissipated could be replaced by a few sandbags or quick work with shovels as soon as the firing stopped.

By the time heavy guns could be emplaced, the enemy usually had plenty of time to dig in securely and although shells probably had a certain morale effect, casualties were few despite thousands of pounds of metal hurled over the landscape.

For instance, the First Great Bombardment of Fort Sumter saw about 6,800 projectiles — mainly 100 and 200-pounders — thrown at the fort within 16 days. Yet casualties were light — two men killed and 50 wounded. **W.R.**

300-pounder Parrott after bursting at the muzzle.

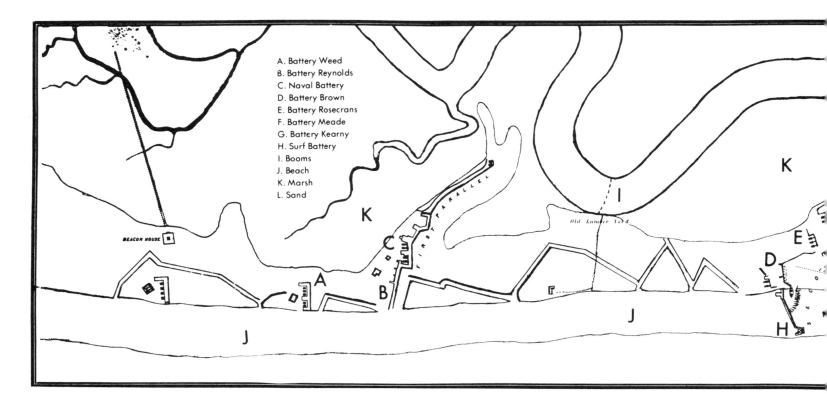

A. Battery Weed
B. Battery Reynolds
C. Naval Battery
D. Battery Brown
E. Battery Rosecrans
F. Battery Meade
G. Battery Kearny
H. Surf Battery
I. Booms
J. Beach
K. Marsh
L. Sand

Yankees

Union troops, licking their wounds from two disastrous attacks against Battery Wagner, laid siege to the Confederate work on Morris Island and set out to take it by a surer method.

The process was hard, dirty and dangerous but it promised success in the end.

Basically, it consisted in digging an entrenchment parallel to the face of Wagner. Using this as a base, the engineers, or sappers, would start another "parallel" a little closer to the Confederate work. This would be improved until it in turn could be used as a base for another move forward.

Eventually, a parallel would be close enough to Wagner for a sudden rush to overwhelm the Confederates before they could man their defenses.

Two methods were used in establishing a new parallel. In the beginning, while still some distance from Battery Wagner and the Confederate outposts, Union engineers would crawl under cover of darkness

Federal shelter in 2nd Parallel. Confederate 'torpedo' right of entrance. (Above)

Sap-roller protected engineers digging toward Battery Wagner. (Right)

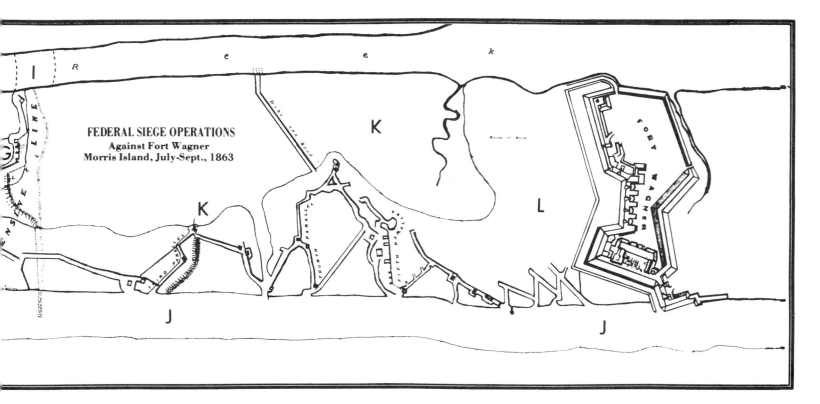

FEDERAL SIEGE OPERATIONS
Against Fort Wagner
Morris Island, July-Sept., 1863

Dig Toward Battery Wagner

to the site of a new parallel several hundred yards in front of the existing line.

Part of the force would serve as a guard, but the sappers would be unarmed. Each man carried a shovel in his right hand and in his left grasped a rope which had been marked at 6-foot intervals.

Led by an officer holding the end of the rope, the group crawled until orders were whispered to halt. Dropping the rope, each man started digging a hole, throwing the sand on top of the rope. The holes were then connected to form a reasonably straight trench, the sand properly thrown up on one side for a parapet, although the entire operation had been accomplished in the dark.

The second method, used when the lines neared Wagner and both shelling and rifle fire became intense, was much slower but was necessary to provide some protection for the diggers.

The main equipment was a 4 by 9-foot cylinder known as a sap-roller. This was made of bundles of small saplings, or fascines, banded together with iron hoops. It would stop bullets and shell fragments and served as a barricade behind which a few sappers could dig.

The sap-roller both concealed and protected the sappers and was rolled forward a few inches at a time as the trench progressed. The sand was thrown up on the sides to give added protection.

Most digging, even when the sap-roller was used, was done at night. Despite this, casualties were high since Confederate snipers inconsiderately drilled any tired engineer who carelessly exposed a head or arm during the daylight, or even bright moonlight, and artillery fire, night and day, made life uncertain.

Union soldiers soon learned to spot shells from Forts Johnson or Sumter and the shout "Cover, Sumter" or "Cover Johnson" would send them scurrying to the nearest hole. But with guns only a few hundred yards away, before a man could yell "Cover, Wagner," he or his audience was dead.

To keep down this fire, heavy cannon ashore and afloat were turned on Wagner. They did considerable damage, too, wrecking guns and killing gunners and snipers. But the Confederates countered this move by protecting artillery embrasures with sandbags. A few bags would be removed, the gun fired, and the bags shoved quickly back into place.

They also used mortars and these were dreaded more than the guns for the Southerners learned to drop shells precisely over the head of the sap where the

charge exploded sending lethal fragments of metal whining around the hard-working shovelers.

Siege operations were started on Morris Island immediately after the disastrous repulse of July 18 convinced Northern commanders that Wagner was too tough to be carried by frontal assault. That same night, an existing Federal position, Battery Reynolds, was converted into a defensive line and thereafter was known as the First Parallel.

It was 1,350 yards from Battery Wagner and during the next few days was turned into a strong line with an obstacle of inclined palisading, or spiked stakes, in front, Requa batteries (a rapid-fire weapon) on the flanks and a bombproof magazine as well as positions for various guns and mortars.

The work was completed July 23 and that night the Second Parallel was substantially completed and the First abandoned. The new line was protected by an

obstacle of inclined palisading and wire in front. It mounted a number of cannon and was considered as strong as Battery Wagner.

Aug. 9 the Third Parallel was opened 330 yards in advance of the right flank of the Second Parallel and 540 yards from Wagner.

At this point, the Yankees believed further approach to Wagner would be unnecessary. Breaching batteries were being emplaced to fire on Fort Sumter and it was felt the fort would be pounded into submission. If so, a prolonged defense of Morris Island would be senseless for the South since Wagner would already have failed in its primary mission — to prevent breaching of Sumter from Morris Island. With Sumter out, the monitors could sail into the harbor and prevent supply of Morris.

In addition, Federal guns already had stopped supply

(Continued On Page 60)

Union troops throw fragments of shells to explode 'torpedo.'

(Continued From Page 59)

YANKEES DIG

of the Wagner garrison by day and the use of calcium lights and a system of small boats, it was thought, would soon do the same at night thereby forcing surrender or evacuation of the work.

However, Union hopes were premature. Fort Sumter did not surrender. The lights and boats disrupted but failed to halt supply of Morris Island. Moreover, Wagner's fire began to play havoc with the breaching battery crews.

Consequently, by Aug. 18, the Federals were hard at work again digging and on the 21st established the Fourth Parallel 350 yards from the Confederate earthwork.

Paying a heavy price in dead and wounded, the engineers inched their way toward the Confederate stronghold — a glacier-like movement that could be delayed by cannon and rifle fire, but never stopped for as soon as the shelling slackened, the Yankees were busy again shoveling their way through the yielding sand.

It was hot, deadly work. The ground was low and heavy rains or storm tides flooded the trenches. Sand drifted from where it was wanted to where it was not.

It swept into the trenches and blew from the parapets erected to protect men and equipment, necessitating repairs almost as soon as work was completed.

Nearing Battery Wagner, the sappers ran into mines which the Confederates had buried leaving the detonators barely exposed. At first these "torpedoes," as they were called, created a nervewracking problem. Then the Yankees discovered they could be disarmed or destroyed by various methods. One of the most succesful was to bore a hole into the wooden device and pour in water until the powder was too soaked to explode.

Another problem, while not dangerous, was extremely distasteful. The diggers began to uncover the bodies of soldiers and civilians. The former had been buried after the July 11th and 18th attacks and the latter in the days when Morris Island was used as the city's "Pest House," or quarantine station. Some of the bodies had to be buried, then reburied as they were uncovered again and again by shellfire or continuing work on the parallel.

Finally, the sappers hit on a solution. They simply reburied the bodies in the parapets of the trenches where they remained undisturbed as the sap ground toward Wagner.

Aug. 26 saw the opening of the Fifth, and final,

Parallel. It was 105 yards in front of the Fourth and was within 245 yards of Battery Wagner. A shallow trench ran off it to within 100 yards of the earthwork.

By Sept. 5, Wagner's fall was imminent. The Confederates knew it as well as the Yankees who were widening the trenches to accommodate troops for an assault. A heavy bombardment was opened on the fort from guns and mortars. Thirteen of the former and 17 of the latter kept up a continuous fire while during the day the New Ironsides steamed close to add its shells to the stream of metal pouring into the work.

This was perhaps the safest period for the sappers. Wagner replied only sporadically during the bombardment and the Yankees were too close to the work for James Island and other batteries to fire without risk of hitting their friends.

Orders were issued to take the fort by storm at 9 a.m. on the 7th. But the Confederates saw no point in needless sacrifice of the garrison.

Quietly, during the night of Sept. 6, Wagner and Morris Island were evacuated.

The fort had done its job. Its garrison had held almost two months against overwhelming odds — time bought with blood to build an inner ring of defenses to protect the city against further advance by the enemy.

W.R.

Northern officers and men examine interior of main entrance to Battery Wagner bombproof.

Batteries Wagner, Gregg Abandoned

Speed and silence were Confederate watchwords on Morris Island the night of Sept. 6, 1863 — the Southerners were pulling out.

The island and its two batteries, Wagner and Gregg, were being abandoned to the enemy after nearly two months of heroic defense.

The Yankees had landed on the island July 10. Since then, the Confederates had repelled two vicious assaults against Wagner and slowed siege operations to a crawl.

Now the end was near. Yankee trenches had been pushed almost to the walls of the earthwork where a sudden rush could overwhelm the garrison. Wagner was in its death throes. Constant shelling had rounded the walls, filled in its ditches and uncovered sections of the bombproof.

Exposure of the bombproof was a serious blow to the defenders. The bunker was crowded. Moisture dripped

from the ceiling. The air stank of too many unwashed bodies. But it was safe, the only spot in the work where a man could almost forget the pressure of death. For weeks, tons of sand atop its wooden roof had stopped shells and bolts with a facility as satisfying to the Confederates as it was frustrating to the Yankee gunners.

But now it was the enemy's turn. Like huge dragons, the guns roared night and day, tongues of flame licking their mouths, snorting and bellowing at the dying foe. Since the morning of the 5th, the bombardment had been continuous. Shell after shell had slammed into the sand protecting the bombproof, each blasting away a little until the constant gnawing seriously jeopardized the bunker. Repairs were impossible. No man could live in that storm of screaming shell fragments.

Confederate leaders decided that further resistance would accomplish little but the sacrifice of the garrison. Wagner was no longer tenable and a Federal

attack — one already had been set for 9 o'clock the following morning — would sweep across the work and probably roll over Gregg and Cummings Point before it stopped.

They issued orders to abandon the island and the evacuation got under way about 9 p.m. of the 6th. It was carried out while the flash of cannon and exploding shells flickered light over the rubble of battered Wagner, catching briefly the tense faces of tired men slipping silently out of the work.

First the wounded were loaded aboard small boats at Cummings Point. The major part of the garrison withdrew next, leaving the earthwork to a small rear guard who were to hold it until the main body had escaped the island, then fall back after destroying all possible equipment.

(Continued On Page 61)

View from sea face of Battery Wagner.

(Continued From Page 60)

BATTERIES

By 11:30 p.m. only 35 men remained at Wagner. During the next hour, they were busy laying fuses to the magazine, firing rifles from the parapet to make the fort appear fully garrisoned, and spiking the cannon.

This last chore proved quite a problem for the vents had been enlarged through weeks of heavy firing and two or three spikes had to be used. To complicate the problem, silence was mandatory to prevent the enemy from discovering the move, so the spikes had to be covered by a haversack partially filled with sand while they were being hammered into the vents.

Finally, all guns had been spiked except a 10-inch columbiad which had been double charged and prepared for bursting.

With arrival of the courier notifying the rear guard that the main body had escaped, all personnel but four officers and an orderly sergeant were dispatched to Cummings Point.

One of the officers, a lieutenant, picked up the end of a long lanyard which had been run from the 10-inch columbiad.

The rear guard commander gave the order: "The last gun from Battery Wagner, fire!"

The lieutenant yanked the lanyard — nothing happened. The primer had failed. Several times more the gun was primed and tried, but with negative results.

They even worked one of the spikes out of another gun and tried that, but a "last gun" from Battery Wagner just wouldn't fire.

Time was growing short. Attempts to fire the guns were given up and the commander lit the fuse to the magazine, all of his companions watching to be sure that it was burning properly.

While the flame sparked along the fuse toward the magazine, the last Confederates left Battery Wagner and headed for Cummings Point. There, with a similar group from Battery Gregg, they boarded small boats for the pull to Fort Sumter, ears and eyes strained for explosions timed to go off simultaneously in both batteries.

The watch was in vain. Apparently the fuses were defective for the explosions never came.

Entrance to Battery Wagner bombproof.

By 1:30 a.m. of the 7th, the entire garrison had been evacuated safely with exception of two boats, containing about 46 men, which were captured while trying to get to Fort Sumter.

Not long after the Confederates left, a deserter arrived at the Federal lines and brought word that the Southerners had gone.

Union troops moved hesitantly into Wagner. Meeting no opposition, they continued toward Cummings Point and before daylight had occupied the entire island — a bloodless end to one of the bitterest campaigns of the war.

W.R.

Stranded Ship Diverted U.S. Attack.

Competition between commanders for the glory of capturing Fort Sumter was one reason that casualties were high among Union soldiers and sailors at Charleston in the fall of 1863.

Adm. John A. Dahlgren, the Navy commander, and Gen. Quincy A. Gillmore, the Army commander, were both taken by surprise at the sudden and successful escape of the Confederate garrison at Fort Wagner. Both responded to the startling news with similar selfish thoughts; to seize for their service the distinction of hoisting the Stars and Stripes over Fort Sumter.

The Navy was the first to react. Dawn, Sept. 7, had barely begun to lighten the broken ramparts of Wagner when signals to the fleet began to move out of the cabin of the flagship Philadelphia. Adm. Dahlgren was ordering an attempt to break through the Confederate obstructions in the channel north of Sumter. In essence, it was the same old plan that had been tried before and failed. The only refinement was a directive to the monitor Weehawken to enter the narrow channel which fringed the northern end of now friendly Morris Island and "cut off communication by that direction" with Sumter.

In his haste to get moving on Sumter ahead of the Army, Adm. Dahlgren was yielding to more than one pressing consideration. Besides concern for the Navy's fair share of any prestige that might come out of joint operations with the Army, he had also to think about his own reputation.

Dahlgren was a desk admiral who had contrived to replace salty old Samuel F. DuPont after the latter's failure to capture Sumter. Since hoisting his flag in July, he had driven himself and ships hard to achieve what DuPont had not. Yet he had not done enough.

On the morning of Sept. 7, with Wagner fallen and Sumter apparently about to fall, it seemed as if too little time remained to do what had to be done for the sake of John A. Dahlgren and the Navy.

Weehawken was a sister to the original Monitor.

Dahlgren's mind raced to the attack ahead of his ships. With no more than a superficial glance at the new strategic situation, he jumped to a dangerous conclusion.

Sumter was indefensible. Since this was so clear to Adm. Dahlgren, it must be obvious to the Confederates, too. Hence, Dahlgren told himself, the wise Southerners would now have nothing but "a corporal's guard" in Sumter.

Having decided this, the admiral got off a message to Charleston. Surrender Sumter.

After a decent interval which the Confederates put to good use strengthening their positions, came the reply: "Inform Adm. Dahlgren that he may have Fort Sumter when he can take and hold it."

In truth, Adm. Dahlgren need not have worried so much about the Army's getting ahead in the race to Sumter. Gen. Gillmore shared the Navy view that Sumter was now helpless. On Morris Island, he was making more leisurely plans of his own. Soon enough, these were to mature in bloody confusion, but in the meantime all that the Army could do was watch the Navy.

In spite of his early start on Sept. 7, the best that

Adm. Dahlgren could do was to get into action late in the afternoon. About 6 p.m., the New Ironsides and five monitors moved into action with Fort Moultrie. There was a bitter two-hour exchange. Then darkness put an end to the fighting. Casualties on both sides were minor.

While the shooting was going on at Sullivan's Island, however, the Weehawken, a mile away, was in desperate trouble in the shallows between Sumter and Morris Island. Her captain, Comdr. E.R. Colhoun, had taken his unwieldy ship into the narrow ditch which bordered Cummings Point. There, early in the morning, she had touched bottom. Freed by the rising tide, she had begun to make her way carefully back to deeper water. Suddenly she sheered to port and went solidly aground in 11 feet of water.

Throughout the afternoon of the 7th, Colhoun and his crew labored to get their vessel off. Coal and ammunition were taken out. A tug was summoned. Nothing had worked. Colhoun and his crew could only pray for time and work harder.

(Continued On Page 63)

While the battle raged, USS Weehawken lay aground near Fort Sumter.

(Continued From Page 62)

STRANDED SHIP

On the morning of the 8th, their luck ran out. The Confederate gunners at Moultrie looked across toward Cummings Point and saw the Weehawken lay uncommonly high in the water. Slowly and deliberately they opened fire, aiming for the exposed hull where it showed beneath the overhang of armor.

Twenty-four times Confederate shells exploded aboard the helpless monitor — a credit to Southern gunnery but not to the quality of their ammunition. The Weehawken suffered only minor damage. Eventually, the tide rose high enough to float her and she limped away.

Despite their chagrin at seeing their prize escape, the Confederates were high in their praise of the Yankee sailors who had labored so cooly under fire to save their ship.

The Federals rejoiced to have the Weehawken safely at her anchorage again, but her difficulties on the sandbank had wrecked Dahlgren's plans to capture Charleston that day.

What had started out as a naval assault on the forts had degenerated into a covering action. Fearing to lose the precious monitor, Dahlgren diverted his energy from attack to salvage. For five hours on the morning of the 8th, the forts and ships slugged away at one another. But behind the roar of the Federal cannons, there was nothing more than an urge to save the Weehawken. Dahlgren was so busy getting her off he could not spare the time to press the attack.

About 2 p.m. the tide rose, and the Union ships withdrew.

Dahlgren's hastily conceived attack had failed. Two whole days of the precious time the admiral needed to gather glory had been wasted.

A.M.W.

Weehawken shell caused explosion in Fort Moultrie.

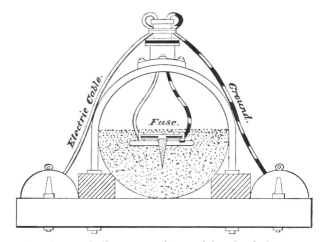

Electric, or boiler, torpedo used by Confederates.

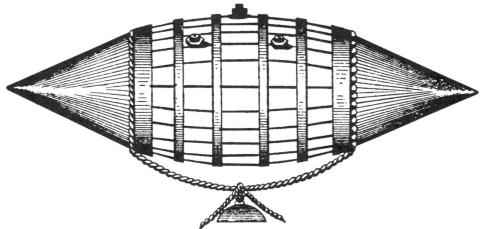

Barrel torpedo, a type used in Charleston Harbor.

Yankee Fleet Feared Torpedoes

"Torpedoes" reported to lie unseen beneath the waters of Charleston Harbor were far more frightening to Federal naval officers planning to capture the city than the frowning forts which guarded the harbor entrance.

Tales were told in the North of the efficiency and ingenuity of the Confederacy in the new medium of underwater warfare. They circulated among the ships of the fleet off Charleston and exerted a depressing effect upon its leaders.

As far as can be determined from the records, the Union officers believed most of the stories told about torpedoes — except when someone, as occasionally happened, tried to tell them the truth.

The Federal commanders saw torpedoes everywhere. Even after the war was over and they had a chance to judge for themselves the feebleness of the mine defenses, they continued to believe the scuttle-butt rumors which had helped preserve Charleston from capture until the war was nearly over.

As far as the Northern public could tell from reading newspapers, it was Southern guns which kept the fleet at bay. But it was not really the guns, although the Federals made much of them, too. It was the mines or, rather, their sinister reputation.

"There are many," wrote Maj. John Johnson, CSA, after the war, "who will always believe that if a gun had not been fired by the forts on the 7th of April, 1863, the whole (Federal) squadron would have turned back with the same alacrity as was shown by the leading vessel."

One of the things that impressed Maj. Johnson was that at no time during the whole long siege did the Union Navy take steps to seriously examine the obstructions it was so much afraid of.

The "Torpedoes" that the Confederacy used with such success were of two general types. Both would be readily recognized by modern mine warfare experts.

Some were what would now be called controlled mines. They exploded on command by an electric current from a position ashore. Others were "contact mines" — moored or drifters — armed with fuses which caused them to explode if they touched the hull of a ship.

Within these two families, there was an infinite variety of torpedoes. Some were quite ingenious. Not a few were devilish. None were used in large numbers at Charleston.

In April 1863, as Adm. Samuel F. DuPont prepared for a thrust into the harbor of Charleston, a few contact mines were waiting for him. None lay in the channels themselves.

Far inside the entrance, near Castle Pinckney, the Southerners had sunk queer contraptions they called "frame torpedoes."

These were arrangements of heavy timbers fixed together in a form not unlike a flimsy raft. At one end of the raft, point upwards, were fixed a series of containers shaped very much like modern artillery projectiles. Each held perhaps 25 pounds of gunpow-

(Continued On Page 64)

(Continued From Page 63)

YANKEE FLEET FEARED

der. At the pointed end of each of these "shells" were contact fuses.

The rafts which supported the torpedoes were towed into position and sunk. One end was anchored firmly to the bottom. The other end, with the explosives attached, was allowed to rise a few feet until the mines were only three or four feet beneath the surface.

Frame torpedoes were clumsy contrivances. They could be used only in shallow water. In the spring of 1863, they seemed to be the best type available.

The Confederates supplemented the meager protection afforded by the frame torpedoes by sinking a huge controlled mine in the Main Ship Channel off Morris Island. This affair, consisting of an old boiler 18 feet long and three in diameter, contained a ton and a half of powder. From it, to an observation station at Fort Wagner, led wires intended to deliver an electric spark.

As the cable was being paid out from the steamer which laid the mine, the ship drifted. A mile of wire

which the electricians had not planned for was added to the firing circuit. When the time came to explode the mine on April 7, the Confederates were bitterly disappointed to find that it would not go off.

The official explanation for this failure — which saved the valuable armored frigate New Ironsides from destruction — was that a wagon carelessly driven along the beach had cut the wires. The engineers, however, knew the truth: the extra mile of wire had sapped the strength of the spark.

A few frame torpedoes, the big mine outside the harbor and a second boiler mine hastily sunk near White Point — this was the extent of the minefields the Federals so greatly dreaded.

As it turned out, the Southerners suffered more than the Yankees from the mines. In April 1863, their own steamer Marion encountered a frame torpedo and sank at once.

Although the Federals did not know it, no effective steps were taken until 1865 to close the harbor entrance with mines. By this time, the tightening blockade had all but choked off the trickle of shipping. There was no longer any need to keep the channels safe for the sorely needed blockade runners.

Accordingly, in the winter of 1864-65, 16 barrel torpedoes — barrels filled with powder and equipped with contact fuses — were laid between Sumter and Moultrie.

They formed a line across the Main Ship Channel.

On Jan. 15, 1865, the U.S. monitor Patapsco was sent into the harbor entrance to cover the operations of small boats searching for obstructions.

She struck one of the newly laid mines.

There was a shock, a cloud of smoke, and within less than a minute, the Patapsco was gone.

Fewer than half of her 109 officers and men survived.

Although the Patapsco's loss was caused by mines which had existed for only a few days, her sinking satisfied the Federals that their worst fears were justified. Another attempt being planned to penetrate the harbor was called off.

This was virtually the full extent of the Confederate torpedo efforts in Charleston.

Far fewer than the enemy dreamed, the mines were also far more effective than anybody could reasonably have expected them to be.

A.M.W.

Matter Of Courage

Union Tools Crude In War On Mines

Naval mine warfare was two years old in the spring of 1863 but the Union Navy off Charleston had little more than harsh words and grappling irons to cope with the Confederate torpedoes.

The Navy worried a good deal about the mines which it believed were sown in the approaches to Charleston but it did not come up with reliable countermeasures.

At the end of the war, the job of detecting and destroying mines remained just about what it had been at the beginning: an affair of crude tools and cold courage.

Generally speaking, there were two problems to be solved if the Navy was to feel secure in its anchorages or move with reasonable safety about the rivers and inlets off the coast.

The first was how to clear mine barriers from the channels. On the solution to this problem, the fleet believed, depended the success of the strategy to capture Charleston.

Every prisoner gleaned from the Confederacy, every deserter who came over from the South, was closely interrogated as to the nature and extent of the minelaying. Some of the prisoners were sailors who had participated in such activities. Some were remarkably well informed. The records show their testimony was frequently accurate and comprehensive. It was not very useful, however, because the Federals preferred to rely on other sources, some of which were merely rumor.

Despite evidence that there were not many mines in the entrance to Charleston Harbor, the Navy took troublesome precautions against them. When Adm. Samuel F. DuPont ordered the ironclad squadron to get under way to attack Charleston on April 7, 1863, his leading ship was hopelessly encumbered with a monstrous mine-sweeping device.

(Continued On Page 65)

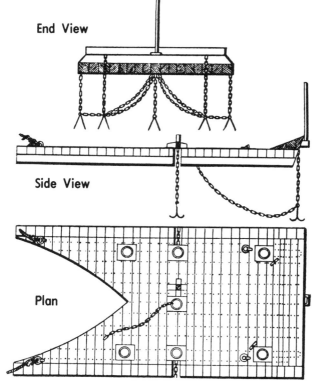

End View

Side View

Plan

The 'Devil,' or Ericsson Raft, for minesweeping.

U.S. seamen remove Confederate torpedo. Operation took more courage than skill.

(Continued From Page 64)

UNION TOOLS CRUDE

This was a raft designed by Capt. John Ericsson to "catch torpedoes." It fitted across the bows of the monitor Weehawken. Festooned with grapnels and heavy chains, it looked like nothing ever seen in war before. When it washed up on the beach after the battle, the Confederates found it and puzzled over it. In their reports, they called it "The Devil."

The Devil was 50 feet long and 27 wide. It represented the most ambitious of the Federal attempts to sweep mines. Three of these rafts were built but two were lost before they got to Charleston. The one attached to the Weehawken did more harm than good.

First it fouled the monitor's anchor chain, holding up the advance of the whole squadron. Then it proved so unwieldy that it had to be cut loose.

From time to time during the course of the Charleston campaign, the fleet experimented with other minesweeping devices but none offered much promise. In the end, the Navy was forced to fall back on the primitive method of sending small boats to explore ahead of ships venturing into dangerous waters. With grappling irons or rope, or wire sweeps, the boats would search for mines beneath the surface.

If one was found, the boats would sometimes try to pull it loose from its moorings. Sometimes the sailors would lash knives to long poles and saw through the mooring cables. When the mines rose to the surface, they would be drawn along side. Then the brave men in the boats would gingerly remove the fuse, hoping they would not accidentally blow themselves up. Often, as a precautionary measure, mines cut loose would be fired at with muskets to open the casings and let water in to dampen the powder.

It was a touchy and dangerous business.

As a rule, moored mines were the most feared. They were hard to spot. Occasionally, a ripple in the water at low tide would mean a mine below the surface. More frequently, the first warning came when a ship exploded one.

The second major problem in defense against mines was protection of vessels in their anchorages off shore or in the swift rivers whose mouths the Federals controlled.

Drifting mines, launched upstream and carried down by the current, were a hazard familiar to every gunboat crew. The drift mines were favorite devices of the Confederates and they came in many sinister forms. Some were cleverly disguised as flotsam. The best protection against them was a bright and suspicious lookout. The Union sailors learned to look twice at every floating tree branch, no matter how harmless it might seem. There might be a mine underneath.

On August 16, 1863, the USS Pawnee, lying in the Stono, was the target of Confederate engineers using drift mines of a particularly ingenious design.

Each consisted of a canister of powder, a loaded musket and a float. The muzzle of the musket was inserted in the canister of powder. The float supported the breech of the musket clear of the water. Four trigger arms were attached to the musket. If one brushed the side of a ship, the musket would fire into the powder charge.

Several of these were sent down by twos, attached to each end of a 250-foot rope. Fortunately for the Pawnee, the lookout on a nearby mortar schooner spotted them coming downstream. A boat was sent out and all were hauled ashore and disarmed.

Occasionally a moored mine would break loose from its anchor and become a drifter. The crew of the Nahant spotted one of these Sept. 13, 1863, in the Main Ship Channel off Charleston.

The Nahant retrieved the mine and found it to be a 25-gallon beer barrel, coated with tar, pointed at the ends and loaded with 35 pounds of powder. For some reason, it had no fuse, only a pine plug driven into the bung hole.

The people aboard monitors were particularly touchy about mines in any shape because their ships had little reserve buoyancy. When a monitor hit a mine, it went down in a hurry. For this reason, the officers of the monitors thought more about mine defense than some of their colleagues in wooden ships. They devised torpedo nets, clumsy affairs of cord or wire, which could be lowered over the side to form barricades around ships at anchor. Under way, the nets were hoisted clear of the water.

On Jan. 15, 1865, the monitor Patapsco, moving cautiously about the approaches to Charleston, hit a mine in an area where mines were believed not to be. As a matter of fact, they had not been there a few days before. Her captain was saved because he happened to be on deck when his ship sank under him. He testified he had taken care to keep clear of danger zones. Also he had put out scout boats. Neither of these precautions paid off and the Patapsco sank in 50 seconds.

After Charleston fell, in February 1865, the war was over for everyone in the fleet except those assigned to minesweeping. Long after the guns were silent, the civilian contractors and the sailors assigned to help them were busy with their grappling irons trying to locate and destroy the torpedoes in Charleston Harbor.

A.M.W.

Confederates (upper left) pour fire into Union sailors attacking Fort Sumter from small boats.

Easy Job Proves Tough

Small Boats Attack Fort Sumter

Yankees attacking Fort Sumter Sept. 9, 1863, found the fort in ruins, but a long way from beaten.

Twenty-five small boats containing some 400 men rowed silently toward the dark pile of bricks and rubble into which the fort had been pounded by weeks of shelling.

Suddenly the mass blazed with small arms fire. Heavy guns soon flashed from nearby forts and incoming shells turned the scene into a nightmare of flying metal.

Thirty minutes later Sumter was still again. The battle was over. The Yankees in retreat — those who were able.

It was a bitter, unexpected blow to Rear Adm. J.A. Dahlgren, commander of Union naval forces off Charleston. He had expected an easy victory — one that would plant the American Flag once again over the symbol of rebellion that Sumter had become; a decided boost to the Northern cause — and a feather in the cap of the man who achieved it. The fall of Sumter also would eliminate the rifle fire which threatened any attempt to remove rope and torpedo obstructions believed to be blocking entrance of the admiral's ironclads into Charleston Harbor.

Dahlgren wanted Sumter badly and he made his first try for the fort within hours after learning of the evacuation of Morris Island by the Confederates.

Convinced that the bastion was untenable now that heavy United States guns were within point-blank range, he sent a note to the Confederates demanding surrender.

Unfortunately for the admiral, the Confederates didn't agree defense was hopeless. He was politely informed that he could have Sumter when he could take — and hold — it.

Consequently, Dahlgren on the afternoon of Sept. 7, sent the ironclads toward Sumter to reconnoiter and perhaps pass the channel obstructions.

However, his plans went astray. One of the monitors, the Weehawken, had grounded during the morning, so Dahlgren abandoned his mission and came to her aid by shelling the Sullivan's Island forts until dark made shooting inaccurate.

The next day, falling tide exposed the vulnerable hull of the Weehawken beneath the armored overhang and the Southern forts began to take advantage of the vessel's plight with carefully aimed fire.

This forced Dahlgren to commit his other ironclads, in an effort to save his stricken monitor, and precipitated a three-hour engagement with the forts.

The attempt was successful and fire was diverted from the Weehawken. She floated with the rising tide and the fleet was withdrawn.

Dahlgren now determined to launch a small-boat attack against Sumter that night. Plans were hastily laid and an assault commander selected. This worthy later stated he had tried to decline the dubious honor, but had been assured by Dahlgren that only a "corporal's guard" held the fort and all the Federals had to do was "...go and take possession...."

In planning for the attack, Dahlgren learned that his were not the only eyes on Sumter. The Union Army commander, Brig. Gen. Quincy A. Gillmore, had prepared an attack for the same night. Neither had bothered to notify the other and each was confident his force was sufficient to do the job.

They learned of the dual plans when Dahlgren tried to borrow Army boats. This led Gillmore to request that it be made a joint venture, but Dahlgren refused unless it would be under Navy command. The general took a dim view of this, so both sides went ahead with preparations agreeing, however, upon a password to prevent a collision between the assaulting forces.

As it turned out, there was no danger of a collision, for the Army's boats were left high and dry by low tide until after the Navy attack had failed. It was then prudently called off.

The Navy force, composed of volunteers from the fleet and including a contingent of Marines, set out at 9:30 p.m. Sept. 8 in tow of the tug Daffodil and after several delays enroute was within a quarter of a mile of Fort Sumter early in the morning of the 9th.

Despite considerable confusion upon being released, most of the boats set out for Sumter. Part of the group was to create a diversion on one side while the main party stormed another.

It was the assault commander's intention to hold the main attack until the feint had started, but when the diversionary force pulled away, so did most of the other boats.

This lack of control apparently persisted throughout for some of the boats landed while others did not.

Those men who got ashore discovered that an overhang prevented them from scaling the walls and coming to grips with the Southerners.

They wound up huddling in shell holes and behind the rubble through the rain of bursting shells, unable to retreat to the boats through the heavy fire.

Those in the boats fared even worse — they sweated out the battle with little or no protection.

Fort Sumter had proved a hard nut to crack. Many factors contributed to its strength, but perhaps its main resource was its garrison. It was composed of hardened infantrymen who had relieved the artillery units when the guns were removed. These were experienced, tough fighters led by a dedicated officer, Maj. Stephen Elliott Jr. He had taken command of Sumter with the firm conviction of holding it — or not coming back to explain why it fell.

Elliott knew perfectly well he would be attacked, and the Union Navy apparently had made no effort to conceal its preparations.

Consequently, the Southerners were waiting when the two lines of boats appeared about 1 a.m. Much of the garrison had been strategically located to defend the fort's weak points, and the remainder constituted a strong reserve ready to be sent where needed.

The major, when the Yankees appeared, was on the parapet where he had been trying to watch the grounded Weehawken. He immediately brought up his reserve to within supporting distance and had all his men remain silent until the attackers started to land.

Then the Confederates opened a devastating fire which drove the Federals under the projecting masses of the walls. Even there, safety was short-lived for the Southerners began tossing hand grenades and before long the surrounding forts opened against the base of Sumter's walls and the surrounding water.

Elliott reported he had only 104 men engaged in the fight and they apparently had a field day for not a single one was injured.

They inflicted 21 casualties on the attackers and captured 106 prisoners. (Dahlgren admitted three killed and 114 prisoners). In addition, the Southerners picked up five boats and five stands of colors.

The Federals, those who escaped, came away with nothing — but renewed respect for Fort Sumter.

W.R.

Smoke pours from embrasures of Fort Sumter as shot and shell land near the beleaguered fortification.

Inside The Fort

Confederate Artillery Shells Sumter

Fort Sumter, Charleston's strongest bastion in 1861, had a weak point which proved fatal during the bombardment of April 12-13.

The Achilles heel in this case was wood — the roofs and interior partitions of barracks and other buildings within the heavy brick walls. They were a major factor in the downfall of Maj. Robert Anderson's command.

Anderson, who had slipped over to Sumter Dec. 26, 1860, had spent the intervening time mounting the fort's guns, filling unusued gun embrasures, and in general putting the fort into first-class condition to fight off attack.

He was short of food and almost entirely out of fuel, but the fort itself was in shape to give an excellent account of itself — except for the wood.

This, Anderson apparently either ignored or did not realize existed for it would have been entirely possible for him to have ripped the wood from the barracks and officers' quarters during the months of "cold war" prior to the actual shooting and to have bunked his men inside the casemates.

The signal shell starting the bombardment of Sumter burst over the parade ground at 4:30 a.m. April 12, 1861. Confederate guns encircling the fort opened immediately and shot and shell smashed into the silent fort looming dimly in the darkness — spattered by the quick light from bursting shells.

Anderson, who was short of cartridge bags, held his fire until daylight. Then, after breakfast, Capt. Abner Doubleday fired the first shot from Sumter. It was aimed at the Iron Battery on Cummings Point.

In order to protect his men, Anderson ordered them to use only the guns in the casemates (32 and 42-pounders) instead of the heavier weapons on the exposed barbette tier which might have done damage to Southern defenses.

The fire continued heavy throughout the day, was slackened by the Confederates and stopped entirely by Anderson during the night, then resumed at daylight of the 13th.

Several times during the first day of the bombardment, hot shot or bursting shells set fires in the

(Continued On Page 18)

Charlestonians watch bombardment from rooftops.

(Continued From Page 17)

CONFEDERATE ARTILLERY

wooden buildings of Fort Sumter. Each time the blaze was extinguished within a short time.

It was a different matter on the morning of the 13th.

A Confederate hot shot set fire to the officers' quarters and the blaze spread to the barracks.

The defenders had time to remove only a small amount of powder before the magazines had to be closed.

Flames leaped above the parapets and clouds of smoke curled above the fort amid the crack of bursting shells as the Confederates redoubled their efforts.

The smoke seeped into the casemates and slowly the fire of the fort slackened as the gunners, kerchiefs bound over their faces, lay gasping on the flagstone floors or hung limply at the embrasures searching for air.

Although the fire from the fort was cut to almost nothing, as each shot rang out, the Confederates at the different batteries mounted the parapets around their guns and cheered the gallantry of their enemy.

Finally, Sumter's fire stopped. Then about 1:30 p.m. a Confederate shot brought down the flag.

Shortly afterwards, the fort was approached by a Confederate officer under a flag of truce and Anderson agreed to surrender.

Firing stopped pending outcome of negotiations for the surrender.

About 7:30 p.m., the terms were accepted by both sides and the engagement was officially at an end.

The bombardment had lasted 34 hours and although more than 3,000 shot and shell had been hurled at the fort, not a single man on either side had been killed.

The barracks, officers' quarters and other wooden buildings were destroyed, but the walls of the fort suffered little damage, evidence that Anderson might have held out longer had it not been for the wood, and presaging the later struggle of its Confederate defenders against month after month of Federal bombardment.

W.R.

Federal soldiers repair damage to Fort Sumter.

Bad Luck Dogged Relief Fleet

A mixture of bad luck and confusion left the Northern relief fleet sailing in circles off the Charleston bar while Fort Sumter was taken by the Confederacy.

Plans to reinforce or at least to land provisions at Fort Sumter had blown hot and cold for several months after Maj. Robert Anderson moved his command to the island fortification Dec. 26, 1860.

But while the North vacillated, the South did not. Fortifications were thrown up on Morris Island to prevent shipping from using the main channel leading to the harbor and Fort Sumter was ringed with guns which could make it hot for any vessel unloading. In addition, buoys were removed and the channel blocked to any but very shallow-draft vessels.

Since Southern defenses prevented relief of the fort by force and because a request for permission to land provisions had been turned down by South Carolina's governor, President Lincoln decided there was only one way to relieve Sumter — by stealth.

About the middle of March, the President had ordered an expedition prepared and on March 29 gave orders that it be ready to sail by April 6.

Plans for the expedition had been prepared by its leader, Navy Capt. Gustavus V. Fox, and consisted, basically, in the use of two or three shallow-draft tugboats or a number of small launches to run the Southern defenses by night.

The tugs had most of their machinery below the waterline and any above was to be protected by bales of hay or cotton. It was estimated they would pass about 1,300 yards from the batteries and, being on a crossing course and boiling along in the darkness at 14 knots, their chances of being hit would be almost nil.

Just in case they were hit, however, each would be towing sufficient empty launches to carry all personnel. These launches, if the seas were particularly calm, might be used for the entire maneuver instead of the tugs.

The only obstacles remaining were Southern gunboats which could make short work of the unarmed tugs or launches. However, warships in the fleet would take care of any gunboats that ventured across the bar and Fort Sumter was expected to use its guns to clear the channel from the harbor to the vicinity of the bar.

The fleet, insofar as Fox knew, consisted of the armed sidewheel steamer Harriet Lane; the second class screw sloops Pawnee and Pocahontas; the large, paddle-wheel sloop Powhatan; the transport Baltic, on which Fox sailed with some 200 men and provisions, and three tugs, the Freeborn, Uncle Ben, and Yankee.

The ships were to sail individually and in some cases on different dates in order to preserve the secrecy of the expedition.

Fox, in the Baltic, arrived off the Charleston bar before daylight of the 12th after battling a heavy gale down the coast. He discovered at dawn that only two other elements of his fleet were on station, the Harriet Lane and the Pawnee.

Missing were the tugs, the Powhatan and the Pocahontas. With either tugs or the Powhatan, which carried sufficiently large boats to be used in a heavy sea, the operation could go forward. But in the absence of all, Fox was stymied.

His three vessels stood in toward the bar and discovered that the battle for Fort Sumter already was under way. However, the fleet could do nothing except watch during the daylight hours of the 12th.

That night an attempt to send one small boat to Sumter was considered, but seamen felt that the boats carried by the Pawnee and Harriet Lane could never live in the heavy seas. The attempt was given up and Fox steamed slowly near the bar, waiting for the Powhatan, until the Baltic touched ground at Rattlesnake Shoals. She got off easily, but was forced to move out to sea and anchor in deep water.

The next day, an ice schooner was taken over with the idea that it could go in alone on the night of the 13th, but the surrender of Sumter eliminated the necessity of the attempt.

That day, about the time Fort Sumter ceased firing, the Pocahontas came into sight. But the Powhatan and the tugs, the elements really needed, never arrived.

Fox discovered later that the Powhatan had been removed from the expedition in a secret and entirely unorthodox maneuver authorized by President Lincoln to aid Fort Pickens in Florida.

Bad weather had stopped the tugs. The Freeborn, because of the gale, was prevented from sailing by her owners. The Uncle Ben was driven into Wilmington, N.C. and seized by the Southerners. The Yankee was driven past Charleston to the entrance of Savannah and didn't get back up to Charleston until after the Baltic had returned north — carrying Anderson and the defeated garrison of the fort she had come to relieve.

W.R.

The Powhatan. Her failure to arrive hindered the fleet.

Sketch shows Federal artist's conception of Confederate David's attack on New Ironsides.

Torpedo Boat Damages Blockader

Naval operations at the entrance to Charleston Harbor in 1863 were dominated by the ponderous black hulk of the ironclad frigate USS New Ironsides.

Like other armored vessels, the Ironsides never enjoyed the full confidence of Yankee admirals bred to sail. The Confederates, however, looked upon her with wholehearted respect. They competed vigorously for the privilege of destroying her.

Their concern was understandable. The New Ironsides was the most powerful ship in the blockading fleet. To the Confederates, she was the embodiment of seapower in a form their limited resources would never permit them to enjoy.

Nearly 250 feet long, armored with a belt three inches thick all around, with solid plating 4½ inches thick over her sides amidships, the Ironsides shed Confederate shells as if they were marbles bounced across the water. Her battery of fourteen 11-inch smoothbores was more powerful than any fort which guarded the harbor. When the ironsides moved down channel toward the forts, she was irresistible.

The Confederates prided themselves on the strong sand parapets of Fort Wagner, but when the Ironsides came within range, prudent members of the garrison climbed down into the bombproof shelters.

After a few misguided attempts to trade shots with the big ship, the Confederates gave it up as a bad job and suffered in silence.

Gen. P.G.T. Beauregard, the commander at Charleston, had clear views on dealing with Federal ironclads. He considered it a waste of time to try to sink them by shooting at them. The best way, he declared, was to plant a charge against the unprotected areas of their hulls underwater. And the way to do that was with mines or torpedo boats.

The Confederates tried once to sink her with a mine and missed. Then they turned to spar torpedoes — canisters of powder on the end of a boom. Capt. F.D. Lee, a protege of Beauregard's, was also trying to build a fast, small vessel to carry such torpedoes but he was having trouble prying materials loose from other military channels.

When a fellow officer, Capt. James Carlin, asked his help in tackling the Ironsides, however, Lee was exceedingly cooperative. He and Carlin managed to find the hull of a never-to-be-completed gunboat which nobody wanted. They installed a secondhand engine in it and mounted a torpedo at the bow. On the night of Aug. 20, 1863, Carlin went out hunting.

To insure a safe return with his feeble engine, he caught the last of the ebb tide as it ran out past Sumter, hoping to ride back on the flood. At Sumter, he picked up a squad of riflemen to help repel boarders and then he moved out into the darkness toward the bar.

The ebb tide swept him down rapidly upon the New Ironsides.

About midnight, Carlin sighted her lying across the channel a few hundred yards east of Morris Island, her bow toward the island, swinging to the changing tide.

Keeping her on his port bow, Carlin steamed up abreast the frigate and put his rudder hard left, intending to charge in.

Then misunderstandings and mechanical trouble set in. Orders to the helm passed too slowly. The attack missed. As the Ironsides continued to swing to the tide, the Confederates found themselves tangled in her anchor chain. To their horror, their engine stopped.

For five minutes, while the sleepy frigate shook herself awake, the Southerners struggled to get their vessel moving again. Finally, the screw began to turn. It was too late.

Followed by a scattering of musket balls and a couple of poorly aimed shells, the Confederates scurried for home.

Gen. Beauregard chose to overlook the failure. Tactfully, he congratulated the unsuccessful torpedomen on their gallantry — and then he looked around for someone else to challenge the big Yankee frigate.

He did not have to look far. The semi-submersible torpedo boat David, built up the Santee river 35 miles from Charleston, had come down to the city and was awaiting orders.

Thirty feet long, her blue-gray hull deep in the water, the David was a formidable weapon. She also had a formidable crew — four men notable both for skill and courage. The commander, Lieut. W.T. Glassell, was an officer of the "old Navy" who had served a time in a federal prison for refusing to take the oath of allegiance to the U.S.

The engineer in charge of the little steam boiler and reciprocating engine was J.H. Tombs, assistant engineer of the gunboat Chicora. With him to the David, Mr. Tombs brought a fireman — James Sullivan. Navigation was in the hands of J.W. Cannon, pilot of the CSS Palmetto State.

On the night of Oct. 5 these four boarded the David. Soon after dark the little ship was under way, pushing a scarcely discernible ripple along the surface of the dark harbor as she steamed down the channel. About 9 p.m. she was off Morris Island.

Lieut. Glassell steered along the outer edge of the channel. From his post in the tiny cockpit of the steamer, he could see the Federal ships inshore, silhouetted against campfires on the beach.

In their midst lay the New Ironsides, drowsing at anchor, not one whit the wiser for her earlier brush with disaster.

Glassell ordered full speed and turned toward his target, rigging the torpedo boom for action. With 300 yards to go, there came a hail from the deck of the frigate. Glassell picked up the only firearm aboard, a shotgun, and responded with a blast of buckshot.

The frigate's officer of the deck fell mortally wounded. Confusion reigned aboard as the David struck her amidships. There was an explosion. Water soared high into the air and cascaded down into the open topsides of the David. The fires under her boiler were put out.

Although the David was now helplessly drifting under enemy guns, the crew of the Ironsides was unable to sink her.

The blast of the torpedo had shaken their ship from stem to stern. Below decks, men and furniture were scattered in confusion. Several sailors were injured. The shaken gunners, manning their pieces amid the uproar, could see nothing to shoot at. Topside, Marine riflemen picked out a dark shape drifting by and opened fire. Eventually the dim form disappeared into the darkness.

Although the Federals did not know it, they missed a splendid chance to capture the one weapon the Confederates might use to break the blockade.

When the engine stopped, the commander of the David had ordered "abandon ship." He and his companions went over the side. Glassell and Sullivan made it to one of the blockaders and were taken prisoner.

Cannon, however, could not swim. Afraid to strike out, he held on to the drifting torpedo boat. As he hung there, Engineer Tombs suddenly showed up. The two men climbed back aboard. Patiently they sought to rekindle the fires. After a few minutes, they were successful.

While the alarm was still spreading through the blockading fleet, the little David, half her crew gone, crept slowly back into Charleston Harbor.

The Ironsides did not sink. In spite of fairly extensive damage, she lived up to her reputation of invulnerability, keeping her station for eight more months.

From that time forward, however, there was no more sleeping on station in the blockading fleet.

A.M.W.

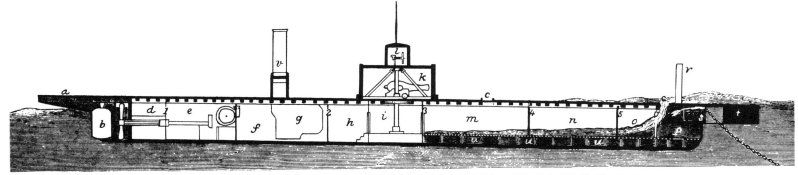

Diagram shows how water poured into Weehawken as she lay at anchor off Charleston.

(a. Overhang protecting propeller; b. Rudder; c. Hatches; d. Engineer's storeroom; e. Engine room; f. Fire room; g. Boilers; h. Coal bunker; i. Turret chamber; k. Turret; l. Pilot house; m. Men's quarters; n. Officers' quarters; o. Captain's cabin; p. Anchor chamber; r. Ventilator; s. Anchor well; t. Ram; u. Lockers for stores; v. Smokestack; 1-5. Watertight bulkheads.)

Monitor Sinks Off Charleston

Three months, almost to the day, after she had narrowly escaped disaster on a sandbank in Charleston Harbor, the U.S. monitor Weehawken plunged suddenly to the bottom of Charleston Ship Channel.

Remembering the punishment the little iron ship had taken while she lay helpless under the guns of Fort Moultrie on Sept. 8, the Confederates gleefully accepted part credit for her sinking. Union naval officers, too, at first suspected that the Southern gunners had something to do with the loss of their valuable ship. Later on, however, they accepted with embarrassment and sorrow full responsibility for an accident which cost Admiral John A. Dahlgren an irreplaceable fighting unit and the lives of three score officers and men.

Of all the sailors in the U.S. Navy, few endured more risks and hardship than the men who served in the sea-going monitors. These low-lying little ships were designed to endure maximum punishment but they also enjoyed a minimum of reserve buoyancy.

It was no jest to say that monitors, particularly the Passaic class monitors — those employed at Charleston — singularly resembled floating coffins. One difference was that it was easier to escape from a coffin than from a sinking monitor.

Heavily armored, laden with burdensome weapons, crammed with machinery, the monitors could afford few openings which might let in sea water.

Hatches were kept to a minimum and tightly shut in action.

Escape, if any, was via a narrow ladder which led into the turret. If for any reason anything happened to rupture the sealed box in which the crews lived and fought, one man, with luck, might escape up the ladder.

Because of their inability to survive any loss of watertight integrity, monitors were particularly susceptible to mines.

But explosion was not the only risk. Almost as great a hazard was the sea itself. The original Monitor, the conqueror of the Virginia, had drowned in a storm at sea.

From this, the Union Navy had learned the vital importance of restricting monitor operations to sheltered waters for safety's sake.

At Charleston, however, circumstances compelled the monitor crews to accept exposure to wind and wave. Most of the operations against the outer forts, in which the monitors were the backbone of the fleet, were conducted in placid waters, but there were occasions when the sea inside the bar ran high and dangerous.

It was on such a day, Dec. 6, 1863, that the Weehawken went down in the midst of the fleet and before the gaze of the astonished Confederates.

The Weehawken was well known to both friends and enemies. Ever since April, when she had led the fleet in the first assault of Sumter, she had been prominent in the Navy's activities at the gates of Charleston.

On this day she was lying at anchor off the Beacon House at the south end of Morris Island. A moderate gale was blowing in from the northeast, the wind was strong, the sea lumpy and uncomfortable.

As far as the other units of the fleet could observe from their anchorages nearby, there was nothing to indicate that the Weehawken was in distress until

Sailors climb through hatches and leap from stricken ship.

Survivors are hauled from water by crewmen of rescue boats.

about 2 p.m. when she suddenly hoisted the signal: "I require assistance."

In the fleet, there was an immediate stir of activity. From the New Ironsides, anchored nearby, boats put out.

Before they could reach the laboring monitor, however, she was sharply down by the head. Before her signal had been in the air for five minutes, the Weehawken heaved her stern into the air. Then she dove to the bottom, carrying part of her crew, leaving the rest struggling in the rough water.

Since she had been one of but four monitors on the station, Adm. Dahlgren was appalled by the unexpected loss of the Weehawken. He immediately set about preparing plans to raise her.

The question that faced the salvors was: What made her sink? If her hull was ruptured, if it had parted at the point where the armored deck met the underwater portion in a wide overhang, she might be impossible to bring to the surface.

From the survivors it was difficult to piece together a helpful report. The Weehawken's captain had been absent when she sank. Many of the engineers who had been working to stem a sudden inflow of water had gone down with their ship. The others did not have a coherent story to tell.

Gradually, a board composed of captains from the remaining monitors pieced together a painful tale of faulty design and poor seamanship.

The Weehawken, it appeared, had recently taken aboard an extra supply of ammunition. It had been stored well forward. Because of this, her normal trim of 12 inches down by the stern had been altered. She was slightly deeper forward than was normal.

As the gale blew up, a hatch which gave access to the anchor windlass room in the bow had not been secured.

Neither had precautions been taken to make watertight the hawse pipe through which the anchor cable passed into the ship from the sea.

The sequence of events as reconstructed by the board of investigation and Adm. Dahlgren was this:

Rough seas had found their way into the ship through the open hatch.

Because of the Weehawken's slightly down-by-the-head attitude, not all of this water flowed aft where it could be picked up by bilge pumps and discharged over the side.

As water gradually accumulated forward, the open hawse pipe was submerged.

A flood suddenly swept into the Weehawken.

In five minutes she was on the bottom, only her stack showing at high tide.

The loss of the Weehawken, although she was only one of many ships at Dahlgren's disposal, helped to further depress the spirit of the Navy which had been so long baffled by the defenses of Charleston.

Adm. Dahlgren's plans to raise her came to naught as she settled into the soft mud of the channel bottom. Eventually, though reluctantly, she was given up for lost.

A.M.W.

Magazine today (1). Line leads to entrance (2).

Small Arms Magazine Explodes

Fort Sumter, hard hit by Northern bombardment, was enjoying a rare respite from bursting shells during the second week of December 1863.

By Friday, Dec. 11, the week's report showed only seven rounds had rumbled in from Yankee cannon on nearby Morris Island or the ever-present ironclads blockading the harbor.

Seven, compared to a daily ration which sometimes ran into the hundreds, seemed like a holiday.

Men off duty crawled from the rubble to bask in the December sun, outwardly relaxed but keyed to quick movement at the first sound of a gun.

Around them, work continued on repairs to the fort, but at a more leisurely pace than the frantic sandbagging of shell damage under fire.

Many of the garrison were queued up to draw rations from the fort's commissary, a seemingly harmless pursuit that suddenly turned into terror and death.

The commissary had been placed in what was considered a safe spot — at least safe from enemy fire.

It was located in one of the fort's original magazines which consisted of two rooms. The inner was still used as a magazine — for small-arm and howitzer ammunition. The outer housed the commissary.

The Confederates realized this dual use of a magazine was far from safe, but felt it was necessary due to the shortage of storage space and the necessity for keeping the rations safe.

The rooms, at parade ground level of the gorge near the left flank, were now covered by tons of debris from the battered gorge wall which protected them from the fire of Morris Island guns. Heavy brick work stood between them and any shells thrown by the fleet. The brick work was threaded by narrow, angular passageways leading to the left flank casemates and the parade ground.

These passages, so carefully designed to keep out enemy fire, became a trap for the line of men drawing rations that December day.

What caused the explosion of ammunition in the magazine — amounting to some 150 pounds of black powder — is still a mystery.

Certainly, it was not due to enemy action for no shells had been fired that day at the fort.

Perhaps a lantern in the commissary was carelessly knocked over. Maybe a spark from static electricity, even spontaneous combustion. Those left alive were too far back in the passageways to know what happened. Those who knew, were too close to the blast to live.

It is known that flame and smoke suddenly erupted from the inner chamber about 9:30 a.m. The commissary officer and his men died instantly along with the first soldiers in the line.

Concussion and flame were funneled into the passageways striking down men in the lines until, effect lessening with distance, those at the ends staggered out of the smoke into the parade ground.

Inside the magazine was an inferno. Smoke and heat thwarted all efforts to get at the flame. An attempt to block the passageway to the left casemates with wet sandbags was stopped by the intense heat and stifling smoke. Finally, nothing could be done but block all entryways, embrasures and other openings to reduce the draft and let the fire die of its own accord.

The ceiling of the magazine had collapsed filling the space with debris from the gorge wall and leaving a gaping crater on top of the debris. However, since this subsidence occurred almost instantaneously and since the noise of the explosion was muffled, the blast was not at first noticed by the Yankees.

However, within minutes, smoke began oozing from the various openings to rise above the fort signaling the enemy that something was amiss.

The Federals opened fire pouring some 200 rounds into the fort to add to the problems of rescue and firefighting efforts.

Later in the day, the Confederates counted their casualties — 11 dead and 41 injured.

Much of the fort was out of action. The area surrounding the magazine, including the casemates on the left flank, were closed. The lower casemates were filled with smoke and hot air. Those on the upper tier, where a number of men were quartered, were also evacuated, the men being forced to descend via ladders to the ground outside the fort.

By noon, the fire had consumed everything combustible in the upper left flank casemates and by nightfall had burned out in the lower. Timbers of about half the passageway leading to the parade ground were destroyed. The rest were saved by sand which fell from above and arrested the flames.

Copious watering permitted access to the upper casemates by the time provisions and replacements for the casualties arrived that night. But the lower casemates, through which was the fort's sally port, were still hot. Consequently, all supplies had to be carried up ladders from the wharf to the second tier of casemates, up more ladders to the brick arch forming a roof, then down the rough footing of the debris slope of the gorge.

During the next few days, the casemates and passageways slowly cooled. Debris and sand were removed from the passageways and the burned areas gradually repaired.

By the 18th, men were able to penetrate to the commissary despite material still smouldering on the floor.

The small-arms magazine was not entered and remained closed until excavated by Fort Sumter National Monument personnel in 1960. At the time, they found a quantity of shot and a number of musket barrels, several of which, securely fused together by the heat, were left in place against the side of the wall.

Although casualties were heavy, the main danger of the explosion to the fort was the elimination of badly needed space. This forced extreme crowding of the garrison and created such an unhealthy condition that Maj. John Johnson, writing in 1890, was led to assert that had the enemy continued for a single week the intense bombardment opened when the fire started, the Confederates would have been forced to abandon the work.

W.R.

Marblehead, right; Pawnee, left, and mortar schooner in the center.

Marblehead Escapes Trap

Attack On U.S. Gunboat Fails

As 1863 neared its end, the Confederates in Charleston saw the Northern tide eating steadily away the ramparts that defended their city.

It had been a year of grim defense, relieved from time to time by a bold and brilliant stroke. Although they did not decisively — or often seriously — affect the course of events, such feats as the capture of the USS Isaac Smith and the attacks on the New Ironsides served to bolster the martial spirit which served the Confederates so well in lieu of adequate numbers of men and weapons.

It was time now for another morale-building coup.

Gen. P.G.T. Beauregard, whose energy and imagination were chiefly responsible for the good fight the Southerners were putting up at Charleston, laid plans to repeat his brilliant success in capturing the Isaac Smith.

He ordered a Christmas visit to the Union Navy in Stono River.

It was not as easy, however, in December 1863, to arrange a gunboat trap as it had been 10 months earlier.

The capture of the Isaac Smith had taught the U.S. Navy a thing or two about masked batteries.

The Smith, an old river tub, had been caught napping at anchor in the midst of enemies far from her consorts in the fleet.

Nowadays, the river patrol was in the hands of two regular gunboats, the Pawnee and Marblehead, solidly built, heavily armed and habitually alert.

When these professional warriors moved upriver, they went warily, guns manned, on the lookout for trouble.

When they were not on the prowl, they lay downriver, where friendly troops controlled the banks.

To attack one of these vessels was a far more ambitious undertaking than the expedition against the Smith had been.

As dawn broke on Christmas Day, therefore, it found nearly 1,000 Confederates concealed on the south bank of the Stono a few hundred yards below a strong Union outpost in the little old settlement called Legareville.

Three strong fieldworks erected at night or when the enemy was looking the other way, sheltered twelve guns ranging from 8-inch siege howitzers to light fieldpieces.

Between Legareville and the guns, behind a hedge which ran across the narrow peninsula on which Legareville was built, was a regiment of infantry. The soldiers lay with their eyes toward the village, waiting the signal to open fire so that they might advance and capture the 150-man Union garrison.

As the morning mist drew away from the river banks, the black hull of a gunboat loomed into the sight of the eager Confederates. It was the Marblehead, lying at anchor a quarter of a mile, more or less, upstream. The Pawnee was not to be seen.

Soon the haze had thinned enough for the Confederate gunners to lay their pieces. Shortly after 6 a.m. a gun in the "upper" battery, nearest the village, roared. The other guns promptly joined in. The trap was sprung.

Lt. Comdr. R.W. Meade Jr., captain of the Marblehead, was just as surprised as his colleague in command of the Isaac Smith had been when Confederate shells suddenly began to rain around his ship. In some ways Meade's predicament was even worse than that of the captain of the Smith had been. One of the Marblehead's boilers was shut down for repairs.

Instead of falling into confusion, however, the Marblehead's skipper and his crew reacted with cool precision. For a few minutes, while the seamen scrambled to their guns and the engineers built up steam pressure in the remaining boiler, the gunboat lay placidly at anchor.

To the puzzled Confederates it seemed as if the Marblehead was ignoring them. The gunners, believing their shots were flying wide, hastily corrected their aim. Their officers strained their eyes, searching for evidence of hits.

The shells were hitting, all right, even if the Confederates couldn't see them. They drummed against the Marblehead's sides and tore at her bulwarks. Her maintopmast came tumbling down. Here and there a sailor collapsed, blood streaming from wounds.

It was 15 minutes before the engine room signaled "ready to answer bells." Then the Marblehead slipped her cable and stood calmly downstream, shooting as she went.

Up from the south, where she had lain in the mist at the mouth of the river, came the Pawnee, attracted by the shooting. Instead of steaming up to join the Marblehead, however, she swung into the mouth of the Kiawah River where it joined the Stono a few hundred yards below the Confederate position. Her anchor went down. The river current swung her to bring her starboard battery to bear on the flank of the Confederate batteries. Across the Southern position from right to left swept a hail of iron like nothing the Confederate gunners had ever experienced.

Caught in the crossfire from the Marblehead in front and the Pawnee on their right, the batteries suffered. Only one man was killed but more than a dozen valuable horses were cut down.

The Confederates, misled by the cool behavior of the little Marblehead, believing she was beyond range, now had no stomach for a fight with the bigger, heavier armed Pawnee.

Hastily, the guns were hauled out — those for which teams remained. Then the infantry, which had never gotten started toward its objective, was withdrawn.

Shortly, the whole force dispirited and shaken, two of its guns missing, was back at Abbapoola Bridge, leaving the field to the gunboats.

While the Confederate commanders framed reports blaming one another for the fiasco, the triumphant Federal sailors landed on the river bank and carried away the guns.

Upon Lt. Col. Del Kemper, commanding the artillery, fell the weight of official Confederate displeasure.

"Expedition failed through bad firing of our batteries," Gen. Beauregard reported to Richmond.

To the Union sailors, busy repairing damage to the Marblehead, it did not look like "bad firing." In the sick bay lay four of their messmates dead, others severely wounded. They counted more than 30 places where their ship had been struck in her hull and topsides. Eighteen shots had cut up her rigging.

If the Confederates had been able to read Capt. Meade's report, they would have seen where the real blame lay — with the miserable ammunition with which the Southern batteries were supplied.

It was not Col. Kemper's gunners who were to blame for the collapse of Old Bory's plans, but shells that would not explode when they hit and shot too small to hurt.

A.M.W.

Union Base Held Many Structures

Forage house was one of several sizeable storage buildings.

Morris Island, which saw some of the most vicious fighting of the Civil War, today presents a desolate scene to the visitor.

Erosion steadily eats away the beach — cutting stretches down to what apparently was once marsh and mud.

At highwater mark in some sections, thousands of cleanly-washed, bleached oyster shells have been thrown up in even rows as though by a huge road grader. In other parts, eroded dunes are putting up a poor defense against the tides.

About the center of the island, a small clump of pine and palmetto trees is fighting a losing battle against the sea. This forlorn area, site of a Federal breaching battery, once teemed with men feeding the guns which helped crumble Fort Sumter into ruins.

The island is narrow here, but near the Cummings Point end it widens a bit to present, inland from the beach, a tangle of scrub undergrowth and cacti which is far from tempting to the tourist.

Yet 100 years ago, Morris Island was a beehive of activity. Tents and wooden buildings dotted the landscape, especially after the island was evacuated by the Confederates and became a Yankee base for bombardment of Charleston and its surrounding forts.

Supply of the Union garrison was no small problem and numerous wooden buildings were thrown up throughout the island, especially on the southern, or Folly Island, end.

A complete list of buildings is not available but references in the Official Records and photographs show there were carpenter and paint shops, Army and Navy boat building or repair shops, a gas manufacturing plant, ice house, blacksmith shop, and a forage house for storing food for horses brought to the island.

There were also quartermaster and commissary storehouses, ordnance and engineer depots, each with several buildings, and a number of headquarters and administrative structures. Doubtless there were others.

All, to judge by the photographs, were crude, wartime structures of no architectural beauty. They served a temporary purpose, were abandoned when the troops moved on, and disappeared through ravages of time, wind and sea with perhaps a helping hand from human vandals and scavengers.

W.R.

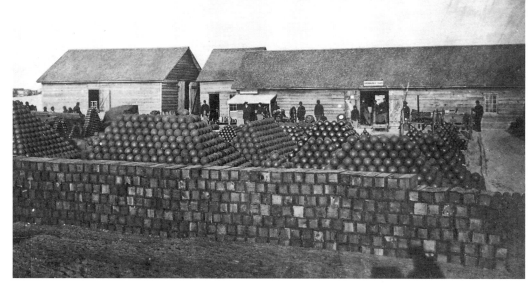

Ordnance yard fed Yankee cannon firing on Charleston and Southern forts.

Blacksmith shop made field repairs to Federal equipment.

Neatly lettered sign proclaimed the carpenter shop.

Morris Island gas manufacturing plant.

Hunley Attacks Housatonic

Submarine Sinks U.S. Warship

On a bright moonlit night early in 1864 a band of incredibly brave Confederates in a clumsy submarine made the last significant attempt to break the Federal blockade of Charleston.

The Confederate Navy with mines and surface torpedo boats had already fully opened a new era of warfare, but it remained for the Army to supply the means to take the fighting into a new element — under the sea.

For this venture, the Navy was willing to stand aside for soldiers.

The naval officers looked at a strange craft the Army had brought up from Mobile on flat cars and labeled it, truthfully enough, a "veritable coffin."

It was between 30 and 40 feet long, made of boiler plate, and from 4 to 5 feet in diameter — in essence a tube of iron, closed at both ends, with two hatches whose coamings were raised above the hull and provided with portholes. It was named, prosaically, H.L. Hunley for the man who built it. It was a true submarine.

The Hunley could, if properly handled — with luck — sink beneath the surface and journey as far beneath the water as her crew, turning a hand-powered propeller, could drive her. To submerge was simple: one turned a valve and admitted water to a ballast tank. To rise again was equally simple: one turned another valve and pumped out the water.

A dreadful complication to this routine was that the operation sometimes had to be carried out in foul and treacherous darkness. Men locked up in the Hunley grew fuzzy-headed from lack of oxygen. The candles they kept burning in their boat guttered and grew dim. A whole platoon of heroes died in the Hunley because it was so hard to find the right valve to turn.

Some died under the eyes of Lt. George E. Dixon, an Alabama soldier who had helped build the Hunley at Mobile and had commanded her on trial trips there. Dixon was on a pier at Charleston with Engineer Tombs of the Navy when the Hunley, her builder at the helm, tried to dive under the Confederate receiving ship

The Housatonic under sail and steam.

Indian Chief. The Hunley submerged, leaving an ominous stream of bubbles and did not come up. A week later, salvage crews pulled her from the bottom.

"They failed to close the after valve," Dixon said laconically and proceeded to take charge of the boat.

Dixon's friend Tombs had already had experience with the Hunley himself. He was no coward — he had been in the David when she had attacked the New Ironsides — but he wanted no part of the Army's "fish boat." He had seen her go down once with her crew and he knew she had killed three other crews, one at Mobile and two at Charleston. All told, the Hunley now had about 25 dead men to her account, all of them Confederates.

On trial trips in Charleston Harbor, Tombs had been in charge of the tug assigned to haul the Hunley back and forth. He and his tow had gotten mixed up with the Hunley's torpedo which trailed on a long line astern.

There had been a narrow escape from an explosion.

Tombs reported to his superiors the Hunley was a bad risk, cranky, dangerous and probably unable to survive the blast of her own torpedo.

Tombs passed his views on to Dixon who listened but refused to yield a conviction that the Hunley could be used effectively against the enemy.

Dixon had been in on the original trials of the submarine at Mobile, the series of tests in which the little ship had killed a crew for the first time. He knew as well as anybody that she lacked both buoyancy and power. But he did not alter his plans.

"He is a brave and coolheaded man," Tombs wrote in his journal.

Brave as he might be, Dixon was apparently not exceptional. Every soldier and sailor on the waterfront

(Continued On Page 73)

Housatonic heels under blow as exploding charge of Hunley torpedo deluges her decks with water.

Painting shows Confederate submarine Hunley on dock at Charleston.

(Continued From Page 72)

SUBMARINE

knew about the Hunley and her murderous record, yet when Dixon set out to collect yet another crew, he had no trouble getting volunteers. Six sailors and an army officer agreed to try a crack at the blockaders.

Dixon then got reluctant permission from Gen. Beauregard to take the fish boat out. Nobody in the South was more anxious than the general to break the blockade. He had been the man who brought the Hunley to Charleston in the first place.

But Beauregard had also witnessed the return of the Hunley from one of her disastrous dives and he well remembered what he had seen when her hatches were opened by the salvagers.

"The unfortunate men were contorted into all sorts of horrible attitudes...the blackened faces of all presented the expression of their despair and agony," he wrote.

The general stipulated there would be no more dives; any attack Dixon wanted to undertake would have to be made on the surface.

This limitation compelled Dixon to accept another change of technique.

Since the Hunley could not dive under her target, the towed torpedo had to be eliminated. A conventional spar torpedo on a long pole at the bow was substituted.

There were any number of targets available for the spar torpedo. Close offshore, in a long line stretching down to the south and away to the north, lay the blockaders. Anchored in a strategic berth, near the entrance to the Swash Channel, was the handsome sloop USS Housatonic. Unlike most of her sisters on the blockade, she was a regular warship, built for sea duty, with the rakish lines of a cruiser and the rig and armament of a small frigate. She was a genuine menace to any blockader looking for a safe path into port.

On the clear night of Feb. 17, with the swift ebb tide to supplement the exertions of her human machinery, the Hunley slipped out of Breach Inlet and turned her bow south, toward the Housatonic. At Battery Marshall, the Confederate fort which guarded the inlet,

lanterns were set in readiness to guide her home again.

In the bright moonlight, the spars and funnels of the blockaders shone clearly. It was easy to pick out the Housatonic's silhouette. Moving silently, with only her bulbous hatches showing, the Hunley stole toward the Federal ship.

Aboard the Housatonic all was quiet, but the watch was alert. Adventures with the Davids had taught the Federals the need for staying awake. Guns were cast loose and provided. Steam pressure was up and at the throttles. In a moment the chain anchor cable could be broken at a convenient shackle and the ship could be under way.

Shortly after 9 p.m., Master Crosby, the officer of the deck, and his lookouts saw something stir on the waters a few yards away. It looked like a log.

Crosby hesitated and took another look. The log cruised toward the Housatonic's starboard quarter, streaming a wake from two curious projections.

Crosby called an alarm. Drums rolled action stations. The anchor cable splashed overboard. A bell rang in the engine room and the Housatonic began to gather sternway.

Within three minutes, the big ship, her crew at quarters, guns trained out — in vain because they could not be brought to bear — smoke rolling from her stack, was underway, ready to fight.

It was not soon enough. The "log" bored into the starboard quarter, just abaft the mizzenmast. There was a stunning crash, a muffled explosion, like the shock of a 12-pounder howitzer, and a severe shock. A dark column of smoke rose in the sky. Pieces of timber soared as high as the mizzenmast head.

The spar deck — upper deck — crumbled aft and fell away. The engines stopped. The ship dipped her stern. In less time than it took to tell the story later, she was on the bottom in 30 feet of water.

Her crew, except five killed by drowning or explosion, scrambled into the rigging and looked around for help.

None came. The rest of the fleet lay serenely at anchor. The fierce attack had gone unnoticed beyond the decks of the Housatonic.

As soon as he could recover his wits, Capt. Charles

C. Pickering mustered a crew for one of the ship's boats which had drifted free. With their dazed and bruised captain, the men rowed over to the USS Canandaigua, a few hundred yards away. The Canandaigua got under way and steamed over. She plucked 21 officers and 137 men from the shrouds of the Housatonic.

Later on, a court was convened to study what had happened to the Housatonic. The members sat briefly and reported what everybody knew already: a "queer looking craft" had rammed the Housatonic. There had been an explosion. Nobody was to blame.

A diver went down. He did not find any evidence of a torpedo boat, but he reported the explosion had been a formidable one. Everything abaft the mainmast of the Housatonic was smashed. The spar deck was gone, bulkheads shattered, cabins destroyed, furniture, muskets and coal were scattered everywhere. Rudder post and screw were broken. The Housatonic, in short, was a total wreck.

The Confederates, who held the secret of the attacker, were left in the dark themselves. They knew only that the Hunley had not returned. The lights held in readiness at Battery Marshall had been put away after a while, but there had been a mixup in communications between headquarters and the outposts and Gen. Beauregard had not been told the Hunley was missing.

It was the 27th of February before a group of talkative Yankee prisoners spilled the story to the Confederates.

Looking out to sea on the 18th, the Southern lookouts had been unable to spot anything amiss in the fleet.

In Charleston there was a brief flurry of excitement. Beauregard put out an order commending the Hunley and her brave crew and giving them up for lost. The Daily Courier cried "glorious victory" but was slow in telling its readers that the victors had not come home.

When everything had settled down again, the blockade was on as usual. Nothing had been changed by Dixon and his men — except history.

A.M.W.

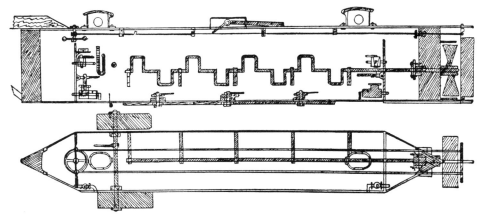

Diagrams show interior of the Hunley.

Cross section of Confederate submarine.

Torpedo Sinks USS Patapsco

Throughout the war, the bogey of Confederate torpedoes commanding the approaches to Charleston had haunted the Union Navy. The end was close at hand, however, before they were able to report solid evidence at hand to support their fears.

On Jan. 15, 1865, the USS Patapsco, standing boldly into the gap between Fort Sumter and Fort Moultrie — the threshold to Charleston Harbor — hit a mine and sank.

In the little plume of smoke hovering above the spot where she vanished in a swirl of water, carrying more than half her crew with her, the Federal admirals were pleased to read a message which justified their reluctance over the years to test with determination the defenses of Charleston.

It was, the admirals said, just as they had said all along — the rebels and their infernal machines were more than a match for the ironclad fleet. The loss of the Patapsco proved it.

If the sinking proved anything, however, it was not the accuracy of Union intelligence but the low state to which Southern spirit had fallen by this time.

Eighteen months before, when the Keokuk had gone down off Morris Island, after a spirited if reckless point blank duel with Fort Sumter, the Charlestonians had gone into raptures over her loss. Staff officers turned out reams of correspondence concerning the significance of the sinking of one little tin-clad teapot and editors hailed the sight of her smokestack above the waves off Morris Island as evidence of a great victory.

The view of the Patapsco's smokestack midway between Sumter and Moultrie, however, conjured up no such visions of conquest, led to no such exultation.

By this time, the Confederates were too wise to mistake the sinking of an ironclad for supremacy at sea and too tired to celebrate.

The event rated a paragraph in the Courier under a headline "The siege of Charleston — 157th Day" to the effect that a Yankee monitor had gone down suddenly and some of her crew had been heard calling for help. The official reports disposed of the matter in scarcely more detail and neither editor nor military commander bothered to explain how it was that the Union Navy these days felt so free to steam boldly into the gap between the two forts.

The truth was that in the winter of 1864 and early 1865 not only ironclads were operating right in the entrance to Charleston, but men in rowboats as well — all busy seeking what the Union commanders were so sure was there — the torpedoes.

They were there all right on the night that the Patapsco found them, but they had been there less than 24 hours. A few days before, Capt. John A. Simon, the officer in charge of the Torpedo Service at Charleston, had been busy in the harbor entrance laying torpedoes where none had ever been laid before — in spite of the elaborate reports which traveled to Washington from off Charleston Bar. Simon had anchored 16 barrels filled with gunpowder across the main ship channel between the two forts, arranging them to float about five feet below the surface of the water at low tide. The last went down on the night of the 14th.

Early in the evening of the 15th, the Patapsco, a veteran of long service off Charleston, got underway and steamed slowly toward the harbor entrance.

The Patapsco had been one of the seven ironclads which engaged in the first great assault on Charleston from the sea in April 1863, the same fight in which the Keokuk had been mortally wounded. She was a sister of the Weehawken which had foundered in a storm off the bar.

Her crew had survived the tedious boredom of the blockade as well as the Confederate shot and shell. Old hands in the crew could read in the increasing boldness of their captain as they moved in a little closer each night in their patrols, the signs of flagging Confederate resistance. The Johnnies were giving out and the Yankee sailors knew it.

On this night, the Patapsco's captain, Lt. Comdr. S.P. Quackenbush, did not even bother to seek shelter in his armored conning tower as his ship moved in toward Sumter to offer fire support to the boats' crews looking for mines.

In the darkness, he gathered the picket and scout boats about his ship and from the position at the railing atop the conning tower called down orders. Boats equipped with grapnels were to pull ahead of the slow-moving monitor, searching for mines. The other boats were to stay on the beams and quarters of the Patapsco under the shelter of her guns.

Thus the Patapsco and her flock drifted slowly in between the forts until nearly on the line between Sumter and Moultrie. Then the monitor moved out again a short distance, stopped engines and drifted slowly in on the tide once more.

Three times this procedure was repeated, Quackenbush conning his ship from atop the turret, giving orders in a low voice to Acting Ensign A.P. Bashford and the quartermaster of the watch.

At a few minutes after 8 p.m., the Patapsco was ready to get under way once more for her run out towards the sea.

There was an explosion. To Lt. W.T. Simpson the executive officer below decks, it sounded like a hit from a shot. Water pouring in from a great hole on the port side, 30 feet from the bow, promptly proved otherwise. Simpson and his shipmates ran for their lives.

To Lt. Comdr. Quackenbush, the explosion was a shock. He had been absolutely sure there was no danger from mines. As soon as he recovered his presence of mind, he ordered the engine room to start pumps. The words were hardly out of his mouth when he realized his ship was going under.

He issued his second and last order — "man the boats."

That one could not be carried out either. The Patapsco's only boat, hanging from its davits abaft the turret, was already afloat as the ship sank under it. Providentially, said the captain, he and the men who had been standing with him on the turret, wound up in the boat. Thus saved to direct rescue operations, Quackenbush managed to save 43 of his officers and men. Sixty-two more died in the ship.

The Confederates listening in the darkness were deprived of most of the pleasure of witnessing the end of one of their most despised enemies.

The cries of the men in the water carried clearly through the night but the Southerners, now reduced to utmost economy in the conservation of ammunition, did not even risk a few trial shots at the source of the noise.

Not until daylight came and they discovered the Patapsco's smokestack poking up through the water were they able to find out what happened.

A.M.W.

USS Patapsco Monument at Fort Moultrie.

Interior of Fort Sumter in December 1863.

Fort Weathered 11 Bombardments

Fort Sumter, symbol of Southern resistance throughout the Civil War, stood up under three major and eight minor bombardments which pounded the brick walls into rubble, but failed to force its surrender.

The First Major Bombardment was initiated not long after Yankee troops stormed ashore on Morris Island July 10, 1863. In attempting to possess the entire island, they tried two major assaults on Battery Wagner which was considered an outpost of Fort Sumter.

With the disastrous failure of both attacks, the Federals determined to reduce Sumter anyway. They brought up heavy breaching batteries and Aug. 17, 1863, began pounding away at the fort over the heads of Wagner defenders who were powerless to do anything about it.

The bombardment was in two phases. The first, Aug. 17-23, was the most intense with some 5,000 rounds being fired. The second, marked by desultory fire during much of it to prevent repairs to the fort, culminated Sept. 1-2 in a night attack by the monitors hurling 11 and 15-inch shells. The fort suffered this attack in grim silence — there was not a single gun in condition to reply.

With the bombardment's end Sept. 2, Sumter's gorge wall was in ruins and the fort's offensive power, to all practical purposes, had been destroyed. Yet despite an estimated 6,800 shot and shell fired at the fort, only two men were killed. An additional 50 were wounded.

Morris Island was evacuated Sept. 7 and the following night the Union Navy decided to occupy Sumter which appeared ripe for the taking.

However, the Federals discovered Sumter still could sting and their small boat attack was decisively smashed. They withdrew to lick their wounds and for almost three weeks the front was relatively quiet.

The end of September brought a resumption of fire with the First Minor Bombardment, Sept. 28-Oct. 3. Casualties were light — one killed and two wounded. Damage was hardly perceptible. A Confederate count placed the number of Federal rounds at roughly 570.

The guns fell silent after the 3rd while the Yankees worked on batteries established on the Cummings Point end of Morris Island and the Confederates strengthened Sumter — particularly with the addition about the middle of October of a battery of three guns on the right face.

The work led to the Second Major Bombardment in which the Union attempted to destroy the new battery, or disrupt work on it, by cutting down the fort's right flank and taking the channel casemates in reverse.

The bombardment lasted 41 days, Oct. 26-Dec. 6, at close range from guns on and near Cummings Point. It was characterized primarily by a high portion of mortar fire which was particularly vigorous at night.

Casualties mounted gradually, but the heaviest loss of life occurred early in the morning of Oct. 31. A detachment of 13 men were sleeping in a first-floor room of one of the old barracks. The floors above had been wrecked, but ceiling girders were thought strong enough until a chance shell brought down the overloaded floor wiping out the unit instantly and burying the bodies beneath tons of rubble.

During the last three days of October, the fort received some 3,000 rounds, the heaviest firing of any period of its existence.

Throughout the 41-day period, between 18,000 and 19,000 rounds were fired at the fort. Casualties were roughly 100, a third of them dead.

Damage was extensive, but repairs had continued throughout the bombardment. The right flank, at which the fire had been mainly directed, was cut from 40 feet in height to 20 but the rubble formed a solid base for the lowered wall. Continuing the line of fire beyond, the shells had taken the left face in reverse and turned it into a mountain of jagged masonry about 25 feet high.

Yet one of the major aims of the bombardment, destruction of the Three-Gun Battery, was defeated. The guns were still serviceable.

There was only a brief respite from the end of the Second Major Bombardment until the Second Minor Bombardment. This was a one-day affair touched off when, for some unexplained reason, the small arms magazine in the fort exploded about 9:30 a.m. Dec. 11.

There had been no firing that day until the sudden blast. Then, smoke rising over the fort announced the tragedy, and Federal guns opened a heavy fire. Casualties, mainly from the explosion, were 11 dead and 41 wounded. During the bombardment, 220 rifle and mortar shells were counted.

The remainder of 1863 and start of 1864 were relatively quiet. Then at 9 p.m. Jan. 28, the Third Minor Bombardment was opened. It lasted through the 31st, with firing mainly during the daylight hours. Casualties were light (two wounded) and damage slight. Not quite 600 rounds were fired.

February and the first part of March brought only desultory shelling. Then March 15 the Federals opened the Fourth Minor Bombardment. This was another short one — a single day — and was brought about by the discovery of work designed to protect the Three-Gun

Bombardments Listed

No. And Class Of Bombardment	Dates	No. Casualties Confederate	No. Rounds Fired (Approximate)
First Major	Aug. 17—Sept. 2, 1863	52	6,800
First Minor	Sept. 28—Oct. 3, 1863	3	570
Second Major	Oct. 26—Dec. 6, 1863	100 (Approximately)	18,000
Second Minor	Dec. 11, 1863	52	220
Third Minor	Jan. 28—31, 1864	2	600
Fourth Minor	March 15, 1864	5	140
Fifth Minor	April 28—May 4, 1864	1	510
Sixth Minor	May 13—17, 1864	6	1,150
Seventh Minor	May 30—June 5, 1864	1	220
Third Major	July 7—Sept. 4, 1864	81	14,600
Eighth Minor	Sept. 6—18, 1864	6	570
		---	------
TOTALS (Approximate):		309	43,380

(Continued On Page 76)

Fort Sumter in 1865 shows evidence of extensive Confederate repairs.

(Continued From Page 75)

FORT WEATHERED

Battery. Only 140 or so rounds were fired. Five men were wounded and the results of the Confederate labor splintered and partly demolished, but the battery itself was undamaged.

The afternoon of April 28, 1864, saw the opening of the Fifth Minor Bombardment which continued through May 4. Some 510 mortar shells were lobbed toward the fort in an effort to discourage Confederate repair work.

Only one man was wounded and damage was slight. The bombardment is noteworthy primarily for the volley firing of mortars.

In the past, the 10 and 13-inch Federal mortars had been fired singly. Now, they were touched off in a volley at irregular intervals. Consequently, the Confederates, accustomed to ducking one shell at a time, now found seven descending on them at almost the same instant.

The Sumter garrison had a few days of quiet after May 4. Then, on the 13th, firing picked up again with both land and naval guns shelling the fort. This was the Sixth Minor Bombardment and it lasted through May 17. Casualties were light — one dead and five wounded. The number of rounds was estimated at 1,150. The bombardment is notable for being almost the last firing on Fort Sumter by the monitors.

The Seventh Minor Bombardment was even less spectacular than the Sixth. Starting May 30, it lasted through June 5. Roughly 220 rounds were fired at the fort, mainly from mortars with a sprinkling of Parrott shells including an occasional 300-pounder. This gun dismounted a 24-pounder flank casemate howitzer, but other damage was slight. There were no deaths and only one man was seriously wounded.

Desultory fire continued through the rest of June, then July 7 the Federal batteries opened the Third Major Bombardment of Fort Sumter.

The fire had been ordered by Maj. Gen. John G. Foster who had assumed command of the Department of the South. Foster had been captain of engineers in Fort Sumter under Maj. Robert Anderson and now determined to try his hand at taking the bastion which he had once defended.

He decided the fort had never been properly demolished and set out to correct this oversight. As a first step, he proposed to breach the walls with artillery fire, then, when weakened, to shake them down with the explosion of torpedo rafts floated against the fort.

The collapse of the walls, he believed, would provide an easy slope for assaulting infantry. However, it is difficult to fathom why Foster thought additional slopes necessary when former bombardments already had pounded the gorge and left flank walls into easily mounted rubble.

The bombardment, which also was designed to stop repair work on the fort, was opened July 7 and by afternoon the Confederates reported it was as damaging as any that year.

Initial firing apparently was directed against the gorge angles and the log boom which prevented small boat attack on the fort. The boom had to be destroyed to permit the torpedo rafts access to the base of the walls.

The intensity of the bombardment at first alarmed the Southerners, especially since the laboring force at the fort had been reduced during previous slack periods. However, as soon as sufficient laborers were on hand, the damage done during the day was repaired each night and life settled into the routine of previous bombardments.

By July 21, the Confederates reported that the boom had been broken in two places and the gorge wall, particularly the angles, damaged.

During the bombardment, the Federals began firing incendiary shells but with little effect other than to force movement of one of the magazines as a precaution.

The shelling continued through July and August, but with slackening intensity as supplies of ammunition ran low and breaching guns, damaged by continuous firing, were put out of action.

The 60-day bombardment came to an end Sept. 4. It had cost the South 16 dead and 65 wounded, and the North more than 14,600 rounds of ammunition plus a number of guns. The much vaunted torpedo rafts had exploded harmlessly a short distance from the fort which came out of the shelling somewhat battered, but as strong, or stronger, than it had been when the guns began to fire.

The Eighth, and final, bombardment — a minor one — followed closely after the Third.

Starting Sept. 6, it ended Sept. 18 with a total of six casualties (two dead and four wounded) and some 570 rounds. Lack of ammunition brought it to a halt although intermittent firing continued almost until the fort was evacuated five months later.

During the long siege, breaching batteries and ironclads hurled an estimated 3,500 tons of ammunition at Fort Sumter, but failed to defeat it.

Finally, it fell to a distant maneuver it was powerless to prevent — Gen. W.T. Sherman's march through South Carolina which flanked the entire Charleston area.

Then, during the night of Feb. 17-18, the garrison quietly filed aboard boats. They abandoned — not surrendered — Fort Sumter.

W.R.

Charleston Is Abandoned

When the time came, in the early spring of 1865 to yield Charleston to the Federals, the decision proved almost more than the unhappy Confederates could bear.

Time and again, the soldiers and sailors at Charleston and the civilian men, women and children besieged with them, had been exhorted to fight to the last. To each call they had responded cheerfully, knowing that surrender would forfeit a strategic seaport and depress, perhaps beyond recovery, the spirit of independence which was a mainstay of the war.

With the arrival of Sherman's Army at Savannah, however, and the evidence that it might soon start northward to split the Confederacy yet again, the defense of Charleston became secondary to the preservation of the trained and disciplined soldiers who served the guns about the city. To Gen. Beauregard, who thoroughly appreciated the importance of Charles-

ton to the South, the safety of the garrison was paramount. It represented a substantial part of the force he hoped to muster somewhere in front of the invaders to keep Sherman from marching to Virginia and joining Grant in front of Lee.

There was this single chance of stopping Sherman: Beauregard must correctly divine where the Union Army, marching from Savannah, would attempt to breach the "river line," the expanse of swamps and waterways that formed a natural defense line across the state.

At that point, drawing on all his manpower resources from Charleston to Augusta, a battle might be fought which would divert the Union thrust toward the coast where its spearhead might be pinned against the sea and broken.

There were many contingencies which might arise to make this plan a failure. The single certainty was that, once it went into execution, Charleston would be lost

for to effect the concentration, Beauregard envisioned, would require every man in the Charleston lines.

In the early part of February, Gen. Beauregard sought to balance the requirement that Charleston be held as long as possible in the interest of national morale against the overriding need of withdrawing the garrison for service in the field.

To insure against premature abandonment, Beauregard warned Gen. Hardee, the commander at Charleston, of the city's vital importance both materially and psychologically to the South. Then he sought to prepare Hardee for eventual abandonment.

The two agreed that "whenever it was no longer practicable to hold Charleston, Gen. Hardee should abandon the place, removing all valuable stores and hasten to form a junction in front of Columbia with the

(Continued On Page 77)

Troops of the 55th Massachusetts Colored Regiment singing as they march through Charleston streets.

(Continued From Page 76)

CHARLESTON

forces of Gen. Beauregard, who would have to cover Columbia and take up the Congaree as a line of defense.''

Beauregard himself planned in detail the evacuation of the city — the withdrawal of the troops from James Island across the Ashley and up the Neck; the abandonment of the Christ Church lines, the march out of Charleston itself and, finally and saddest of all, the stealthy removal of the garrison of Fort Sumter.

The Federals on the surrounding islands could not read Beauregard's confidential orders, but they nevertheless scented impending victory. For weeks they had been scanning the city and its defenses eagerly, looking for positive indications that the Confederates might be pulling out.

Much of this curiosity was stimulated by the activities of the signalmen attached to the headquarters of Brig. Gen. Alexander Schimmelfennig on Morris Island. They had been busy reading the exchanges between the Confederate signal stations. After years of studying one another's flags across a few miles of sand and water, each side had learned to read the other's simple codes and ciphers. Communications security was so loose that Schimmelfennig had been compelled to make his own men case their flags and put out their lanterns and torches and confine themselves to watching the enemy's.

Into Schimmelfennig's tent poured a stream of reports, mostly trivial. When the trivialities were put together, however, they made a recognizable pattern.

The Confederate commissary at Sullivan's Island was to reduce his stocks to 40 days rations.

An aide to Col. Alfred Rhett, commanding at Sumter, went over to James Island to inspect a wagon train for Col. Rhett's brigade.

A surgeon at Fort Moultrie asked about sending sick to the city and was told that hospitals were being moved away from Charleston into the interior.

Forty days rations?

Wagon trains for men who had never traveled a quarter-mile from their guns?

Hospitals moving out?

In Schimmelfennig's mind it meant preparation for evacuation. As the observant general cocked an ear in the still night he could hear noises which tended to confirm his suspicions — trains puffing in an out of the city at unusually short intervals, as if the Southerners were sending off their valuables.

Despite the alertness of the Federals, however, the Confederates slipped away like shadows on the night of Feb. 17. The evacuation was silent and smooth, as planned. When it was over, only the hulk of a city peopled by the very young, the aged, the infirm and — in some cases — the disloyal, remained for the Union Army.

Until the last, the Southerners maintained a stout front, keeping their outposts solidly manned, going routinely about military business, exchanging invitations to cockfights, in general behaving as if they intended to stay forever and leaving the Yankees to make what they could of the bits of information they picked out of the air and presented to their generals.

Schimmelfennig missed the point of the one bit of ceremony the Confederates permitted themselves as they prepared to give up the city they had held so long.

On the morning of the 17th, a brand new Confederate ensign replaced the customary tattered garrison flag on the flimsy flagstaff at Sumter. It was a final gesture of sentimental defiance. At sunset, as the garrison watched, it was hauled down. Solemnly, the last evening gun pealed across the waters of the harbor. The soldiers marched to waiting boats and rowed away into the darkness.

At daybreak the next morning, though Confederate flags flew from the other staffs around the harbor, none appeared at Fort Sumter. Lt. Col. A.G. Bennett, 21st U.S. Colored Troops, on Morris Island, heard about this and hurried out to take a look. Capt. Samuel Cuskaden, the regimental recruiting officer, rode up on a horse. Bennett told him to take a boat and some men and go over to Fort Sumter and take a look. Cuskaden suspected what had happened and he sent an orderly to his tent on the double to fetch a U.S. flag he kept there.

Flag in hand, he ran down to the waterfront. There he found a boat full of Rhode Island artillerymen setting out on a similar reconnaissance mission. Cuskaden piled in with them. As the rowers pulled past Sumter at a discreet distance, another boat hove in sight, coming the other way.

To Cuskaden's astonishment, it proved to be the Confederate band from Sullivan's Island, left behind by the retreating defenders. The unhappy bandsmen gladly told all they knew about the evacuation but they flatly refused to go over to Sumter. The place was mined, they said. Cuskaden arrested them and took them back to Cummings Point.

Col. Bennett, however, did not worry about the mines. He got in the boat himself and ordered ''Pull for Sumter!'' On the way across, another boat, manned by Maj. John A. Hennessey of the 52nd Pennsylvania Volunteers, came up with them. The two boats made a race of it to Sumter. Maj. Hennessey was first ashore and hoisted a U.S. flag on the southeastern angle.

Then the officers and their corporal's guard pulled boldly into the harbor. At Fort Ripley, built on piles halfway between Sumter and The Battery, they found a ''Quaker gun'' and a Confederate flag. They hauled down the flag and hoisted the Stars and Stripes.

Finally, about 10 a.m., after a five-mile row, the five officers and 22 soldiers reached the Cooper River piers and climbed ashore, the first Federals to set foot in Charleston except as prisoners, since 1861.

Now that they had arrived, however, they hardly knew what to do. There was fire and explosion in the city. The Confederates had left a large quantity of damaged powder in the Northwestern Railway depot. A crowd of looters gathered about the depot. A small boy playfully lit off a quantity of loose powder. A shattering blast leveled the building and eliminated a large number of the looters.

On the other side of the city, somebody put a torch to the Ashley River Bridge. The fires met in the middle of town. There was nobody to stop them.

Some of Col. Bennett's officers and men wanted to go farther into the city, where they could see the fires burning and where they could hear shouts and cries that showed people were still present.

Bennett thought of his tiny force and hesitated. From Mills Wharf he wrote a note conveying the impression he had a brigade with him instead of a couple of squads.

Impressively headed ''Headquarters, U.S. Forces, Charleston, S.C.,'' it called on the mayor, if he were still there, to surrender without delay.

Mayor Charles Macbeth was indeed still there and shortly he came, kicking aside piles of trash left by looters, stepping around the broken glass that littered the streets, wading through papers left by fleeing merchants, and made a formal reply. Mayor Macbeth did not stop to count the ''U.S. Forces.'' He surrendered promptly and asked for help in fighting the fires and protection against the mobs that were roaming the city.

By noon, the harbor was beginning to fill up with naval vessels. A few companies of the 52nd and the Third Rhode Island Volunteer Artillery arrived to join Col. Bennett.

Bennett marched uptown to The Citadel, where he established a new and more impressive headquarters. A guard was sent to the old U.S. Arsenal. Stray Negroes were rounded up and put to work on the fire engines. Pickets were set up around the few large buildings which housed supplies. Mostly there was only cotton and rice. The rice was passed out to the poor.

By 5 p.m., things were mostly under control. The streets were quiet. Capt. Cuskaden, the recruiter, was happily signing up Negroes for the army. Some of the Union soldiers were getting drunk.

The Stars and Stripes were back to stay.

A.M.W.

Path cut by fire

1865

After the fall of Charleston, Union cameramen recorded the distress of a city laid prostrate by fire within and cannon without. The pictures on the following pages are the face of Charleston under military rule in 1865.

In 1865, when the Federals moved into Charleston, the city still wore the look of ruin left by the fire of 1861. Looking northwest from the Mills House, the camera recorded a portion of the path cut by the fire. The view is across King Street and shows the Unitarian Church and St. Johannes Lutheran (St. John's) Church in background.

St. Michael's Church at the historic center of the old city, was a ranging mark for Federal guns fired from Morris Island. This 1865 photograph shows the steeple in drab war paint to make it less conspicuous. Federal soldiers lounge under portico.

City Hall was converted into a military guardhouse for use by troops occupying the city. These soldiers have stacked their muskets on the pavement along Broad Street.

Cathedral of St. John and St. Finbar, named for the Bishop of Cork who was reputed to have made the sun stand still, was a victim of the 1861 fire. It was still in ruins in 1865. Rebuilt without its steeple, it is now called Cathedral of St. John the Baptist. View is from Legare Street.

St. Michael's Church

City Hall

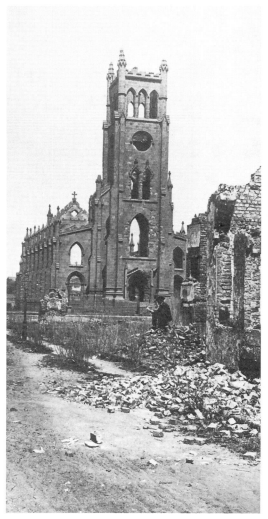

Cathedral

Battery Ramsay was erected in White Point Garden as one of the fortifications in the city's inner line of defense. Post-war photograph shows Federal warships peacefully anchored under the battery's guns which were disabled by Confederates at the evacuation of the city in February 1865.

Castle Pinckney as it appeared after Confederates had reinforced the walls with sand for protection against artillery. Chimneys are on buildings inside the work. Light on scaffold was erected after the war as a navigation aid. Small building in foreground is a privy.

Vendue Range looking west. Colonnade at right overhung sidewalk in front of an office building. Columns are gone now, but building remains.

Battery Ramsay

Castle Pinckney

Vendue Range

East Battery

East Battery in 1865 looked substantially as it does today. At the south end of the street are fortifications of Battery Ramsay in White Point Garden.

Shortly after the war, Meeting Street exhibited a large hole a short distance north of South Battery. The excavation may have been part of an incompleted fortification.

Battery James, also known as Half-Moon No. 2, was at East Bay and Cooper Streets. Faber House (with cupola) in distance was near Half-Moon No. 1, or Battery Augustus Smith.

Meeting Street

Battery James

The Mills House

The fire of 1861 swept along Queen Street but spared the Mills House, the hotel where Robert E. Lee, then a colonel, was boarding. This 1865 view shows the swath of the fire as it moved west. War conditions made restoration impossible.

St. Philip's Church dominates this view of Church Street. Dock Street Theatre now occupies building with balcony at left. Huguenot Church is at right.

St. Andrew's hall lay in ruins after the fire of 1861. Building — where decision was made to secede from the Union — is gone. Iron fence still stands on Broad Street.

St. Philip's Church

St. Andrew's Hall

Post-war photograph shows houses along King Street near Vanderhorst. Old Citadel buildings are in background and the Second Prebyterian Church at far right rear.

The City Lines of fortifications stretched across Charleston Neck approximately at the level of modern Magnolia Cemetery. Designed for 25 guns, the lines held only six when the city surrendered.

East Bay Street at Broad, looking south. The Exchange Building (left) lost its cupola in the earthquake of 1886. Building opposite, north of Broad, was destroyed by fire in 1963. Adjoining structures to the north have secumbed to parking lots.

Old Citadel

City Lines

East Bay at Broad

Houses along South Battery

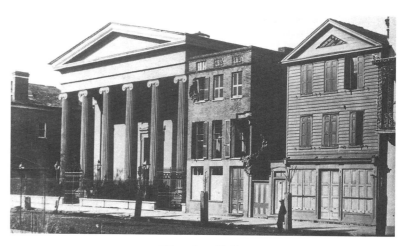

Hibernian Hall

Houses along South Battery were occupied by Federal officers after the fall of Charleston. Camera is looking toward Cooper River from King Street.

Hibernian Hall as seen from the east side of Meeting Street about opposite the Mills House. Damage to buildings appears to be the result of Federal shells. Fire of 1861 missed this area by a few yards.

View looking west along Broad Street toward State. Office building now occupies site of porticoed structure. Building with peaked roof and eagle has been occupied by the same bank since 1834. The bank also has occupied and preserved the next two buildings. The others burned in 1963.

East Bay Street at Broad. View is toward Exchange Street. With exception of cupola on Exchange Building, which fell during earthquake of 1886, this scene has changed little in more than a hundred years.

Broad and State

East Bay at Broad

Circular Congregational Church

The Charleston Hotel

Ruins of the Circular Congregational Church which was in the path of the disastrous fire which swept across the city in 1861. St. Philip's Church is in the background.

The Charleston Hotel in Union hands. Camera caught the Stars and Stripes flying from the historic Meeting Street hotel. This magnificent building, with its splendid columns, was torn down in the 1950s.

Calhoun Street Battery was armed with a rifled and banded 8-inch columbiad. It was one of several Charleston defenses that overlooked the Cooper River.

Calhoun Street Battery